IDEALS
INSTITUTE FOR JEWISH
IDEAS AND IDEALS

A SYNAGOGUE

COMPANION

Insights on the Torah, Haftarot,
and Shabbat Morning Prayers

Rabbi Hayyim Angel

KOD

Cover design by Benjamin Motola
Text designed and typeset by Olivestone, Inc.

Distributed by Kodesh Press
www.KodeshPress.com
kodeshpress@gmail.com
New York, NY

Dedications

～

I thank my dear friends for their support of the publication of this book. Your friendship and commitment to Torah are eternally appreciated.

Joshua Angel
in memory of his wife, Rita Angel

Sam and Vicki Katz
in honor of Sam's parents, Rabbi Joseph and Elana Katz, for over a century of commitment and dedication to Jewish education

Roysi Erbes and Volfi Mizrahi
in honor of their children,
Jessica Ida and Joshua Samuel Mizrahi

Tikva and Irwin Ostrega
in memory of Tikva's father, Ezra Zion Shohet,
who had a dedication and zeal for prayer
and the study of Torah

Norris and Judy Wolff
in loving memory of Louis and Molly Wolff (Lupu)

In memory of Ansel David Rosenfield and Murray M. Romer

Anonymous

Sephardic Publication Foundation

Norman Benzaquen Publication Fund
of the Institute for Jewish Ideas and Ideals

S. Daniel Abraham

～

A SYNAGOGUE
COMPANION

CONTENTS

Introduction   *vii*

I ⟶ TORAH   1

Bereishit—Genesis   3
Shemot—Exodus   63
Vayikra—Leviticus   109
Bemidbar—Numbers   135
Devarim—Deuteronomy   167
Selected Bibliography: Torah   207

II ⟶ HAFTAROT   217

Shabbat Haftarot   223
Haftarot for Holidays and Special Days   277
Selected Bibliography: Haftarot   303

III ⟶ PRAYER   307

Topics in Prayer   309
Shabbat Morning Prayers   321
Selected Bibliography: Prayers   348

Introduction

One of the miraculous success stories in world history is the continuity of the Jewish people. Generation after generation of Jews has built family and community around the vision of the Torah, lived its laws, and transmitted its observances and religious experiences. Today, we live in a complicated world. Inundated with information and often given insufficient rooting in Jewish tradition to navigate through our world, we may lose sight of our values, commitments, and even basic identity. There is a profound thirst among so many Jews to connect to the vision of the Torah, but many find the process daunting or inaccessible.

The Institute for Jewish Ideas and Ideals is one of the great beacons of light for promoting a vision of the Torah that is authentic, passionate, reasonable, and embracing of people of all backgrounds. Thanks to the membership and support of people around the world who identify with our vision, we provide teaching, writings, resources, and ongoing opportunities to make Torah more accessible and inviting to people of every background. Our goal is to bring Torah to real life, and to bring our real-life experiences into our Torah study.

This *Synagogue Companion* is written in this spirit. It is comprised of brief essays on the Torah, Haftarot, and Shabbat morning prayers. The essays draw from the best of traditional and contemporary scholarship, and attempt to make the synagogue experience more relevant, inspiring, and understandable.

For the book's cover, I selected a photograph taken by my wife Maxine during our honeymoon in January 2010. It was taken from within the synagogue of Rabbi Joseph Karo in Safed, Israel. The image suggests that one's vision developed inside the synagogue should radiate outward to one's experiences outside the synagogue, and one's experiences from outside should influence one's synagogue experience when in communion with God through prayer and Torah study. The picture also suggests a broad, outward-looking vision emanating from within the walls of Jewish tradition. Torah illuminates our innermost thoughts and feelings, and also prods us to share this light with the world. I thank my friend Benjamin Motola for his creativity in designing the cover for this book.

This book did not just happen. It required the dedication of like-minded individuals who support the dissemination of Torah. Thank you to my friends Joshua Angel, Sam and Vicki Katz, Roysi Erbes and Volfi Mizrahi, Tikva and Irwin Ostrega, Norris and Judy Wolff, and two couples who have chosen to remain anonymous. Thank you also to S. Daniel Abraham, the Sephardic Publication Foundation, and the Norman S. Benzaquen Publication Fund of the Institute for Jewish Ideas and Ideals. Their support enables our Institute to spread its vision to people and communities across America and beyond.

Thank you to my father, Rabbi Marc D. Angel, for supporting the publication of this volume. It has been a pleasure working with him as the National Scholar of the Institute for Jewish Ideas and Ideals, which he founded in 2007. Thank you also to my sister, Ronda Angel Arking, for her exceptional editing of this volume.

Special thanks to the Sephardic Publication Foundation for its co-sponsorship of this volume, and for its help and support in publishing my original books on Prayer (*Know Before Whom You Stand: Thoughts About Prayer*, first edition 2010, second edition 2011) and Haftarot (*Prophetic Sermons: Thoughts on the Haftarot*, 2011). The material from those shorter books has been edited and augmented for this publication.

Most importantly, I thank my family for their constant love and support: Mom and Dad, Ronda and Dan, Elana and James, Grandma, Jake, Andrew, Jonathan, Max, Charlie, Jeremy, and Kara, JoAnn, Matt, Erin, Molly, Emily, Nate, Mimi, and Papap. *Ve-aharonim havivim*, I thank my wife Maxine and our twin daughters, Aviva Hayya and Dahlia Rachel.

I welcome your comments and questions, and look forward to continuing these Torah conversations with you. You can contact me at hangel@jewishideas.org.

Finally, I pray that this volume will help readers gain greater access to our eternal and sacred texts, so that we may grow religiously through study and experience of the Torah, the Prophets, and Prayer—both in the synagogue, and in all aspects of our lives.

Hayyim Angel
FIRST NIGHT OF HANUKKAH, 5774
NOVEMBER 27, 2013

תורה

Torah

Bereishit
בראשית
Genesis

Bereishit

Torah and Science

There are several traditional approaches to clashes between the literal reading of the Torah and the findings of modern science. Rabbi Chaim Navon at Yeshivat Har Etzion explores several leading approaches.

One approach casts doubts on science. For example, the late Lubavitcher Rebbe, Rabbi Menachem Mendel Schneersohn, insisted that there is no way to disprove the possibility that dinosaurs lived only 6,000 years ago. Even if that could be fully proven, perhaps God created the world and inserted fossils to make the world look older than it really is. Therefore, he maintained that the world is in fact less than 6,000 years old, as per the literal understanding of the Torah. It is difficult to refute such an argument—although it raises serious questions regarding the way God operates in the world. More broadly, it is difficult to identify with these arguments, because we rely on science in nearly every aspect of our lives.

A second approach takes the opposite stand. It does not reexamine the validity of the assertions of science, but rather our understanding of the Torah. A classic example of this approach is what Rambam writes regarding the question of the eternity of the world. Aristotle maintained that the world is eternal, that is, it was never created. Although Rambam did not think that Aristotle had proven his case (long before the Big Bang theory), he argued that were science to conclusively prove the eternality of the world, we would interpret the Torah creation narrative less literally (*Guide for the Perplexed* II:25). Many in our generation have followed this path, attempting to reinterpret biblical verses in line with modern science.

A third approach makes no attempt to reinterpret the Torah or to raise doubts about the validity of science. Rather, it argues that the Torah and science relate to two different realms. Science generates facts, and religion teaches us values and commandments. The nineteenth-century commentator Shadal (on Genesis 1:1) insists that the Torah is not a science text-book. The Torah teaches goodness and justice, and belief in God's Providence.

Rabbi Abraham Isaac Kook similarly stressed that the Torah's religious teachings are far more important to us than how the world and species came into being (*Iggerot Ra'ayah*, I, letter 91, p. 105). There is no need to be upset by the theory of evolution. Although it may appear to contradict the literal sense of Scripture, the verses do not pretend to teach us science, but rather spiritual ideas.

Professor Yeshayahu Leibowitz agreed: "If the Holy Scriptures were sources of information, it would be difficult to see where their sacredness resided...The idea that the Shekhinah (God's Presence) descended on Mount Sinai in order to compete with the professor who teaches history or physics is ludicrous, if not blasphemous" (*Judaism, Human Values, and the Jewish State*, p. 140).

Rabbi Chaim Navon, *Genesis and Jewish Thought*, translated by David Strauss (Jersey City, NJ: Ktav in association with Yeshivat Har Etzion, 2008), pp. 29–41.

SOME LESSONS OF CREATION

*I*n his opening comment on the Torah, Rashi wonders why the Torah does not begin with the first law to Israel (which appears in Exodus, chapter 12). He concludes that Genesis teaches that God created the world, so God therefore has the right to give the Land of Israel to the Jews. Rabbi Jonathan Sacks explains the idea underlying Rashi's comment. What type of literature is Genesis? Is it history or legend; chronicle or myth? The answer: It is Torah—teaching, law, instruction, and guidance. It is about how we live, and its narratives must be understood in this context, also.

Strikingly, there is no allusion to Israel or the Temple in the creation narratives. Adam and Eve live in Mesopotamia. Jerusalem is not mentioned by name in the entire Torah. The creation narrative has no political motive to prove Israel's centrality or superiority.

The central message of the creation narrative is that people are created in the image of God (1:26). Nahum Sarna (*JPS Commentary on Genesis*, p. 12) observes that in Mesopotamia and Egypt, kings often were described as being in the image of the gods. For example, the name Tutankhamen means "in the living image of (the god) Amun." The Torah democratizes this concept to all humanity. The Torah also repudiates racism, since we are all one species descended from Adam and Eve, created in God's image and God is everyone's God (see *Sanhedrin* 37a).

God saw that the creation was very good (1:31). This outlook was a radically different understanding of the universe from any other nation's creation narrative. History is purposeful, and society can have direction. Human impotence as described in Mesopotamian creation narratives is replaced by human nobility and responsibility in the Torah. Belief in the goodness of the universe can lead to a covenant with God and ultimately the messianic ideal.

Of all creation, only two things are not described as "good": the firmament separation, and people. This anomaly suggests that these two creations are incomplete, and their becoming good is an ongoing process (Rabbi Joseph Albo, *Ikkarim* III:2). Rabbi Shmuel Goldin further suggests that these two elements are linked. People can achieve their goodness potential to the degree that they unite heaven and earth through living a life of holiness.

In Greece, the study of cosmogony belonged exclusively to elite philosophers. In Israel, the youngest children study the Torah and its lessons. One midrash (*Exodus Rabbah* 30:12) states that Aquilas converted to Judaism because he was so impressed that Genesis and its lessons are accessible to all.

Rabbi Shmuel Goldin, *Unlocking the Torah Text: An In-Depth Journey into the Weekly Parsha: Genesis* (Jerusalem: Gefen Publishing House, 2007), pp. 6–8.

Rabbi Jonathan Sacks, *Covenant & Conversation: A Weekly Reading of the Jewish Bible, Genesis* (New Milford, CT: Maggid Books, 2009), p. 16.

THE GARDEN OF EDEN

*T*here were two trees at the center of Eden. The Tree of Life seems magical. Were Adam and Eve to eat from it, they would become immortal. Studying the mythology of the ancient Near East, Professor Umberto Cassuto found that nearly every ancient mythology had a tree, a plant, or a fountain of life. The quest for immortality was an obsession of the ancient world.

In contrast, the Torah decisively downplays the Tree of Life. It becomes significant to the plot only after Adam and Eve sinned by eating from the Tree of Knowledge and were expelled from the Garden of Eden. God then sends angels called Cherubim to protect the Tree of Life.

To understand why the Torah would diminish the role of the Tree of Life, we must consider the tree that is central to the narrative: the Tree of Knowledge. Adam and Eve must have had some sense of good and evil before eating from the Tree of Knowledge, as they knew that it was forbidden to them. However, that knowledge was external to their psyches, since they had never experienced sin or its consequences. Prior to their sin, they were like children. God took care of all their needs, and they had minimal responsibilities in return.

By prohibiting the Tree of Knowledge, God gave Adam and Eve a choice. They could obey and remain like children forever, or they could rebel by taking control of their lives, and responsibility for their actions. After Adam and Eve ate from the Tree of Knowledge, their concept of wrongdoing became internalized.

Whereas the Tree of Life appears magical, the Tree of Knowledge appears to be a regular fruit tree. The Sages of the midrash suggested that the Tree of Knowledge was a normal fruit, whether a fig, grapevine, wheat, or an etrog (*Genesis Rabbah* 15:7). The effects of the fruit derived from God's prohibition, rather than from any inherent magical property.

The Tree of Knowledge could be understood as "The Tree of Growing Up." Adam and Eve became conscious of sexuality. They lost the protection they received in exchange for minimal responsibilities. The "punishment" of the woman was pain in child bearing and sexual dependence. The "punishment" of the man was in working hard to feed his family.

These so-called punishments simply are the difficult aspects of adulthood. The positive aspects are marriage, creating new life, and contributing constructively to society. Had they remained in Eden, Adam and Eve would never have grown up.

Even though the Tree of Life was prevalent in other ancient literatures, the Tree of Knowledge is otherwise unattested. The Torah is a revolution in human history, shifting focus away from nonexistent magical solutions for immortality and replacing them with an emphasis on an adult relationship with God. It teaches that we must live morally, and take personal responsibility for our actions.

—

CAIN AND ABEL

hy did God reject Cain's sacrifice? After all, Cain brought the first sacrifice in world history on his own initiative. Rashi and several later commentators observe that the Torah emphasizes the goodness of Abel's offering: "Cain brought an offering to the Lord from the fruit of the soil; and Abel, for his part, brought the choicest of the firstlings of his flock" (Genesis 4:3–4). One may deduce that Cain brought poor, or perhaps mediocre quality produce.

"The Lord said to Cain, 'Why are you distressed, and why is your face fallen? Surely, if you do right, there is uplift. But if you do not do right sin couches at the door; its urge is toward you, yet you can be its master'" (4:6–7). Cain needed to use his free will more positively in the future. If not, evil always would lurk. According to this interpretation, Cain's commitment was insufficient, leading to divine rejection and his eventual moral downfall.

Although this reading has a textual basis, it presents difficulties. The Torah does not emphasize the flaws in Cain's commitment. Moreover, if Cain's offering was not ideal, let God accept his initial offering and then teach him, rather than creating a jealousy that would lead to the world's first homicide.

Jon Levenson (Harvard University) notes further that this reading may be overly microscopic. Cain brought sacrifice "to the Lord," whereas the Torah does not say the same for Abel. Had God accepted Cain's offering we likely would read this point in as well (*The Death and Resurrection of the Beloved Son,* 1993, pp. 72–74).

Rabbi Haim Sabato submits an alternative reading to that of Rashi. God rejected Cain's offering as a test to see how he would respond to rejection. Instead of acknowledging rejection, Cain turned selfish and violent. God then told him that sin crouches at door. In this reading, Cain's failure was not in the quality of his original offering but rather in his horrible response to unfair rejection. According to Rabbi Sabato, the story addresses our moral responsibilities in a seemingly unfair world.

Rabbi Jonathan Sacks suggests that we can learn something significant about Cain's motivations only after his response. If one gives a gift and it is refused, the giver can wonder if he or she did something wrong, or the giver can get angry at the recipient. If the latter, this indicates that the original gift was selfish, more of a bribe than a genuine gift.

It also is noteworthy that while God rejects Cain's offering, God also approaches him with prophecy. This demonstrates that God has not rejected Cain. God also did not punish Cain for his sacrifice, teaching him to improve without inflicting any harm.

However, the Torah's emphasis on the superiority of Abel's offering does appear to create a contrast. Each side of this interpretive circle addresses important aspects of the story, but also falls short of comprehensive interpretation. Regardless, this narrative stresses that we are indeed our brother's keepers.

Rabbi Haim Sabato, *Ahavat Torah* (Hebrew) (Tel Aviv: *Mesorah la-Am, Sifrei Aliyat ha-Gag,* 2000), pp. 15–20.

Rabbi Jonathan Sacks, *Covenant & Conversation: A Weekly Reading of the Jewish Bible, Genesis* (New Milford, CT: Maggid Books, 2009), p. 31.

THE LONGEVITY OF THE EARLY GENERATIONS

*O*ne of the enigmatic aspects of the early chapters of Genesis is the incredible longevity of the people. At the beginning of the sixteenth century, Abarbanel quoted those who suggested that a "year" in those sections of the Torah must mean what we call a "month." This would mean that Methuselah's staggering 969 years really was a little under 81 years.

Abarbanel rejects this convenient answer. The Torah knows how to use the terms "month" and "year." Additionally, some people on these lists had children at age 30. If the numbers refer to months, these individuals would be fathers at age two and a half. Fair interpretation demands that these numbers refer to actual years.

Rambam (*Guide for the Perplexed* II:47) suggests that these individuals must have been righteous, and probably ate a healthful diet. Abarbanel similarly suggests that they were vegetarians and had children later in life. Granting that one who tries these techniques today would not live to age 969, Rambam and Abarbanel add that there also must have been divine intervention. God wanted these early generations to live long lives so that they would be able to develop science and philosophy to pass on to future generations.

Adopting a more naturalistic perspective, Ramban and Sforno speculate that there was a cataclysmic climate change as a result of the flood. Professor Nathan Aviezer of Bar-Ilan University also recently proposed a scientific hypothesis. Although it always had been thought that aging is a function of wearing out, there likely is a gene for aging. Certain turtles, birds, and fish do not age.

The safest age for human beings is between the ages of 10 and 15, with a .05 percent mortality rate in Western nations. In a world without aging, disease and accidents would kill equally, regardless of age. If all people had a .05 percent mortality rate, 95 percent of the population would reach age 100, and the average lifespan would be about 1,300 years. Additionally, men and women would be able to bear children throughout their lifetimes.

It is possible that the early generations had aging genes that would eventually lead to death at around age 900. This would explain why most of these individuals died between the ages of 895 and 969, with the exception of Enoch (365) who is said to have died prematurely. It took 10 generations for new aging genes to spread throughout the population, causing a gradual decline of the average age—something that can be predicted genetically.

Although this theory sounds intriguing, I consulted a geneticist at Johns Hopkins University who dismissed the hypothesis as incredibly unlikely. According to this geneticist, Aviezer's theory requires divine intervention, in which case we no longer have a scientific genetic theory but a modernized Rambam-Abarbanel approach—combining some naturalistic ideas but bringing divine providence to the forefront.

How will future interpreters explain the longevity of the Torah's early generations? We may not know yet, but it is exciting for all of us to be an active part of that next generation.

Nathan Aviezer, "The Extreme Longevity of the Early Generations in Genesis," Bar-Ilan University, Noah 5759/1999, at http://www.biu.ac.il/JH/Parasha/eng/noah/avi.html.

TEN GENERATIONS FROM ADAM TO NOAH

*C*hapter 5 of Genesis chronicles the 10 generations from Adam until Noah. In its description of Seth's family, the Torah adds considerably more detail than it had for Cain's progeny in chapter 4. Chapter 5 specifies the age of each person when he had the son who would be a direct progenitor of Noah, how many years that individual lived after having that son, and the total number of years that person lived.

Noting that the Hebrew *enosh* is synonymous with *adam*—both meaning "humankind," Umberto Cassuto demonstrates that with only minor variations, the name lists of the descendants of Cain and Seth are identical. These similarities highlight the fundamental religious differences between the descendants of Cain and of Seth prior to the flood.

Whereas Seth's family prayed to their Creator (4:25–26), Cain had proclaimed to God "I must avoid Your presence" (4:14). Seth's family advocated a direct relationship with God. Cain's chose a life devoid of religion, and sank to the depths of immorality as reflected by Lamech—Cain's only descendant with a biblical voice (4:17–24).

At the time of the two Lamechs, the world was divided into two groups: the godless, immoral Cain group; and the God-fearing descendants of Seth. At the beginning of chapter 6, however, we learn of a change in the status quo: "When men began to increase on earth and daughters were born to them, the divine beings saw how beautiful the daughters of men were and took wives from among those that pleased them. The Lord said, 'My breath shall not abide in man forever, since he too is flesh; let the days allowed him be one hundred and twenty years'" (6:1–3).

Who were these "divine beings"? Ibn Ezra suggests that they were those people who had followed a Godly existence, namely, the descendants of Seth. In contrast, the earthy Cainites are referred to as the daughters of men. Based on this interpretation, chapter 6 pinpoints the underlying cause of the moral corruption of humanity. When Seth's descendants intermarried with Cain's descendants, the godless immorality of Cain came to dominate the entire society. At this tragic point, God decided to start a new world stemming from the only individual whose faith was strong enough to withstand the intermarriages with Cainites—Noah.

Rather than interrupting the story of the development of humanity, the genealogies of chapters 4 and 5 in fact provide the underlying story of the cause of the flood. The details gleaned from the two lists convey a deeper understanding of how humanity moved into a life of depravity and lewdness—eventually leading to near-extinction.

Hayyim Angel, "*Elleh Toledot*: A Study of the Genealogies in the Book of Genesis," in *Haham Gaon Memorial Volume*, ed. Marc D. Angel (Brooklyn: Sefer Hermon Press, 1997), pp. 163–182; reprinted in Angel, *Through an Opaque Lens* (New York: Sephardic Publication Foundation, 2006), pp. 111–126.

Noah

NOAH'S RELUCTANCE TO BUILD A NEW WORLD

*G*od brought the flood because humanity had become evil. God's goal was to restart creation with the most righteous family (Radak on Genesis 9:1). Rabbi Samson Raphael Hirsch (on Genesis 7:4) suggests that the flood lasted 40 days, parallel to the time it takes for a fetus to form. The catastrophe led to a rebirth of humanity.

When the flood was about to begin, God told Noah, "You shall enter the ark, with your sons, your wife, and your sons' wives" (Genesis 6:18). A midrash concludes that God prohibited marital relations during the flood (*Genesis Rabbah* 31:12). It would be insensitive and selfish to engage in pleasure and future-building while the rest of the world was being destroyed. The Torah follows this order of all the men followed by all women—rather than Noah and his wife, and then his sons with their wives—when they enter the ark (Genesis 7:7, 13).

Following this logic, the midrash suggests that after the flood, God wanted husbands and wives to resume marital relations and procreate (*Genesis Rabbah* 34:6): "God spoke to Noah, saying, 'Come out of the ark, together with your wife, your sons, and your sons' wives. Bring out with you every living thing of all flesh that is with you: birds, animals, and everything that creeps on earth; and let them swarm on the earth and be fertile and increase on the earth'" (Genesis 8:15–17).

God commanded Noah to get off with his wife, his sons with their wives, and the animals to disembark in pairs. However, Noah does not follow this order: "So Noah came out, together with his sons, his wife, and his sons' wives" (8:18).

Abarbanel (elaborated on by Rabbi Chanoch Waxman) suggests that Noah did not want to rebuild a new world. His righteousness was sufficient to save himself and his family, but he had no vision for the future. Consequently, men disembarked with the men, then women with women.

This deviation from the divine command was emblematic of Noah's intent to avoid procreation.

God repeated the command to procreate in 9:1 and 9:7. Instead, Noah got drunk, cursed his grandson Canaan, and faded from the text instead of building a better society. His descendants appear to have been little better than those who perished in the flood, culminating with the soaring arrogance and paganism of the community that built the Tower of Babel.

The Sages therefore idealize the religious worldview of Abraham, who dedicated his life to teaching his children and spreading his vision to build a better society.

Rabbi Chanoch Waxman, "Survival and Revival: On the Righteousness of Noach," Yeshivat Har Etzion Virtual Beit Midrash, Noah 5762, at http://www.vbm-torah.org/parsha.62/02noach.htm.

For a survey of rabbinic sources that contrast Noah and Abraham, see Nehama Leibowitz, *Studies in Bereshit (Genesis)*, translated and adapted by Aryeh Newman (Jerusalem: Eliner Library), pp. 59–66.

—

VEGETARIANISM

raditional commentators generally assume that the generations before the flood did not eat meat, since God blessed humanity to eat only plants: "God blessed them and God said to them, 'Be fertile and increase, fill the earth and master it; and rule the fish of the sea, the birds of the sky, and all the living things that creep on earth.' God said, 'See, I give you every seed-bearing plant that is upon all the earth, and every tree that has seed-bearing fruit; they shall be yours for food'" (Genesis 1:28–29). Even animals initially were blessed to eat only plant life (1:30).

In contrast, God permitted meat after the flood: "'Be fertile and increase, and fill the earth. . . . Every creature that lives shall be yours to eat; as with the green grasses, I give you all these'" (Genesis 9:1–3). Why did God change the original course and permit meat after the flood?

Abarbanel (on Deuteronomy, chapter 14) suggests that Adam was on a high spiritual level and therefore was forbidden from eating meat. Carnivory breeds cruelty and materialism. After humanity lapsed into immorality at the time of the flood, God permitted meat. This transition may be likened to a doctor who has given up on an ill patient and therefore allows him to eat whatever he wants.

The fifteenth-century Spanish thinker Rabbi Joseph Albo (*Ikkarim* III:15) speculates that Cain did not offer an animal sacrifice because he wrongly thought that men and animals were equals. When God accepted Abel's offering, Cain saw that it was acceptible to kill animals and mistakenly concluded that it must be acceptable to kill people as well. Therefore, he murdered his brother. Cain's act began the breakdown of the social order. After the flood, God permitted meat in order to impress upon people the superiority of humans over animals.

Rabbi Abraham Isaac Kook takes the discussion in a different direction. In his view, vegetarianism is the ideal state. When the Messiah comes, people will no longer eat meat. Today, one who wishes to abstain from meat may do so. However, there are far greater moral problems in our society such as racism, hatred, and many others that good people should focus on first.

In Torah law, the only meat that every Israelite *must* eat is one olive's worth of lamb of the Passover sacrifice. Although meat from kosher animals prepared in accordance with halakhah is permissible, the discussion of the origins of carnivory in the Torah should refine our moral sense toward our relationship with the animal kingdom.

Rabbi J. David Bleich, *Contemporary Halakhic Problems*, vol. 3 (New York: Ktav, 1977), pp. 237–250.

Rabbi Yehudah Nachshoni, *Studies in the Weekly Parashah*, trans. Shmuel Himelstein (Brooklyn: Mesorah Publications, 1988), vol. 1 pp. 20–26; vol. 5 pp. 1261–1269.

Rabbi Elhanan Samet, *Iyyunim be-Parashot ha-Shavua* (third series) vol. 1 (Hebrew) ed. Ayal Fishler (Tel Aviv: Yediot Aharonot, 2012), pp. 11–38.

THE TOWER OF BABEL

he nine-verse narrative of the Tower of Babel is the only narrative story in the 300-year period from the flood until Abraham. Therefore, it is a significant aspect of the Torah's description of world history. Evidently, the human population, concentrated in Babylon, did something wrong, and God scattered them and created diversity in language. What was their mistake?

"They said, 'Come, let us build a city, and a tower with its top in the sky, to make a name for ourselves; else we shall be scattered all over the world'" (Genesis 11:4). Early interpreters saw this act as a rebellion against God (see *Sanhedrin* 109a). The key is in the concluding sentence of the narrative: "That is why it was called Babel, because there the Lord confounded (*balal*) the speech of the whole earth" (11:9). However, Babylonians called *themselves* Babel. They would not have referred to themselves as "the confused ones," or used a Hebrew term.

Professor Umberto Cassuto explains that in every ancient Babylonian city, there were temples built to their gods accompanied with a tower called a ziqqurat (from Akkadian *zaqaru*, "to rise up high"). The most famous was in city of Babylonia, the temple of Marduk. It appears that this temple originally was built in Hammurabi's time (eighteenth–seventeenth centuries BCE). The Babylonians took such great pride in this temple that in their mythology they attributed its building to their gods.

The ruins of the Temple of Marduk were found between 1889–1917 by German archaeologists, and its size was truly enormous for the ancient world. It was some 300 feet high, rising from a square base of equal size. Given that the Torah's story is set in the city of Babylonia, there is little question that it is describing this tower.

The purpose of building ziqqurats was to create a human-made mountain, thought of as a meeting place between the gods and people. The building of such structures was a deeply religious gesture, built on the hopes that the gods would descend and establish contact with people. The Babylonians called themselves Babel from the term *bab-ilim*, "the gate of the gods." They called the Temple of Marduk *etemen-an-ki*: the center of the heavens and earth.

The Torah mocks this theology. It says, "Although you think that you are the gate of the gods, you are confused." Idolatry is when you create gods and maintain that you are the highest power in the world. The Torah belittles and condemns the surpreme arrogance of the Babylonians and all pagan culture, which insisted that it could control the gods through magical acts. Although contructing a ziqqurat may have appeared to be a religious act, it was ultimately a self-serving project.

In contrast, Abraham was able to look beyond himself and know he was not the highest power. Rather than creating artificial structures, he chose the more difficult path of forging a genuine relationship with God.

Hayyim Angel, "The Tower of Babel: A Case Study in Combining Traditional and Academic Bible Methodologies," in *Where the Yeshiva Meets the University: Traditional and Academic Approaches to Tanakh Study*, ed. Hayyim Angel, *Conversations* 15 (Winter 2013), pp. 135–143.

Umberto Cassuto, *Commentary on the Book of Genesis* (Hebrew) (Jerusalem: Magnes Press, 1987), pp. 154–169.

Rabbi Elhanan Samet, *Iyyunim be-Parashot ha-Shavua* (first series) vol. 1 (Hebrew) ed. Ayal Fishler (Ma'aleh Adumim: Ma'aliyot Press, 2002), pp. 21–30.

Nahum Sarna, *Understanding Genesis: The Heritage of Biblical Israel* (New York: Schocken Books, 1966), pp. 63–80.

THE TEN GENERATIONS FROM NOAH TO ABRAHAM

After the flood, Noah plants a vineyard, becomes drunk, and fades from prominence. Chapter 10 then lists 70 descendants of Shem, Ham, and Japeth. After the story of the Tower of Babel (11:1–9), the Torah lists the generations of Shem's family, leading to Abraham.

Although the genealogies in chapters 5 and 11 are similar, there are notable distinctions between the two lists. First, Seth's lineage includes some details about the family and its members (they prayed to God; Enoch was righteous; Lamech named Noah to bring hope to humanity). This is not the case in Shem's family. Until Abraham's father Terah, the Torah provides no details. This distinction appears to belittle the collective contribution of Shem's descendants, as they bestowed nothing of lasting value to the world.

Additionally, in Seth's lineage, the Torah specifies that each person died. In Shem's lineage, this seemingly obvious fact is omitted. Prompted by this inconsistency, Sforno (on Genesis 11:11) observes that all of Seth's descendants listed in chapter 5 died before the flood. Perhaps they were so righteous that God felt they did not deserve such an extreme punishment as the rest of humankind. For this reason, the Torah emphasizes that they died, that is, before the flood. In contrast, when Abraham was born, Noah was still alive. In fact, *all* of Shem's descendants listed in chapter 11 were alive. Sforno asserts that God wanted everyone—even the righteous Noah—to witness a truly superior individual.

Abraham's concern for others and for the future distinguished him from Noah. This upgrade in righteousness is reflected in the list of Shem's descendants. After going from Shem until Terah without distinguishing any descendant, the Torah marks Terah off by stressing "this is the line of Terah." Abraham represents a clean break from Noah's descendants. Abraham would herald a new spiritual era in the world.

Abraham's nation develops through Isaac and Jacob. When the children of Israel go to Egypt, the Torah (46:8–27) enumerates their families: They had 70 family heads, as did Noah's family in chapter 10. The 70 nations of the world are thus paralleled by the 70 Israelite families.

The Talmud (*Sukkah* 55b) asks why 70 sacrifices were brought throughout the Sukkot festival (see Numbers 29:12–34). It answers that the offerings were offered to atone for the 70 nations of the world. The Jewish people, represented by their own 70 families, continued to pray for the 70 nations of the world—Noah's descendants. By prescribing the 70 Sukkot sacrifices, God reminded the Israelites of their ongoing responsibility to be involved in both the physical and spiritual welfare of all people.

Hayyim Angel, "*Elleh Toledot*: A Study of the Genealogies in the Book of Genesis," in *Haham Gaon Memorial Volume*, ed. Marc D. Angel (Brooklyn: Sefer Hermon Press, 1997), pp. 163–182; reprinted in Angel, *Through an Opaque Lens* (New York: Sephardic Publication Foundation, 2006), pp. 111–126.

Lekh Lekha

THE CHOSEN PEOPLE

*A*dam and Eve failed by eating of the Tree of Knowledge and were thus exiled from Eden. Cain murdered his brother, and he, too, was exiled. The following generations became corrupt to the point where the entire human race was overwhelmed by immorality.

At this point, God rejected most of humanity and restarted human history with Noah, the "second Adam." After the flood, God explicitly commanded several moral laws (Genesis 9), which the Talmud understands as the "Seven Noahide Laws" (also referred to as ethical monotheism). Noah should have taught these principles to all his descendants. Instead, the only recorded story of Noah's final 350 years relates that he got drunk and cursed his grandson Canaan. Although Noah was a righteous man, he did not transmit his values to succeeding generations.

The Tower of Babel represents a societal break from God. It marked the beginnings of paganism and unbridled human arrogance. At this point, God appears to have given up on having the entire world perfected and instead chose Abraham—the "third Adam"—and his descendants to model ethical monotheism and teach it to all humanity. This synopsis of the first 12 chapters of Genesis is encapsulated by Rabbi Ovadiah Sforno in his introduction to Genesis.

The remainder of the Book of Genesis revolves around a selection process within Abraham's family. Not all branches would become Abraham's spiritual heirs. By the end of Genesis, it is evident that the Chosen People is comprised specifically of all Jacob's sons and their future generations.

Can other nations be chosen again by reaccepting ethical monotheism? The answer is a resounding "yes." Prophets look to an ideal future when all nations can again become chosen. For example, Zephaniah envisions a time when all nations will speak "a clear language," thereby undoing the damage of the Tower of Babel (Zephaniah 3:9).

One is chosen *if one chooses God*. For a Jew, that means commitment to the Torah and its commandments. For a non-Jew, that means commitment to ethical monotheism. God longs for the return of all humanity, and the messianic visions of the prophets constantly reiterate that aspiration.

Rather than serving primarily as an ethnic description, the Chosen People concept is deeply rooted in religious ethics. It is a constant prod to faithfulness to God and the Torah, and it contains a universalistic message that addresses the community of nations. All are descendants from Adam and Eve, created in God's Image. God waits with open arms to choose all those who choose to pursue that sacred relationship with the divine.

Hayyim Angel, "'The Chosen People': An Ethical Challenge," *Conversations* 8 (Fall 2010), pp. 52–60; reprinted in Angel, *Creating Space Between Peshat and Derash: A Collection of Studies on Tanakh* (Jersey City, NJ: Ktav-Sephardic Publication Foundation, 2011), pp. 25–34.

GENESIS CHAPTER 12 AND THE EXODUS

*G*enesis, chapter 12 relates that soon after Abraham and his family arrived in Canaan, a famine drove them to Egypt. Pharaoh seized Sarah, but God plagued him and rescued Sarah. Pharaoh then lavished many gifts on Abraham and sent him back to his land.

Midrashim and later commentators recognize that this story foreshadows Israel's enslavement and exodus from Egypt (see, for example, *Genesis*

Rabbah 40:6). A famine drove Jacob and his family to Egypt. The immoral Pharaonic society enslaved the Israelites and drowned their baby boys. God plagued the Egyptians, thereby redeeming Israel. The Israelites left Egypt with great wealth. In this analogy, Israel is the woman (like Sarah) being snatched from her husband as she becomes enslaved to Pharaoh. Ramban (on Genesis 12:6) develops a typological reading of Genesis and explains how the narratives of the Patriarchs and Matriarchs often foreshadow later national narratives.

There is one uncomfortable aspect of this narrative analogy that can be taken in two different directions. Fearing that the Egyptians would kill him and forcibly take Sarah, Abraham asked Sarah to say that she was his sister so that they would spare Abraham. This element appears parallel to Pharaoh's later decree to drown the Israelite boys and to spare the girls.

Assuming that Abraham's fears were correct, then he had little choice. The Egyptians would take Sarah in either case, so at least this way Abraham would not be killed. Given these dire alternatives, most commentators do not think that the text is passing negative judgment on Abraham. The narrative teaches that there are inexplicable tests and sufferings even for covenantal people bearing divine promises of blessing. Though God miraculously rescued Sarah, Abraham could not depend on that intervention and needed to act in the most prudent manner. Similarly, the Israelite slavery is never explained in the Torah. It does not appear to have resulted from any sin, and is depicted as inexplicable suffering, as was that of Abraham and Sarah.

Ramban stands apart from this majority view. He insists that Abraham should have relied on God's intervention and not told Sarah to say she was his sister. Abraham sinned and lacked faith by going to Egypt instead of trusting that God would end the famine, and then by giving away Sarah. Consequently, God punished his descendants with slavery in Egypt.

Yair Zakovitch accepts Ramban's arguments and adds that Sarah's oppressing her Egyptian servant Hagar in chapter 16 (Hebrew *innui*) parallels the later *innui* that Pharaoh inflicted on the Israelites (Exodus 1:11–12). Pharaoh enslaved the Israelites lest they multiply, as Sarah had tormented Hagar when the latter became pregnant. God heard Hagar's cries (Genesis 16:11), parallel to God's later hearing the outcry of the Israelites (Exodus 3:7). That Joseph was brought to Egypt by Ishmaelites (Hagar's descendants) marks the beginning of this cycle of punishment for the sins of Abraham and Sarah.

The typological reading of the Patriarchal narratives to later Israelite history appears evident in the text. How one interprets these parallels sparks a very important textual and moral debate.

David Berger, "Miracles and the Natural Order in Nahmanides," in *Rabbi Moses Nahmanides (Ramban): Explorations in His Religious and Literary Virtuosity*, ed. Isadore Twersky (Cambridge, MA: Harvard University, Center for Jewish Studies, 1983), pp. 107–128.

Barry Eichler, "On Reading Genesis 12:10–20," in *Tehillah Le-Moshe: Biblical and Judaic Studies in Honor of Moses Greenberg*, ed. Mordechai Cogan, Barry Eichler & Jeffrey Tigay (Eisenbrauns, Indiana: 1997), pp. 23–38.

Yair Zakovitch, "Juxtaposition in the Abraham Cycle," in *Pomegranates and Golden Bells: Studies in Biblical, Jewish, and Near Eastern Ritual, Law, and Literature in Honor of Jacob Milgrom*, ed. David P. Wright, David Noel Freedman & Avi Hurvitz (Winona Lake, IN: Eisenbrauns, 1995), pp. 509–524.

—

LOT

*M*oving with his family from Mesopotamia to Canaan, Abraham took along his nephew Lot. Given that Sarah was 65 years old and barren, Lot was heir apparent to Abraham's possessions and also to the Land of Israel. Soon after they arrived in Canaan, however, there was a famine that drove the family to Egypt. Although Lot was not a major character in that traumatic episode, it no doubt it made a deep impression on him.

After Abraham's family returned to Canaan from Egypt, the shepherds of Abraham and Lot quarreled. Abraham told Lot to go left or right, which means either south or north given that people faced east. As they were facing east, Lot looked forward and saw fertile Sodom: "Lot looked about him and saw how well watered was the whole plain of the Jordan, all of it— this was before the Lord had destroyed Sodom and Gomorrah—all the way to Zoar, like the garden of the Lord, like the land of Egypt" (Genesis 13:10). The Jordan Valley reminded Lot of Egypt and the Garden of Eden, in that there was a regular rise of the Jordan River and therefore that region was not dependent on rainfall the way most of Israel is (cf. Deuteronomy 11:10–12).

Rabbi Elhanan Samet suggests that Lot already made this choice while in Egypt, and simply waited for the right opportunity to separate from Abraham. Lot did not want to wait several generations to inherit the land. Abraham thought that it was simply a fight between shepherds, but Lot used that conflict as a pretext to move to Sodom.

The Torah notes at this point that the people of Sodom were very wicked (13:13). Rashi and Ramban understand this verse as a critique of Lot, who moved to Sodom despite knowing they were evil. Lot had seen the same things Abraham saw in Egypt, and chose a secure Egypt-like climate so that he would not suffer in future famines. Lot wanted to opt out of being Abraham's primary heir, preferring instant gain to a long-term covenantal inheritance.

After Lot departed, God reaffirmed the promise of the land to Abraham's heirs: "And the Lord said to Abram, after Lot had parted from him, Raise your eyes and look out from where you are, to the north and south, to the east and west, for I give all the land that you see to you and your offspring forever" (13:14–15). Rashi notes that God comes to Abraham after Lot leaves to teach that Lot has proven himself unworthy of Abraham's legacy.

Instead of attaining the material security he longed for, Lot instead was captured in a war (chapter 14). Ultimately, Sodom was destroyed because of their wickedness, and Lot had to flee with his family (chapter 19). Although Lot thought that abandoning the covenantal family would help him achieve security, he always remained an outsider in Sodom, and gained nothing.

Rabbi Raymond Harari, "Abraham's Nephew Lot: A Biblical Portrait," *Tradition* 25:1 (Fall 1989), pp. 31–41.

Rabbi Elhanan Samet, *Iyyunim be-Parashot ha-Shavua* (second series) vol. 1 (Hebrew) ed. Ayal Fishler (Ma'aleh Adumim: Ma'aliyot Press, 2004), pp. 39–58.

ABRAHAM'S QUESTIONING GOD (PART ONE)

*G*od repeatedly promises the Land of Canaan to Abraham's progeny. Though silent, Abraham must have wondered who those descendants would be. Sarah was approximately 70 years old and still barren. Lot, Abraham's presumed heir at the outset of the narrative, had distanced himself from the family both physically and spiritually by choosing to settle in the depraved city of Sodom.

When God promises reward to Abraham yet again, Abraham finally verbalizes his concerns:

> Abram said, "O Lord God, what can You give me, seeing that I shall die childless, and the one in charge of my household is Dammesek Eliezer!" Abram said further, "Since You have granted me no offspring, my steward will be my heir." The word of the Lord came to him in reply, "That one shall not be your heir; none but your very own issue shall be your heir." He took him outside and said, "Look toward heaven and count the stars, if you are able to count them." And He added, "So shall your offspring be." And because he put his trust in the Lord, He reckoned it to his merit. (Genesis 15:2–6)

It would appear that Abraham, despairing of having children of his own, already had taken steps to adopt his servant Eliezer. God therefore promises that Abraham himself will father children.

Was it appropriate for Abraham to question God? Adopting the simplest reading of the text, Ralbag and R. David Zvi Hoffmann maintain that it was. R. Hoffmann explains that Abraham essentially was saying, "Give me a child," but respectfully did so indirectly by pointing out that he had no heirs.

Netziv likewise understands Abraham's question as it stands in the text, but he criticizes the Patriarch for doubting God's explicit promises. He therefore interprets Abraham's second statement (in v. 3) as a corrective—Abraham inferred from God's lack of response that he had doubted too much (in v. 2).

Several other exegetes share Netziv's uneasiness with Abraham's questioning an explicit promise from God, but they also find God's favorable response proof that Abraham's statement was religiously justified. Consequently, they offer alternative readings of the text that support their own conceptions of faith, and that also vindicate Abraham's behavior.

Rashi, Radak, and Ramban suggest that Abraham was worried that perhaps he had sinned and thereby forfeited God's promises. In this view, Abraham did not doubt God; he doubted himself. Alternatively, Hizkuni, Abarbanel, Sforno, and Malbim maintain that Abraham fully trusted God's promise of progeny but was concerned that his son would yet be too young to inherit by the time the elderly Abraham expected to die. As a result, Eliezer still would emerge as the guardian of Abraham's estate. God responded that this son would be old enough to inherit by the time Abraham would die. The aforementioned readings do not appear to reflect the plain sense of the text. They emerge from these commentators' concerns about Abraham's faith.

ABRAHAM'S QUESTIONING GOD (PART TWO)

*I*n the following vision, God again promises the Land of Canaan to Abraham's descendants: "Then He said to him, 'I am the Lord who brought you out from Ur of the Chaldeans to assign this land to you as a possession.' And he said, 'O Lord God, how shall I know that I am to possess it?'" (Genesis 15:7–8). Abraham's response is astonishing. Moments ago, he trusted God; what would prompt him to doubt God now?

Shemuel (in *Nedarim* 32a) and several other midrashim maintain that Abraham indeed was requesting further confirmation of God's promises. He was wrong for doing so, and was punished: His descendants were enslaved in Egypt as a result. It appears that Shemuel and the other Sages interpret the relationship between Abraham's question and the subsequent divine promise of slavery in verse 13 as one of cause and effect.

However, most commentators do not perceive divine criticism. On the contrary, God makes a solemn covenant with Abraham in the wake of his second question. Although God accepted Abraham's question, these exegetes cannot believe that Abraham would express doubt at this point. Therefore, they suggest no fewer than five alternate readings of the question "how shall I know that I am to possess it."

(1) Perhaps later generations will sin. How can I be assured that this covenant will be fulfilled regardless of the deeds of those later generations? (2) By what particular merit will I inherit the land? (3) In which generation will my descendants inherit? (4) How will my descendants know that the promise has been fulfilled? (5) The "covenant between the halves" (Genesis 15) occurred some five years *before* the beginning of this chapter; therefore, Abraham did not doubt God immediately after conveying his trust in God; he asked this question considerably earlier.

However, these alternatives are difficult to fit into Abraham's words. The common assumption of these interpretations is that the very possibility of Abraham's questioning in this instance is unacceptable. Shemuel and other midrashim accept the plain sense of Abraham's statement, and sharply criticize the Patriarch. The later exegetes reinterpret Abraham's words so that he does not doubt God's promise so soon after having accepted another one.

Nevertheless, the plain sense of the text appears to vindicate a questioning Abraham. One could argue that Abraham already trusted God's promise that he would have a child. Now, he wanted an absolute sign of confirmation that his descendants would in fact inherit the land. God responds favorably to Abraham's request, causing a divine fire to "pass in between the halves." This is how Rashi (on 15:6, first opinion) and Ibn Ezra (on 15:7) understand Abraham's question. Their reading upholds the plain sense of the text on both ends. Abraham questions (as maintained by Shemuel and other midrashim), and God responds favorably (consistent with the majority of later exegetes).

Instead of viewing Abraham's questioning as a sign of little faith, it appears that Rashi and Ibn Ezra find great religious heroism in Abraham's question. He did not question from doubt; he questioned precisely because of his faith and his truthful relationship with God.

Hayyim Angel, "Learning Faith from the Text, or Text from Faith: The Challenges of Teaching (and Learning) the Avraham Narratives and Commentary," in *Wisdom from All My Teachers: Challenges and Initiatives in Contemporary Torah Education*, ed. Jeffrey Saks & Susan Handelman (Jerusalem: Urim Publications, 2003, ATID), pp. 192–212; reprinted in Angel, *Through an Opaque Lens* (New York: Sephardic Publication Foundation, 2006), pp. 127–154.

SARAH'S TREATMENT OF HAGAR

*S*till barren and 75 years old, Sarah believed that she never would have children. She therefore told Abraham to take Hagar as a concubine. Legally, the child of Hagar would belong to Sarah. Emotionally, however, Hagar's pregnancy created family tensions.

Radak explains that Hagar's pregnancy gave Hagar a sense of superiority. Since she would bear Abraham's child, she believed that she would become Abraham's main wife. Rashi submits that Hagar taunted Sarah that, since she was barren, she must have been rejected by God.

Sarah "treated Hagar harshly" until Hagar fled. Radak and Ramban criticize Sarah for her behavior. Aside from their moral sense, they likely derive their judgment in part from the angel's blessing Hagar with a son in the ensuing narrative. They cite additional elements in the angel's blessing to support their arguments, as well. Other commentators disagree with this negative judgment of Abraham and Sarah.

With the more recent discovery of parallel ancient legal codes, this debate takes on different dimensions. According to the Code of Hammurabi (#146), Sarah could have reasserted slavery on Hagar, since Hagar was attempting to break free on the basis of her pregnancy. In the eleventh century, Rabbenu Hananel suggested this point in explaining the debate between Sarah and Abraham. "Harsh treatment" (*innui*) can refer to the deprivation of one's freedom, as it does, for example, in Exodus 1:11–12 when the Egyptians enslaved the Israelites.

Rabbi Elhanan Samet maintains that Sarah was following this ancient practice, and notes further that the angel told Hagar to submit to Sarah's yoke, that is, to become a slave again as per the law back then. The angel also promised Hagar that her descendants would be free and noble. Therefore, Sarah and Abraham acted in accordance with the moral code of their day, and the Torah supports their behavior.

In contrast, Professor Nehama Leibowitz also quotes the Code of Hammurabi but argues that the Torah distinguishes itself from that Code by being critical of Sarah and sympathetic to Hagar as per the readings of Radak and Ramban.

One can combine the best elements of both lines of interpretation. Since there were legal standards governing this case, Hagar was in breach of the law, and Sarah was acting within her right to reassert her servitude. Therefore, the angel ordered Hagar to return. Rabbi Samet's argument has merit.

At the same time, Professor Leibowitz correctly observes that the Torah offers a sympathetic treatment of Hagar. One may argue that although Abraham and Sarah followed ancient legal conventions, the Torah is critical of those conventions. Sarah was legally correct in her time, but God heard Hagar's suffering and blessed her descendants with freedom (Ibn Ezra).

This complex narrative promotes superior conduct that ultimately would form the basis for a new society after God revealed the Torah to Israel.

Hayyim Angel, "Sarah's Treatment of Hagar (Genesis 16): Morals, Messages, and Mesopotamia," *Jewish Bible Quarterly* 41:4 (2013), pp. 211–218.

Nehama Leibowitz, *Studies in Bereshit (Genesis)*, translated and adapted by Aryeh Newman (Jerusalem: Eliner Library), pp. 153–157.

Rabbi Elhanan Samet, *Iyyunim be-Parashot ha-Shavua* (first series) vol. 1 (Hebrew) ed. Ayal Fishler (Ma'aleh Adumim: Ma'aliyot Press, 2002), pp. 31–51.

CIRCUMCISION

*I*n his book on Genesis, *The Beginning of Wisdom*, Leon Kass reflects on parenthood. Adam initially named the woman *ishah* (woman), a word related to *ish* (man): "Then the man said, 'This one at last is bone of my bones and flesh of my flesh. This one shall be called Woman, for from man was she taken'" (Genesis 2:23). Adam viewed Eve as an extension of himself. This is the first element of love, the selfish dimension. Someone is lovable because he or she seems to be like you.

After the sin and punishment in Eden, Adam realized that he would die one day and therefore needed children to continue to live eternally. He then recognized Eve's role as the mother of all living things, and renamed her for that role, rather than just for being an extension of himself: "The man named his wife Eve (Havvah), because she was the mother of all the living (*em kol hai*)" (Genesis 3:20). Parental love of children lies at the very beginning of sanctification of life in the Torah.

This discussion ties into circumcision. Male circumcision had been widely practiced throughout the ancient Near East as a puberty ritual. This ritual was an initiation into the society of males, ending a young man's primary attachment to his mother and household, to the society of women and children.

By moving circumcision to the eighth day of a child's life, the Torah transforms the initiation rite of young males into a paternal duty regarding his son. The Torah thereby redefines the very meaning of maleness. The Torah celebrates not male potency but rather procreation and perpetuation of the covenant. A week after his son is born, the father must begin this transmission. He must prove the worthiness of his own circumcision by passing the traditions to child. By doing so, the father connects to Abraham's eternal covenant. Society is defined by those who remember God and the covenant.

Leon Kass, *The Beginning of Wisdom: Reading Genesis* (New York: Free Press, 2003), pp. 102–119, 313–315.

Nahum Sarna, *The JPS Torah Commentary: Genesis* (Philadelphia: Jewish Publication Society, 1989), pp. 385–387.

—

THE MEANINGS OF THE NAMES ABRAHAM AND MOSES

*P*rior to the birth of Isaac, Abraham considered Lot, Eliezer, and Ishmael as potential heirs. When announcing the forthcoming birth of Isaac to Abraham, God renamed Abraham to herald a change in his life's course: "You shall no longer be called Abram, but your name shall be Abraham, for I make you the father of a multitude of nations (*av hamon goyim*)" (Genesis 17:5).

How does this new name, Abraham, reflect the meaning *av hamon goyim*? Ibn Ezra suggests that Abraham is an abbreviated form of *ABiR Hamon goyiM*, "mighty one of many nations." Although this proposal is ingenious, it is an unlikely acronym; nor does *abir* (mighty one) fit the meaning of Abraham's name as stated explicitly in Genesis.

Shadal proposes an appealing alternative. In Arabic, *riham* means "multitude." Abraham therefore literally means *av hamon*, the father of a multitude. It is reasonable that the meaning of this name change was fully understood by the recipients of the Torah, as Hebrew and Arabic are cognate Semitic languages.

A related example of the use of other languages to shed light on the Torah pertains to Moses' name: "When the child grew up, she brought him to Pharaoh's daughter, who made him her son. She named him Moses, explaining, 'I drew him out of the water (*ki min ha-mayim meshitihu*)'" (Exodus 2:10).

How would Pharaoh's daughter have known Hebrew? Hizkuni and Abarbanel submit that Moses' mother named him. Most commentators, however, assume that Pharaoh's daughter did the naming, as indicated by the smooth reading of the text.

Even if Pharaoh's daughter knew Hebrew, Moses' name should have been Mashui based on his name's etymology. Ibn Ezra is not bothered by the use of Moses instead of Mashui, since biblical names do not always follow strict rules of grammar.

Knowledge of Egyptian, however, can clarify this matter. Netziv learned that "Moses" was a common form used in ancient Egyptian names, meaning "son"—like Rameses and Thutmosis. Consequently, Netziv suggests that Pharaoh's daughter named him Moses—an Egyptian name—reflecting her adopting him as her son. The Torah then makes a Hebrew wordplay on the name Moses.

In addition to signifying his being drawn from water (*mashui*), Moses' name also foreshadows his future role in "pulling" (*Moshe*) the Israelites out of the Red Sea. Isaiah later appealed to this wordplay, as well: "Then they remembered the ancient days, him, who pulled His people out [of the water] (*Moshe ammo*): 'Where is He who brought them up from the Sea along with the shepherd of His flock? Where is He who put in their midst

His holy spirit, Who made His glorious arm march at the right hand of Moses, Who divided the waters before them to make Himself a name for all time'" (Isaiah 63:11–12). The word "*Moshe*" is used to describe Moses as the one who pulled God's people out of the water.

Commentators regularly demonstrate that knowledge of languages can shed light on wordplays, etymologies, and many other words in the Torah. The broader one's knowledge in these areas, the more effectively one may interpret the Torah.

Hayyim Angel, "When Other Languages May Help Us Understand," *Enayim LeTorah*, Lekh Lekha 5767–2006.

⌐

Vayera

SARAH'S LAUGHTER

hree angels tell Abraham that Sarah would give birth in a year. Sarah overhears the strange visitors, and laughs to herself at the absurdity of this prediction (Genesis 18:12). Sarah's response is understandable. She is barren and 89 years old. She likely does not know that the visitors are angels. Why should she believe them?

Despite these potential justifications for Sarah's behavior, God criticizes Sarah for her laughter: "Then the Lord said to Abraham, 'Why did Sarah laugh, saying, "Shall I in truth bear a child, old as I am?" Is anything too wondrous for the Lord? I will return to you at the time next year, and Sarah shall have a son.' Sarah lied, saying, 'I did not laugh,' for she was frightened. But He replied, 'You did laugh'" (18:13–15).

God's rebuke of Sarah seems surprising. What makes this matter even more complicated is that only a short while earlier, Abraham laughs at the same promise—and he *knew* he was speaking with God. "Abraham threw himself on his face and laughed, as he said to himself, 'Can a child be born to a man a hundred years old, or can Sarah bear a child at ninety?'" (17:17). God does not rebuke Abraham. Why?

Several commentators observe that "laughter" can include both joy and incredulity. Since God did not rebuke Abraham, Abraham must have laughed exclusively out of joy, completely believing God's promise. Sarah, in contrast, must have laughed from doubt and therefore received a divine reprimand.

Other commentators reject this interpretation, since Abraham used nearly the same words as Sarah, and God reassured him afterward. Rabbi Saadiah Gaon and several later commentators suggest that by confronting Abraham about Sarah, God was indirectly rebuking Abraham also. God expected Abraham to realize that he too had laughed at God's promise, and should have believed that God would keep His word.

In the end, Sarah has the last laugh. After Isaac was born, Sarah joyously proclaims: "'God has brought me laughter; everyone who hears will laugh with me.' And she added, 'Who would have said to Abraham that Sarah would suckle children! Yet I have borne a son in his old age'" (21:6–7). Abraham learns from God's subtle rebuke, never questioning God's abilities again, and growing ever stronger in his faith.

SODOM

*J*ewish tradition focuses on Sodom's extreme lack of hospitality as the root of its evils. The Talmud relates that "The people of Sodom were haughty on account of the good which God had lavished upon them. . . . They said: Since bread comes out of our earth, and it has the dust of gold, why should we be bothered by wayfarers, who come to us only to deplete our wealth" (*Sanhedrin* 109a–109b).

This rabbinic characterization is rooted in biblical texts. "Lot looked in front of him and saw how well watered was the whole plain of the Jordan, all of it—this was before the Lord had destroyed Sodom and Gomorrah—all the way to Zoar, like the garden of the Lord, like the land of Egypt" (Genesis 13:10). Sodom is likened to the Garden of Eden, having all its physical needs provided with the rising of the Jordan River.

Similarly, the prophet Ezekiel described how the Jews of his day were even worse than Sodom: "Only this was the sin of your sister Sodom: arrogance! She and her daughters had plenty of bread and untroubled tranquility; yet she did not support the poor and the needy" (Ezekiel 16:49).

Following the rabbinic lead, Ramban explains that the Sodomites' attack against Lot's angelic visitors reflects a depraved means of treating visitors to deter others from ever entering their town.

The Sages teach that "[There are] four types of character: One that says, 'Mine is mine, and yours is yours'; this is average. Some say this is a Sodom type. [One that says,] 'Mine is yours and yours is mine' is unlearned; [One that says] 'mine is yours and yours is yours' is pious; and [one that says] 'Mine is mine and yours is mine' is wicked" (Mishnah *Avot* 5:10).

By expressing a view that "Mine is mine, and yours is yours" is possibly like Sodom, this Mishnah teaches the value of sharing as a basic aspect of human decency rather than being something above average. The Jewish legal tradition developed the concept of *kofin al middat Sodom*, we compel people not to act in the manner of Sodom. If someone asks you a favor and it does not hurt you, you must do it or a court can compel you to do that favor lest you resemble a Sodomite who was inhospitable by not sharing.

Returning to the Genesis narrative, chapters 18–19 contrast Abraham as the consummate host and then Sodom at his antithesis. Being part of a community includes a responsibility to be hospitable. We must open our tents as did Abraham.

—

ISHMAEL AND THE PHILISTINES

After Isaac's birth, Sarah sees Ishmael and feels that Isaac's sole inheritance is threatened: "Cast out that slave-woman and her son, for the son of that slave shall not share in the inheritance with my son Isaac" (Genesis 21:9).

Abraham is crushed. How can he banish his beloved son Ishmael? For the first time, he refuses Sarah. However, God sides with Sarah (21:12–13). An angel saves Ishmael, and he goes on to found a great nation.

Despite their painful separation, Ishmael returns when Abraham dies, faithfully remaining a son to the Patriarch more than 70 years after being banished (25:9). This sympathetic picture of Ishmael was sustained throughout the biblical period. Israel generally enjoyed a peaceful relationship with the Ishmaelites.

Another group also plays a role in the Patriarchal narratives, namely, the Philistines. Abimelech requests a treaty with the wealthy Abraham (chapter 21). Abraham agrees to the treaty, but rebukes Abimelech for allowing his servants to steal Abraham's well. Abimelech responds, "I do not know who did this; you did not tell me, nor have I heard of it until today" (21:26). Never does he say, "I am sorry, and as king, I will make sure this never happens again." Abraham gives sheep to Abimelech as part of the treaty, whereas the Philistine king gives Abraham nothing in return.

Only a few years later, Isaac returns to the land of the Philistines—his family's alleged partner in peace—during a famine. Isaac digs wells only for Philistine raiders to seize them by force and to drive him away. Finally, Isaac settles at one well, and the Philistines leave him alone long enough for Isaac to prosper. Sensing Isaac's success, Abimelech again comes to make a peace treaty. Once again, the Philistines deny any wrongdoing, and Isaac pays for the meal (26:27–30).

The Torah's portrait of the Philistines in the Patriarchs' time is consistent throughout biblical history. In the period of the Judges, the Philistines terrorized farmers. Samson, Samuel, and King Saul had some limited success against these raids, but were not strong enough to eliminate them. Once king, David defeated the Philistine armies so that they no longer raided. Whenever Israel's kingdom became weaker, the Philistines returned to plundering and attacking.

There was never a resolution to the Israelite-Philistine crisis. The wars stopped only when the Israelites had an army strong enough to keep the Philistines in check. When they did not, the Philistines attacked and never respected their own treaties. The final resolution of the conflict came when the Babylonian armies swept through the region, devastating and exiling both nations.

The juxtaposition between the Ishmaelites and Philistines reflects two types of Israel's neighbors: peace-loving people who are treated as part of the family, and deceptive thieves who are unreliable in treaties as they inflict harm on Israel.

THE BINDING OF ISAAC (PART ONE)

*R*abbi Joseph ibn Caspi notes that many of Israel's neighbors practiced child-sacrifice, including Phoenicians, Ammonites, Moabites, Egyptians, and Canaanites. The Torah outlawed child-sacrifice as a capital offense (Leviticus 18:21; 20:2–5). Rabbi Samuel David Luzzatto suggests that this legislation was in part an anti-pagan polemic, demonstrating that love of God does not involve the sacrifice of one's child.

In light of the ancient setting, one may argue that the primary test of Abraham was not the killing *per se*; child-sacrifice was a real option for Abraham until God categorically ruled it out. The test had more to do with Abraham's heirs. After Abraham sifted through several potential heirs—Lot, Eliezer, and Ishmael—God informed him that Isaac would be his heir. When God commanded Abraham to sacrifice Isaac, all of the divine promises were in jeopardy.

On a literary level, the Binding of Isaac does not occur in a vacuum. Curt Leviant notes several parallels between the banishment of Ishmael in chapter 21 and the Binding of Isaac in chapter 22. In both narratives, Abraham wakes up early in the morning to follow God's command. During the Binding of Isaac, father and son go to the place where there was a mortal threat to the son. Hagar and Ishmael achieve the same effect as a mother-son team. In both cases, an angel appears at the last minute to save the sons. Both narratives conclude with blessings of large nations. Clearly, the Torah wanted readers to perceive a strong connection between the two episodes, and to highlight Abraham's love of both Ishmael and Isaac. When Abraham dies, Ishmael returns and joins Isaac in burying their father, showing the powerful connection between them, even so many years later.

Rabbi Chanoch Waxman derives a different lesson from the juxtaposition of these stories. The narrative focuses on Hagar and Ishmael in the desert. This focus is intended to contrast with Abraham and Isaac in the Binding of Isaac narrative.

Isaac was aware that something was going on, and asked about the absence of a lamb. No dialogue ensues; only silent, courageous walking together. In contrast, when Hagar is banished, she wanders aimlessly, endangering her son Ishmael. When she despairs, she casts him away and breaks down crying. Ishmael, himself at least 16 years old, also is crying. Abraham and Isaac share a common, shocking purpose courageously. Hagar and Ishmael despair, act passively, and cry apart from one another. Rabbi Samson Raphael Hirsch (nineteenth-century Germany) remarks that Hagar did not exhibit the traits of a "Jewish mother." She left her crying son alone to starve because she did not want to face him.

Abraham and Isaac may have been baffled by the divine command, but this experience brought them together. This is exemplary faith and greatness, teaching how to react in crisis. Whereas the reaction of Hagar and Ishmael represents one response to crisis—becoming more divisive, panicking, and despairing—Abraham and Isaac courageously marched onward together, generating a deep and eternal unity.

Curt Leviant, "Ishmael and Hagar in the Wilderness: A Parallel *Akedah*," *Midstream* 43:8 (1997), pp. 17–19.

Rabbi Chanoch Waxman, "But My Covenant I will Establish with Yitzchak," Yeshivat Har Etzion Virtual Beit Midrash, Vayera 5762, at http://www.vbm-torah.org/parsha.62/04vayeira.htm.

—

THE BINDING OF ISAAC (PART TWO)

abbi Jonathan Sacks suggests that a primary message of the Binding of Isaac is that children are not to be taken for granted. Similarly, Jews never should take anything of value for granted, including freedom. In this manner God and Israel can construct a society where everyone may act freely (*A Letter in the Scroll*, 2000, pp. 113–114). Rabbi Joseph Soloveitchik derives a similar lesson from the brief description of Nahor's family immediately after the Binding of Isaac. Abraham had to wait a lifetime to have Isaac, and then was ordered to sacrifice him. Nahor never had to undergo sacrifice—and he had 12 sons without any struggle. Abraham's test is one of farsightedness, looking beyond contradictions and disappointments of the present (*Rosh HaShanah Machzor*, 2007, pp. 415–417).

After God informs Abraham about the impending destruction of Sodom, Abraham pleads courageously on behalf of the wicked city (Genesis 18:23–33). In fact, what is surprising is Abraham's *silence* when God commands the banishment of Ishmael (Genesis 21:12–14) and the sacrifice of Isaac (Genesis 22:1–3). How could Abraham stand idly by, and not challenge God when it comes to his two beloved sons?

By considering the Abraham narratives as a whole, we may resolve this dilemma. Abraham's actions may be divided into three general categories: (1) responses to direct commands from God; (2) responses to promises or other information from God; and (3) responses to situations during which God does not communicate directly with Abraham.

Whenever God commands an action, Abraham obeys without as much as a word of protest or questioning. When Abraham received promises or other information from God, Abraham praises God when gratitude is in order, and he questions or challenges God when he deems it appropriate. Abraham always follows God's commandments without questioning, but he reserves the right to challenge any information or promises. Therefore, Abraham's silence when following God's commandments to banish Ishmael and to sacrifice Isaac is to be expected. And so are Abraham's concerns about God's promises of progeny or information about the destruction of Sodom.

Richard Elliott Friedman describes several important parallels between the Binding of Isaac and the Revelation at Sinai. Moses told the people to sit here until we come back. These are the same words Abraham told his servants. Both accounts describe viewing *me-rahok*, from a distance. Both use the term *le-hishtahavot* for their prostrating themselves. Both Moses and Abraham go up a mountain. Abraham receives divine praise and reward for going through with the Binding of Isaac. At Sinai the nation similarly pledges obedience to God. The merit of Abraham remains the basis of the nation's acceptance of God's covenant. Abraham's obedience is the model to emulate.

Hayyim Angel, "Learning Faith from the Text, or Text from Faith: The Challenges of Teaching (and Learning) the Avraham Narratives and Commentary," in *Wisdom From All My Teachers: Challenges and Initiatives in Contemporary Torah Education*, ed. Jeffrey Saks & Susan Handelman (Jerusalem: Urim Publications, 2003), pp. 192–212; reprinted in Angel, *Through an Opaque Lens* (New York: Sephardic Publication Foundation, 2006), pp. 127–154.

Richard Elliott Friedman, *Commentary on the Torah* (San Francisco: Harper, 2003), pp. 252–253.

Hayyei Sarah

REBECCA'S FIRST ENCOUNTER WITH ISAAC

*I*n only seven verses (Genesis 24:61–67), the Torah describes the meeting of Rebecca and Isaac. Rebecca rides, looks, falls, and enters the tent of Isaac's mother, Sarah. "Raising her eyes, Rebecca saw Isaac. She alighted from the camel (*va-tippol me-al ha-gamal*) and said to the servant, 'Who is that man walking in the field toward us?' And the servant said, 'That is my master.' So she took her veil and covered herself" (24:64–65).

Many commentators understand the Hebrew *va-tippol* to mean that she alighted from her camel. However, the term *va-tippol* also can mean "she fell," and Netziv explains that Rebecca literally fell off the camel. Isaac had been praying. The spiritual grandeur of Isaac's personality at that moment was so overwhelming, that Rebecca was unable to maintain her equilibrium. She was intimidated and felt unworthy to marry him.

With this analysis, Netziv explains the nature of the subsequent relationship between Rebecca and Isaac, and why it is different from those of Abraham-Sarah and Jacob-Rachel. Rebecca is not a meek or passive person. She chooses to uproot herself from her family to marry an unknown husband. When she has problems in pregnancy, she herself goes to inquire of God (25:22), rather than complain to her husband as Rachel did (30:1).

Most importantly, when she thinks her husband is making a mistake in choosing Esau, she manipulates his blindness to ensure that her choice is preferred. Why does she not simply tell Isaac directly that he was wrong?

Netziv explains that first impressions are powerful. After Rebecca met Isaac the way she did, she had a difficult time confronting him directly. It is not that she accepted that "Isaac knows best." On the contrary, she is sure that she knows better than he.

When addressing him directly, however, Rebecca returns to the young girl who catches sight of her husband-to-be with the presence of God resting on him. Hence, she has to work behind his back, not hesitating to manipulate him, but unable to confront him directly.

Rabbi Yaacov Steinman, "Camel-flage," Yeshivat Har Etzion Virtual Beit Midrash, Hayyei Sarah 5765, at http://www.vbm-torah.org/parsha.61/05chayei.htm.

THE CHILDREN OF KETURAH

*R*abbi David Bigman quotes a midrash (*Genesis Rabbah* 61:3) that plays off of Kohelet 11:6: "Sow your seed in the morning, and don't hold back your hand in the evening, since you don't know which is going to succeed, the one or the other, or if both are equally good."

The Sages of the midrash make a series of conventional analogies. Rabbi Eliezer reads the verse according to its literal sense. A farmer should plant crops at different times in the season since he does not know which crops will succeed.

Rabbi Yehoshua interprets the morning and evening of the verse as literal but explains that one should give charity in the morning and evening since one does not know which ultimately will be more helpful.

Rabbi Yishmael reads the entire verse as allegorical. One should learn Torah when one is young and old, since we do not know what will impact on us more. In a similar vein, Rabbi Akiva explains that one should teach students when one is young and old, since the teacher does not know who will succeed him or her.

One Sage offers a more surprising interpretation. Rabbi Dostai suggests that if one had children when young, one still should have more children in old age since we do not know which will succeed the parents. From whom do we learn this—from Abraham, who took Keturah in his old age and had more children (Genesis, chapter 25).

This interpretation is remarkable. In the Torah, God clearly chooses Isaac. Although the Akedah temporarily threatens Isaac's future, it is clear afterward that he is Abraham's sole heir. When Abraham subsequently marries Keturah and fathers six more sons, he gives them gifts and sends them away since he knows they will not be his heirs. In the midrash, however, Rabbi Dostai suggests that Abraham fathered these children since he still was unsure about the future success of Isaac! He could not be confident in the fulfillment of a divine promise.

This midrashic line ties into a different midrash where God rebukes Moses for lacking faith when he complained after Pharaoh deprived Israel of straw (Exodus, chapter 5). In the midrash, God responded that He had made all sorts of promises to the Patriarchs that were unfulfilled, but they never questioned God. In contrast, Moses complained after only one setback (*Sanhedrin* 111a; *Exodus Rabbah* 6:4).

This midrash takes for granted that God promised things to the Patriarchs that went unfulfilled. Moses failed in faith because he expected certainty in God's promises. The Patriarchs understood that even with explicit divine promises, there are unexplained challenges and setbacks. We trust in God but do not always understand how everything works.

As Rabbi Bigman concludes, uncertainty invests the present with immense significance and we can focus all our energies into it rather than assuming that past will automatically continue into present.

Rabbi David Bigman, *The Fire and the Cloud* (Jerusalem: Gefen, 2011), pp. 3–5.

Toledot

Isaac's Unique Character

A remarkable talmudic passage (*Shabbat* 89b) gives us insight into Isaac's personality: "In the future God will say to Abraham, 'Your children have sinned.' Abraham shall answer Him, 'God, let them be wiped out for the sanctification of Your Name.'" God poses the same challenge to Jacob, who comes up with the same response. God expresses disappointment in both Abraham and Jacob.

God then turns to Isaac. Isaac answers that the average human life expectancy is 70 years. The first 20 years do not count, as people are not held accountable for their actions until that age. Of the remaining 50 years, half are spent sleeping, so only 25 years remain where one may sin. Subtract 12 and a half years for praying, eating, and nature's calls, [and] there remain only 12 and a half years. If You will bear sins for those 12 and a half years, good; if not, let us split the difference. And should You say, they must all be upon me, I offered myself up before You [as a sacrifice]! I can bear it.

What distinguishes Isaac that led the Sages to portray him as an unwavering advocate for future generations? One aspect of his personality explicitly noted is his vulnerability. Isaac had a knife held to his throat. He walked away from that experience transformed.

When Isaac was 40, Abraham's servant returned with Rebecca. The two saw Isaac off in the distance, and he had gone *la-su'ah ba-sadeh*, to meditate in the field (Genesis 24:63). Isaac set aside time alone to clear his mind, unite with God, pray, and develop his true identity.

Isaac also is the first person in the Torah about whom it is said that he loved his wife (Genesis 24:67). This does not suggest that others did not love their wives, but it is significant when the Torah mentions a detail of this nature. The only previous reference to love in the Torah is when God tells Abraham to take his son, whom he loves, Isaac, as a sacrifice (Genesis 22:2). Isaac's vulnerability, introspection and prayer, and his ability to love appear to be linked.

Another significant element of Isaac's personality is his name. He was named Isaac because Abraham and Sarah had laughed when God informed them that they would have a son (Genesis 17:17; 18:12; 21:6), and the Hebrew name Isaac derives from that root. The ability to laugh helps us gain perspective no matter how imperfect the world might be.

Isaac is also famed for his ability to continue Abraham's legacy and transmitting it to the next generation. Abraham was the trailblazer, but it was Isaac who made it possible to continue Abraham's vision. If Isaac walked away after Abraham tied him to the altar, our peoplehood would have ended. In the final analysis, Isaac's unique personality enabled him to advocate on Israel's behalf like nobody else could.

JACOB'S VOICE AND ESAU'S HANDS

Rabbi Yoel Bin-Nun discusses how Isaac's passivity differentiates him from Abraham and Jacob. Isaac was bound to an altar. Others worked to find a wife for him. He emulated Abraham in nearly all of his actions. He was regularly manipulated by Philistines and his own family members.

Abraham and Jacob were shepherd-merchants, whereas Isaac was a farmer. Although Isaac is parallel to Abraham in many ways, there is one key difference. When famine struck, God ordered Isaac to remain in the Land of Israel rather than going down to Egypt as Abraham had done (and as Jacob and his family later would do). As a farmer, Isaac was tied to the land and was the only Patriarch never to leave it. Isaac dug wells and farmed. His success in the land aroused the Philistines' jealousy and even hatred. They persecuted him and drove him from well to well.

When merchants or shepherds confront famines, persecutions, or other dangers, they are mobile. Farmers are the most vulnerable, since leaving their land means abandoning their livelihood and starting all over again. The Philistine persecutions taught Isaac that he needed a strong heir to succeed him, since he could not run away from the Promised Land.

In the following generation, Jacob became a shepherd, while Esau became a hunter. Isaac therefore loved Esau, the heir who could provide security to the fledgling nation. To be sure, Esau was a boor, hardly worthy of the spiritual blessings of Abraham's family. He married Canaanite women, showing an utter lack of concern for the core values of the family. Nonetheless, Isaac was willing to bless Esau because of his physical strength.

Rabbi Bin-Nun explains that when Jacob dressed as Esau and tricked Isaac, Isaac for the first time realized that Jacob was tougher than he had appeared. Perhaps he would be able to stand up for himself and the future nation after all. "The voice is the voice of Jacob, yet the hands are the hands of Esau" (Genesis 27:22). This exclamation reflected Isaac's realization of the ideal balance in a leader: the moral, gentle soul of Jacob, coupled with the physical strength and cunning of Esau necessary to feed and protect the nation.

Jacob needed to learn how to stay in the land. His conflict with Esau initially drove him to flee. When God commanded him to return to the land years later, Esau confronted him. Jacob was afraid, sent Esau gifts, and tried to avoid confrontation. God sent an angel to wrestle with Jacob, teaching him that there are times one must stay and fight. Once Jacob prevailed, God renamed him Israel.

Fighting is against Jacob's nature. God taught him that there are times when one needs the hands of Esau. At the same time, Jacob's moral voice always must be present and central.

Rabbi Yoel Bin-Nun, *Pirkei ha-Avot: Iyyunim be-Parshiyot ha-Avot be-Sefer Bereshit* (Hebrew) (Alon Shevut: Tevunot, 2003), pp. 119–164.

—

Vayetzei

CONSEQUENCES OF DECEPTION

*G*od repeatedly makes promises to protect Jacob, yet Jacob remains terrified. Right after Jacob's lofty vision of the angels on the ladder and God's assurance of protection, Jacob wakes up and says, "If God remains with me, if He protects me on this journey that I am making, and gives me bread to eat and clothing to wear, and if I return safe to my father's house—the Lord shall be my God" (Genesis 28:20–21).

Years later, despite additional divine assurances for his return to Israel, Jacob is terror-stricken upon learning that Esau is approaching. The Talmud asks: Given God's promises of protection, why was Jacob afraid? It answers: He worried that his sins may have undermined God's promises (*Berakhot* 4a).

For the rest of his life, Jacob suffered from his deception of Isaac. Professors Nehama Leibowitz and David Berger trace biblical and rabbinic criticisms of the deception, and its impact on Jacob: (1) Laban deceived him with Leah. (2) Laban deceived him with wages. (3) Jacob's sons deceived him during their sale of Joseph. (4) Joseph pretended not to recognize his brothers, leading to further anguish for Jacob and his sons.

On the psychological plane, Jacob could not even trust in God's promises. He had lost his self-confidence as a result of his past, and the deception haunted him for the rest of his life. He was unable to fully trust anyone, not even God.

When he returned to the Promised Land, Jacob finally had to confront his past. Esau came to greet him after more than 20 years of separation. God forced him to confront the deception directly by sending an angel. After Jacob defeated the angel, God changed his name from Jacob (crookedness, *'-k-b*) to Israel (straightness, *y-sh-r*). This name change signaled the beginning of a healing process through which Jacob could face his past forthrightly, and build a more honorable future for himself and his nation.

Nehama Leibowitz, *Studies in Bereshit (Genesis)*, translated and adapted by Aryeh Newman (Jerusalem: Eliner Library), pp. 264–274.

David Berger, "On the Morality of the Patriarchs in Jewish Polemic and Exegesis," in *Modern Scholarship in the Study of Torah: Contributions and Limitations*, ed. Shalom Carmy (New Jersey: Jason Aronson Inc., 1996), pp. 131–146.

LEAH'S EYES

*T*he Torah's introduction of Rachel and Leah contains the roots of their conflict: "Leah had weak (or soft) eyes; Rachel was shapely and beautiful" (29:17). Clearly, Rachel was the better looking of the two sisters; but why mention Leah's eyes?

From ancient times, eyes have represented a window into one's soul. Leah may not have been as physically attractive as Rachel, but she had a deep personality. The Torah gives Leah a forum to express her passions toward Jacob when she names her children. Reuben: "The Lord has seen my affliction; it also means: Now my husband will love me." Simeon: "The Lord heard that I was unloved and has given me this one also." Levi: "This time my husband will become attached to me" (29:31–34).

It took Jacob a lifetime to discover Leah's inner beauty. Following Rachel's death, Jacob favored Rachel's firstborn Joseph. After the brothers sold Joseph and Jacob thought Joseph was dead, Jacob preferred Benjamin, the last vestige of Rachel's line.

When Jacob saw Judah's willingness to sacrifice his own life for Benjamin, however, Jacob realized Judah's greatness. Judah had lost much by his father's favoring Rachel's children, but he had the courage and love to defend his brother.

On his deathbed, Jacob blessed Joseph, but he gave the kingdom to Judah (49:10). The quiet strength and patience of Leah finally won out over the beauty of Rachel. Strikingly, Jacob was buried next to Leah. Although Rachel enjoyed her husband's love throughout her lifetime, Jacob lies alongside Leah eternally.

Despite Jacob's promise of kingship to Judah, the first king of Israel hailed from the Tribe of Benjamin. King Saul, descended from Rachel, is described as tall and handsome (I Samuel 9:2). When Saul stood before the people, they saw his good looks and stature, and accepted him as king (10:23–24). However, it was not long before he demonstrated that he was unfit for kingship and was rejected.

When Samuel searched for a successor, he immediately favored the stately Eliab. God responded, "For not as man sees [does the Lord see]; man sees only what is visible, but the Lord sees into the heart" (I Samuel 16:7). David, from the Tribe of Judah, then appeared: "He was ruddy-cheeked, bright-eyed, and handsome" (16:12). His eyes were a defining feature, like his ancestor Leah. God chose him, and his dynasty endured through the entire biblical period and beyond.

The rabbis characterized the messianic age with the same pattern. First a Messiah will come from the House of Joseph, but he will fail. Then the permanent redemption will come from the House of David (*Sukkah* 52a–b).

It took Jacob a lifetime to realize the greatness of Leah and her children. Later Jewish history repeated the mistake. The people accepted Saul because he was attractive. Even the messianic age will begin with illusory hopes in Joseph. People almost invariably recognize physical beauty first, but eternity will always be found in the depth of Leah's eyes.

—

Vayishlah

JACOB AND ANGELS

*G*enesis depicts a number of angels, including those who encounter Hagar, Abraham, and Lot. The angels that Jacob encounters appear to shed light on his inner character. After obtaining the birthright through deception, Jacob flees home, fearing Esau's retribution. Jacob dreams of angels ascending and descending on a ladder, but they play no obvious role in the dream. Until now, angels always had been prominent in the narratives where they appear. Rashi explains that as Jacob's protective angels in Canaan were going up, different angels were descending to protect Jacob while away from his homeland.

Jacob does not feel safe, though, bargaining with God for protection when he returns to the waking state. Perhaps the angels have a dual-symbolism. God shows Jacob angels as a sign of protection, but they also reflect Jacob's conflicted feelings over the deceptions he has perpetrated and experienced.

Some 20 years later, as he returns to Israel from Laban, Jacob again encounters angels. "Jacob went on his way, and angels of God encountered him. When he saw them, Jacob said, 'This is God's camp.' So he named that place Mahanaim" (32:2–3). Once again, Rashi assumes that these angels arrived to protect him.

Despite this sign of protection, Jacob panics when he learns Esau is approaching, he sends his brother camps (*mahanot*) of gifts after dispatching messengers (*malakhim*) to Esau (32:4–9). The words used are the same as in the previous passage. Jacob's camps are divided exactly like the camps of angels he encountered.

The climactic angelic encounter for Jacob was his wrestling with an angel. One midrash suggests that it was Esau's guardian angel (*Genesis Rabbah* 77:3). Within this interpretation, the struggle with the angel represents Jacob's conflict with his brother. By prevailing over Esau's guardian angel, Jacob obtains forgiveness and blessing from Esau.

A second midrashic opinion suggests that the angel looked like a shepherd (*Genesis Rabbah* 77:2). It appears that this is a reference to Jacob's inner turmoil, that is, he was wrestling with himself. Jacob ultimately needs to confront his past if he wants to move beyond his deception of Isaac.

Only many years later does Jacob finally internalize that God had protected him all along. When blessing Joseph's sons Manasseh and Ephraim, he says, "The Angel who has redeemed me from all harm—bless the lads" (Genesis 48:16).

Jacob's inner conflicts from deceiving his father affected the way he perceived God and angels. After struggling throughout his life, he realized that God always had protected him and blessed his grandchildren that they should merit the same angelic protection.

———

ESAU'S DESCENDANTS

After Jacob's encounter with Laban, his subsequent reunion with Esau, and his return to Canaan, the Torah lists the descendants of Esau. In chapter 36, verses 1–19 trace Esau's children and family leaders; verses 20–30 record the tribal heads of the Horites—the original inhabitants of Seir; and verses 31–43 record the eight Edomite kings who ruled before the nation of Israel had its first king.

Several midrashim and later commentators wonder why the Torah includes this list. Some observe that a few of the marriages were incestuous. This chapter demonstrates how immoral Esau's family had become (*Tanhuma Vayeshev*; *Genesis Rabbah* 82; Rashi; Abarbanel).

Sforno (v. 31) observes that none of the kings of Edom were native members of Esau's family. Esau did not produce anyone worthy of leading his family. Ramban adds that there were no dynasties among these kings, demonstrating their political instability and unworthiness.

In a different vein, Radak asserts that this passage was written in Isaac's honor. Since Isaac was righteous, the Torah wanted to show that even Esau produced a prestigious family. Alternatively, Rambam (*Guide for the Perplexed* III:50) suggests that this passage has halakhic ramifications. The Torah commands the Israelites to eliminate Amalek (Deuteronomy 25:17–19), but at the same time forbids them from harassing the other families of Edom (Deuteronomy 2:2–8). Esau's lineage specifies the exact family lines so that the Israelites would know whom to kill and whom to spare.

Following midrashic lines, Rashi (37:1) explains the contrast between the lackluster account of Esau's descendants followed immediately by a lengthy account of Jacob's family history. Even though the Torah records Esau's generations, their significance is eclipsed by the longer record of the family that would achieve lasting greatness—that of Jacob.

Hayyim Angel, "*Elleh Toledot*: A Study of the Genealogies in the Book of Genesis," in *Haham Gaon Memorial Volume*, ed. Marc D. Angel (Brooklyn: Sefer Hermon Press, 1997), pp. 163–182; reprinted in Angel, *Through an Opaque Lens* (New York: Sephardic Publication Foundation, 2006), pp. 111–126.

~

Vayeshev

JOSEPH'S DREAMS (PART ONE)

*W*ere Joseph's dreams prophetic? Several commentators assume that they were. However, when we compare Joseph's pair of dreams to the following pairs of dreams later in the Joseph narratives, there are important differences. Each of the dreams of the ministers and of Pharaoh merits an interpretation by Joseph that explains every detail. Joseph's dreams are given no detailed, authoritative solution throughout the story. The Torah relates the full realization of the dreams of the ministers and Pharaoh (40:22, 41:54). With regard to Joseph's dreams, though, there is no explicit testimony as to whether or how they were realized. Joseph emphasizes God's role when interpreting the others' dreams (40:8; 41:16, 25, 28, 32, 38, 39), but God's name is not mentioned in connection with Joseph's own dreams.

Rabbi Elhanan Samet suggests that the Torah may be hinting that the dreams were not properly understood at first. The first dream expresses the brothers' economic dependence on Joseph during the years of famine and during their stay in Goshen. Does the brothers' interpretation of this dream—"Will you then rule over us?"—suffice? It seems that it satisfied Joseph, but he later would realize: "No; rather, the day will come when 'I will provide sustenance for you and your children'" (50:21).

In Joseph's second dream, Joseph is not represented by a symbol. The family is symbolized by the celestial bodies, and those bow to Joseph. It seems that the lights symbolize Jacob's household as the foundation of the chosen nation. This nation is chosen to shed light to the world. Joseph prepares for the exile by having them live apart from the Egyptians so that they may preserve their distinctive identity (46:34).

The meaning of Joseph's dreams, as he understood them, was convenient for the youthful Joseph, for they suited his position in his father's house. The coat that Jacob made for him was a royal garment, and his dreams appeared to him a direct continuation of the same idea.

Over time, Joseph learned that dreams sent from Heaven do not come just to compliment a person and foretell a personal future. Rather, they foretell the future in order that the person prepare himself for a mission that he will have to undertake. Joseph mentions God only in retrospective: "God has sent me ahead of you to ensure your survival on earth, and to save your lives in an extraordinary deliverance" (45:7). "Although you intended me harm, God intended it for good, so as to bring about the present result—the survival of many people. And so, fear not. I will sustain you and your children" (50:19–21).

Rabbi Elhanan Samet, *Iyyunim be-Parashot ha-Shavua* (first series) vol. 1 (Hebrew) ed. Ayal Fishler (Ma'aleh Adumim: Ma'aliyot Press, 2002), pp. 105–113.

JOSEPH'S DREAMS (PART TWO)

Spanning from chapters 37–50, the story of Joseph is the longest continuous narrative in the Torah. God never speaks to Joseph, though He speaks to many people in Genesis, including Hagar, Lot, Abimelech, and Laban. The only time God speaks in the Joseph narrative is when He tells Jacob that it is safe to go to Egypt (Genesis 46:2–4).

Although he never receives prophetic revelation, Joseph is conscious of God's presence and supervision, interpreting the brothers' sale of him to Egypt as divine intervention: "God has sent me ahead of you to ensure your survival on earth, and to save your lives in an extraordinary deliverance" (45:7). "Have no fear! Am I a substitute for God? Besides, although you intended me harm, God intended it for good, so as to bring about the present result—the survival of many people. And so, fear not. I will sustain you and your children" (50:19–21).

As a dream interpreter, Joseph stresses that God is giving the interpretations: "Surely God can interpret! Tell me [your dreams]" (40:8). "Not I! God will see to Pharaoh's welfare" (41:15–16). Even Pharaoh acknowledges Joseph's having the spirit of God: "And Pharaoh said to his courtiers, 'Could we find another like him, a man in whom is the spirit of God?'" (41:38–39).

Some commentators assume that Joseph received some form of divine inspiration to aid his dream interpretation, but there is no indication of this in the text. Perhaps Joseph views himself as an interpreter of the divine will. He exemplifies humility, as he does not want to be viewed as a wise man and never takes credit for his interpretations.

There is something dangerous about interpreting personal events as divine signs, as this does not always lead to higher morality or spirituality. It can lead to arrogance and the shirking of personal responsibility.

Joseph represents an ideal model of bringing God into one's life. He humbly attributes his talents to God, and lives with exemplary morality. Without prophecy, Joseph sees Godliness everywhere and consequently lives a better life and improves his society. He does not become passive, nor does he become arrogant from his successes. He has the integrity to avoid Mrs. Potiphar, and later breaks generations of family conflicts by forgiving his brothers for selling him into slavery.

Joseph, then, is the great character in Genesis whose relationship with God is most similar to ours. We also are not prophets but are asked to bring God into every aspect of our lives.

Hayyim Angel, "Joseph's Bones: *Peshat, Derash,* and in Between," *Intersession Reader 2013* (New York: Tebah, 2013), pp. 83–94.

JUDAH AND TAMAR

*T*here are many heroes and villains in the Torah. Rabbi Mordechai Breuer observes that the story of Judah and Tamar describes a different typology: people who appear to be upright citizens but whose public images do not match their private actions.

After the sale of Joseph, Judah moves away from his family, gets married, and has three sons. Years later, he finds a wife, Tamar, for his first-born, Er. Er dies childless, setting up a levirate marriage wherein Onan, the second son, should marry Tamar and prodcue a child who legally would be considered Er's successor. Onan married Tamar, so the public perceived him to be an honorable brother. However, his bedroom manner demonstrated that he had no intention of fathering a child with Tamar.

After Onan dies, Judah assures Tamar that he will fulfill the law with his son Shelah, but he is yet too young. The Torah tells us that Judah was putting her off, and Tamar eventually figures this out. While wronging Tamar, Judah maintains his noble public image by assuring Tamar that she would marry Shelah.

Tamar needed to act to have children on Er's behalf. Disguising herself as a harlot, she seduces Judah and becomes pregnant (but not before acquiring his identifying seal and staff as a pledge of payment). Later, Judah finds out that Tamar is pregnant, and orders that she be burned.

Why was Judah prepared to mete out such extreme punishment? Ramban suggests that Judah was a prominent member of his community, and Tamar's pregnancy was humiliating to him. He was imposing extra-legal punishment, rather than a legal sentence. One also may posit that Judah unconsciously knew that he was wronging Tamar, and was projecting his self-loathing onto Tamar.

Taken out for execution, Tamar could have shamed Judah by announcing that he was the father. Instead she says that whoever owns the seal and staff is the father. Judah faced a moment of truth. Recognizing that the seal and staff were his, he could have remained silent and allowed Tamar to be executed. Once again, he would be able to maintain his upright public image.

However, Judah finally recognizes that he was wrong and publicly admits it. "She is more in the right than I, inasmuch as I did not give her to my son Shelah" (38:26). From that moment onward, Judah returns to family and takes personal responsibility for Benjamin.

Judah ends up a true hero, and Jacob recognizes this transformation. When blessing his sons on his deathbed, Jacob perceives ultimate greatness in Judah and blesses him with the kingship of Israel.

Rabbi Mordechai Breuer, *Pirkei Bereshit* vol. 2 (Hebrew) (Alon Shevut: Tevunot, 1999), pp. 631–641.

Mikketz

JOSEPH'S TREATMENT OF HIS BROTHERS

*U*riel Simon (Bar-Ilan University) surveys approaches to Joseph's treatment of his brothers, and why Joseph never contacted Jacob after rising to power in Egypt. Rabbi Joseph Bekhor Shor (twelfth-century Northern France) suggests that when the brothers sold Joseph, they made Joseph swear that he would never return or let Jacob know that he was alive. Joseph agreed in order to save his own life. He also addresses the question of Joseph's cruelty: Since Joseph had been sworn to silence, he needed leverage. Therefore, he manipulated events so that Benjamin would come and get captured, so that his brothers would have to tell Jacob themselves.

Rabbi Yehudah he-Hasid (twelfth-century Germany) alternatively suggests that Joseph never contacted Jacob in order to preserve family unity. It was preferable to build up his case gradually to make his brothers feel guilty for selling him. Premature revelation would destroy the family forever, since Jacob would figure out what had happened. Although psychologically appealing, Joseph could not have known that he ever would see his brothers again. Therefore, it is still difficult to understand why Joseph would not contact Jacob once he had risen to power in Egypt.

Regarding why Joseph never wrote home, Ramban (thirteenth-century Spain) rejects the idea that the brothers forced Joseph to swear, and instead suggests that Joseph wanted to help realize his original dreams. This required his family to prostrate themselves before him, but Benjamin and Jacob were missing in the brothers' original trip to Egypt. Joseph also wanted to test to see if the brothers had improved after 22 years. Joseph therefore acted the way he did to force the others to come to Egypt and prostrate themselves.

Abarbanel (fifteenth-century Spain) rejects Ramban's approach, since Joseph clearly was ruling over them already, and hardly needed Benjamin's physical prostration. Abarbanel suggests that Joseph's cruelty to his brothers was fitting punishment for their original cruelty to Joseph. They had accused him of spreading bad reports, and now Joseph accused them of being spies. They had thrown him into a pit (*bor*), and now Joseph threw Simeon into prison, also called a *bor*. He took Benjamin as slave, as they had sold him into slavery. Joseph was encouraged when the brothers admitted guilt for selling Joseph, but he still was unsure how they would relate to Benjamin, Rachel's other son. Therefore, he hid the cup in Benjamin's sack to test their loyalty to him. Were Joseph to have revealed his identity earlier, he could not have implemented a full reconciliation.

Uriel Simon, "The Exegete Is Recognized Not Only Through His Approach But Also Through His Questions" (Hebrew), in *Pirkei Nehama: Nehama Leibowitz Memorial Volume*, ed. Moses Ahrend, Ruth Ben-Meir & Gavriel H. Cohn (Jerusalem: Eliner Library, 2001), pp. 241–261.

Vayigash

HE'S MY FATHER

*A*s Joseph reveals his identity, his first words to his brothers are, "I am Joseph. Is my father still alive?" (Genesis 45:3). From his conversations with his brothers, Joseph knew that Jacob was alive. Why did he ask his brothers a question to which he already knew the answer?

Rabbi Marc D. Angel explains that Joseph had been torn during his years in Egypt apart from his family. Part of him longed for his family, but the other part wanted to move on after they sold him. The question, "Is my father still alive?" should be understood as "Is my father still alive within me?" Joseph understood the answer himself: "Yes he is. I cannot shake off my roots and identity."

We can offer a different interpretation through listening to the music of the text. Judah speaks on behalf of all his brothers. When referring to Jacob, we would expect him to say "*avinu*," *our* father. And in fact, he does twice. Seven times during his monlogue, however, he refers to Jacob as "*avi*," *my* father. Judah's final sentence contains this word twice: "For how can I go back to *my father* unless the boy is with me? Let me not be witness to the woe that would overtake *my father*!" (44:34).

Joseph has been alienated from his family for 22 years, but as a child he enjoyed his father's favoritism. Now at age 39, Joseph reconciles with his family, but faces the terrifying possibility that his special relationship with his father is a thing of the past. "Is *my father* still alive?" Joseph asks. I know that Jacob is alive, but is he still *my* father? He uses that term four times in his reintroduction to his brothers, including twice in his last sentence: "And you must tell *my father* everything about my high station in Egypt and all that you have seen; and bring *my father* here with all speed" (45:13). Joseph never says "*avinu*," *our* father.

The brothers were perceptive, recognizing Joseph's profound desire for the distinctive love of his father even after all these years of separation. After Jacob died, the brothers plead:

"Before his death *your father* left this instruction: So shall you say to Joseph, 'Forgive, I urge you, the offense and guilt of your brothers who treated you so harshly.' Therefore, please forgive the offense of the servants of the God of *your father*." And Joseph was in tears as they spoke to him (50:16–17).

By referring to Jacob "your father," instead of "our father," the brothers give Joseph what he wants. With this gracious gesture, the family paved the way to reconciliation.

Rabbi Marc D. Angel, *Angel for Shabbat: Thoughts on the Weekly Torah Portion* vol. 1 (New York: Institute for Jewish Ideas and Ideals, 2010), pp. 41–42.

Joseph's Treatment of the Egyptians

After Joseph explains Pharaoh's dreams, he offers practical suggestions of how to deal with the seven years of plenty in order to prepare for famine (Genesis 41:33–36). A 20 percent income tax, payable in grain, was levied during the years of plenty, and this grain was brought to storehouses of Pharaoh.

Once the famine began, many Egyptians were starving. They did not save up sufficient food to prepare for the famine. Rashi (on 41:55) suggests that their stored grain rotted, so they had to purchase food from Joseph. Alternatively, Radak maintains that since they were paying 20 percent taxes, they could not save up enough beyond what was necessary to feed their families.

After the dramatic reconciliation between Joseph and his family, Joseph settled his family in the fertile region of Goshen (47:1–12). The Torah then offers a detailed account of how the Egyptians fared during the famine (47:13–27). They exchanged their money, livestock, and finally their land to Pharaoh in exchange for seed, eventually becoming slaves to Pharaoh. Joseph transferred them off of their lands, demonstrating that the land does not belong to them.

Although Pharaoh was behind this decree, the Egyptians remembered Joseph as the one who saved them, but their grandchildren may have remembered that Joseph, a foreigner, took their family inheritance and enslaved them to Pharaoh.

The narrative concludes by shifting focus back onto Israel: "Thus Israel settled in the country of Egypt, in the region of Goshen; they acquired holdings in it, and were fertile and increased greatly" (47:27). The Egyptians must have noticed that Joseph treated his own family favorably while they became slaves to Pharaoh.

Perhaps this narrative helps explain why the entire Egyptian nation was willing to enslave the Israelites in the next generation, resenting that family. The first things the new Pharaoh had the Israelite slaves build were store cities (Exodus 1:11). In saving Egypt, Joseph made the role of Pharaoh too powerful and disrupted Egyptian life.

Rabbi Samson Raphael Hirsch (on 47:22) suggests that the Torah's agricultural laws in Leviticus, chapter 25, were an antidote to Joseph's policies. God owns the land, and therefore there are no permanent land sales. Each parcel of land reverts back to the original family. Moreover, the Egyptian priests were the only people able to own land as everyone else was transferred off of their lands (Genesis 47:22). In the Torah, the priestly class never owned land.

Rabbi Yonatan Grossman, "The Priests of Egypt and the Kohanim of Israel," Yeshivat Har Etzion Vayigash 1998, at http://www.vbm-torah.org/parsha.58/11vayig.htm.

Rabbi David Sabato, "The Land Belonged to Pharaoh: The Root of the Egyptian Slavery" (Hebrew), *Megadim* 52 (2011), pp. 41–57.

Vayhi

WHY JOSEPH DID NOT WRITE HOME

*A*fter he rose to power, why did Joseph never contact his father to let him know he was alive? In Mikketz, we discussed medieval responses to this question. Rabbi Joseph Bekhor Shor (twelfth-century Northern France) speculates that when the brothers sold Joseph, they made him swear that he would never let Jacob know that he was alive. Joseph accepted this oath in order to save his own life. Rabbi Judah he-Hasid (twelfth-century Germany) proposes that Joseph never contacted his father in order to preserve family unity. Premature revelation threatened to destroy any hopes of a future reconciliation.

Moving this discussion to the end of the twentieth century, Rabbi Yoel Bin-Nun submits that Joseph did not know the aftermath of the sale, when Jacob was fooled by the brothers and mourned inconsolably. We need to remember that not all characters in the story know what we are told by the Torah's narrative. Given that Joseph did not know that Jacob was in mourning and knew nothing about the sale, Rabbi Bin-Nun speculates that Joseph began to wonder, why doesn't Jacob send for me? Why did he send me out to my hostile brothers? Perhaps my father was involved in my brothers' conspiracy!

In Judah's final speech before Joseph's confession, he quoted Jacob as saying "As you know, my wife bore me two sons. But one is gone from me, and I said: Alas, he was torn by a beast! And I have not seen him since" (Genesis 44:27–28). Only at that moment did Joseph learn what Jacob had been thinking all along. He realized that his father never knew about the brothers' conspiracy and had believed him to be dead. Joseph now could reconcile with his family.

Rabbi Yaakov Medan levels several arguments against Rabbi Bin-Nun's hypothesis, including that Joseph knew he was beloved by his father. Would Joseph suspect his father of being a total hypocrite? Moreover, Joseph did not break down when Judah informed him that Jacob was saddened by Joseph's loss. He broke down after Judah said that Jacob would die if Benjamin would not return. Rabbi Medan suggests instead that the story is about repentance. Selling Joseph was a sin. Joseph therefore orchestrated everything to help them repent. Judah demonstrates full repentance when he offers himself in Benjamin's stead, and then Joseph could reveal himself to his brothers.

Rabbi Bin-Nun retorts: Joseph could not have orchestrated this process of repentance in advance, as he did not know that his brothers ever would come to Egypt. Although everything worked out in the end, this was divine providence rather than something Joseph could have planned.

Each theory has its merits, yet the questions that Rabbis Bin-Nun and Medan ask against each other stand. Neither side has made a compelling case. We need to reevaluate all earlier arguments against the text evidence, attempting to determine how these views—or views not yet proposed—fit the text and context of the Torah.

Rabbi Yoel Bin-Nun, "*Ha-Pilug ve-ha-Ahdut: Kefel ha-Ta'ut ve-Halom ha-Gilui—Mippenei Ma Lo Shalah Yosef (Shali'ah) el Aviv?*" (Hebrew), *Megadim* 1 (1986), pp. 20–31.

Rabbi Yaakov Medan, "'*Ba-Makom she-Ba'alei Teshuva Omedim*' (*Parshat Yosef ve-Ehav*)" (Hebrew), *Megadim* 2 (1986), pp. 54–78.

—

JOSEPH'S EGYPTIAN AND ISRAELITE IDENTITY

*A*t the end of his life, Jacob asks Joseph not to bury him in Egypt but rather in Israel. Joseph agrees. Surprisingly, Jacob then makes him swear (Genesis 47:28–31). Joseph later appeals to Pharaoh not only by mentioning the swear but also but speaking to the house of Pharaoh, that is, Pharaoh's underlings (50:4–6). Joseph was second in command, so why did he not go himself?

It appears that this was a moment of truth for Joseph. He had been struggling with his identity ever since he had become second in command some 25 years earlier. Pharaoh gave him the Egyptian name Zaphenath-paneah and married him to a daughter of the priest of On (41:45). Joseph was a success, and Pharaoh made it clear that he now was an Egyptian.

Rabbi Marc D. Angel explains the names of Manasseh and Ephraim in light of this identity conflict. Manasseh represents Joseph's new Egyptian identity: "God has made me forget completely (*nashani*) my hardship and my parental home." Ephraim, on the other hand, reminds Joseph that Egypt never will become his true home: "God has made me fertile (*hifrani*) in the land of my affliction" (41:51–52).

Rabbi Shlomo Riskin explains that Jacob understood that Joseph's identity would be tested severely by this request to be buried in Israel. Therefore, he made him swear. Similarly, Joseph understood that by honoring his father's will, he would be making a public declaration that his family identity belongs to Israel and not Egypt. He was afraid to confront Pharaoh directly.

Of all the characters in the Torah, Joseph is one of the great examples of someone who grows and changes perspective. He transformed from a teenager strutting and dreaming about his own grandeur, to a hero able to forgive and bring family reconciliation after generations of conflict. Similarly, Joseph went through an identity struggle. Many years later, after his family reconciliation, Jacob forces him to confront his true identity, and Joseph realizes that he ultimately is an Israelite.

Joseph addresses his brothers on his deathbed: "Joseph made the sons of Israel swear, saying, 'When God has taken notice of you, you shall carry up my bones from here.'" (50:25). Joseph solidifies his Israelite identity when he makes it clear that he wants to join his descendants in the future exodus.

Rabbi Marc D. Angel, *Angel for Shabbat: Thoughts on the Weekly Torah Portion* vol. 1 (New York: Institute for Jewish Ideas and Ideals, 2010), pp. 41–42.

Rabbi Shlomo Riskin, *Torah Lights: Genesis* (Jerusalem: Urim, 2005), pp. 307–312.

Shemot
שְׁמוֹת
Exodus

Shemot

SHIPHRAH AND PUAH

*T*wo of the heroes in the Book of Exodus are the "Hebrew mid-wives," Shiphrah and Puah, who appear in chapter 1. They defied Pharaoh by secretly sparing Israelite boys instead of murdering them. It is unclear whether "Hebrew midwives" refers to Israelite women (*Sotah* 11b; Rashi, Rashbam, Ibn Ezra, Ramban), or mid-wives for the Israelites, who could have been Egyptians or other non-Israelites (Josephus, Philo, Abarbanel, Shadal, Malbim).

"The midwives said to Pharaoh, 'Because the Hebrew women are not like the Egyptian women: they are vigorous. Before the midwife can come to them, they have given birth'" (Exodus 1:19). From the way Shiphrah and Puah refer to the Israelite women in the third person, it is likely that they were among the first "righteous Gentiles" who risked their lives to save Israelites. They also describe the Egyptians in the third person, so perhaps they were non-Egyptians as well.

It is remarkable that many years pass in chapter 1, but the only char-acters named after Jacob and his sons are these midwives. The Torah does not even name Pharaoh! Shiphrah and Puah are immortalized by the Torah for their morality, God-fearing qualities, and heroism. The great Pharaoh is not remembered by name. The Shiphrah-Puah narrative is longer than the entire description of Israelite slavery, showing what is most important in the story.

Shiphrah and Puah's heroic actions demonstrate that it was possible to defy Pharaoh. This fact makes the rest of the Egyptians who followed Pharaoh's orders and murdered Israelite boys fully culpable (Shadal on Exodus 9:27).

Theirs also was the first act of heroism in the slavery-exodus narrative, with others to follow, including Pharaoh's daughter, and, of course, Moses. Each of these individuals saw beyond their societal reality thanks to their moral convictions and courage.

"And because the midwives feared God, He established households for them" (1:21). As a reward for their heroism, God made Shiphrah and Puah "households," that is, children (Rashi, Bekhor Shor, Hizkuni, cf. II Samuel 7:11–12; I Kings 2:24). Shadal suggests that perhaps they had been barren, and God rewarded their saving Israelite children by giving them their own children. Alternatively, Hizkuni suggests that perhaps God helped them build their own obstetric clinics. At any rate, their moral courage and heroism in the face of an immoral society immortalize Shiphrah and Puah, teaching essential values of moral protest that span the Torah.

PHARAOH'S DAUGHTER

The story of Pharaoh's daughter seems straightforward (Exodus 2:5–10). Nevertheless, midrashim exploit several details in this brief account that do not appear to have bearing on the plain reading of the text. For example, one midrash asks why Pharaoh's daughter would go to the river to bathe. Its answer: Pharaoh's daughter was using the river as a *mikveh* in order to banish paganism from herself, essentially converting (*Sotah* 12a).

The Torah reports that "*she* spied the basket among the reeds." Were there not also maidservants present? Why does the Torah not say that *they* spied the basket? One midrash concludes that of course everyone physically saw the basket. However, the Torah distinguishes between the mindset of Pharaoh's daughter and that of her maidservants. When Pharaoh's daughter wanted to save Moses, her maidservants critically reminded her that her own father had issued the decree of drowning Israelite boys (*Sotah* 12b).

The aforementioned questions and responses still may have bearing on the textual account. There is something remarkable in the courage of Pharaoh's daughter, who defied her own father and society. Midrashically, this combination points to some form of "conversion" from the paganism and immorality of her father, associates, and society.

On a different plane, the Torah reports that a grown Moses left the palace endowed with an incredible moral sense. In short order, he killed an Egyptian taskmaster, intervened in an Israelite quarrel, and protected Jethro's daugthers from harassment. Where did this moral fortitude come from? Seemingly, it derived at least partially from Pharaoh's daughter. Moses' defiance of Pharaoh and his society parallels the heroism of his adoptive mother. Moses also instantly identified with his brethren, the Israelites. Perhaps Pharaoh's daughter, who could have raised Moses as an Egyptian, reminded him who he really was.

When Moses left the palace as a young adult, Pharaoh's daughter forever lost her beloved adopted son whom she had raised as her own. She likely was heartbroken, but also incredibly proud. She had raised a child who shared her vision of looking beyond the pagan immorality that characterized Egyptian society.

From the Torah we will never know who Pharaoh's daughter was or even her name. But her moral courage in rescuing Moses against her father's orders, and her nurturing Moses' moral and Israelite identity, changed the world by enabling her to raise the greatest individual who ever lived.

Hayyim Angel, "Chur and Pharaoh's Daughter: Midrashic Readings of Silent Heroes," in *Mitokh Ha-Ohel: Essays on the Weekly Parashah from the Rabbis and Professors of Yeshiva University*, ed. Daniel Z. Feldman & Stuart W. Halpern (New York: Yeshiva University Press, 2010), pp. 205–213; reprinted in Angel, *Creating Space Between Peshat and Derash: A Collection of Studies on Tanakh* (Jersey City, NJ: Ktav-Sephardic Publication Foundation, 2011), pp. 35–43.

MOSES' HUMILITY AND INSECURITY

*D*uring his revelation at the burning bush, Moses covered his face, awed by his vision. Some Sages (see *Exodus Rabbah* 3:1; *Berakhot* 7a) explain that Moses covered his face as an expression of humility. In their reading, Moses is rewarded by his eventually being able to transcend to the greatest heights. He communicated with God "face to face" (Numbers 12:3–8).

A dissenting Sage views Moses' covering his face as a missed opportunity. After the Golden Calf, Moses appeals to God, "Oh, let me behold Your Presence!" (Exodus 33:18). God responds, "You cannot see My face, for man may not see Me and live" (33:20). This was an ironic response by God: When you had the chance to perceive Me, you covered your face; now, you cannot have what you want. What negativity did this Sage perceive in Moses?

There is a fine line between humility and insecurity. Moses' multi-tiered response to God's challenge is instructive. (1) Who am I to accept such a great mission? God responds that He will help Moses, making the daunting mission possible. (2) What will I tell the people of Israel? This, too, was a fair question, and God answered that He will be with Moses. (3) Why should they believe me? Moses asked another fair question, and God gave him signs to convince the Israelites. (4) I am not eloquent! Here, God responds with some harshness: "Who gives man speech? Who makes him dumb or deaf, seeing or blind? Is it not I, the Lord?" (4:11).

(5) At this point, Moses has exhausted his rational arguments. "Please, O Lord, make someone else Your agent" (4:13). God gets angry at Moses. No longer is this a demonstration of humility. It rather was an expression of fear in going back to Egypt. Abarbanel suggests that Moses was traumatized some 60 years earlier. After killing the Egyptian, Moses had hoped to inspire feelings of freedom among the Israelites but instead received complaints from the quarreling Israelites. Moses was terrified to return to Egypt since the people may be ungrateful and blame him again.

If Moses covered his face at the burning bush out of pure humility, he would have risen above his fears and weighed the situation objectively. His first three questions demonstrate that he was well on his way; the last two showed he still had more to learn.

Both midrashic opinions are necessary to capture the essence of Moses' covering his face. For the most part, Moses was the paradigm of humility. Part of him, however, was running away from a mission because of his own personal fears. Over time, his humility and prophetic level grew to unprecedented heights (Numbers 12:3).

Moses was fortunate in receiving a prophetic vision to jolt him into confronting his insecurities. Were it not for the encounter with God at the burning bush, Moses would have died a shepherd in Midian, living a good life, but not helping his people or transforming history. God provided him with the opportunity to move past his fears and to become a national hero and teacher.

—

WOULD MOSES BELIEVE IN HIS PEOPLE?

*A*t the burning bush, God promises Moses that the Israelites will listen to him: "They will listen to you; then you shall go with the elders of Israel to the king of Egypt" (Exodus 3:18). However, Moses displays no confidence in the people, to the point where God must give several signs to reassure him: "But Moses spoke up and said, 'What if they do not believe me and do not listen to me, but say: The Lord did not appear to you?'" (Exodus 4:1).

Ramban insists that Moses' concern that the people would not listen to him was legitimate. God had promised that Pharaoh would be stubborn (Exodus 3:19). Moses therefore worried that although the Israelites might listen to him initially, as they did in Exodus 4:31, they no longer would heed Moses' words after the anticipated failure with Pharaoh. These reservations were validated by what occurred in chapters 5–6.

In contrast, several midrashim criticize Moses' lack of faith in God's promise (*Exodus Rabbah* 3:12; *Deuteronomy Rabbah* 9:6). Others similarly interpret the miraculous signs of the serpent and skin affliction as God's rebuke of Moses for exhibiting insufficient faith in the people (*Tanhuma Shemot* 23). Following their lead, Rashi maintains that Moses did not believe that the people deserved their redemption. God therefore rebuked him (see also Rashi's comments on Exodus 2:14; 3:11; 4:2–6).

It appears that a balance between the views of Ramban and Rashi lies at the heart of Moses' career. Throughout the Torah, Moses legitimately worried whether his people ever would reach the desired level of faith. At the same time, God constantly prodded Moses to remain with his people, since it is impossible to lead a nation one does not believe in.

It is likely that the signs God gave Moses had symbolic significance in addition to being means of impressing Pharaoh. Perhaps they contained a message for the people. They appeared to be in peril, symbolized by the menacing snake and *tzara'at*, but God will miraculously save them.

Deriving additional meaning from the signs, Rabbi Moshe Shamah quotes Rabbi Suleiman Sassoon, who suggests that the staff symbolizes leadership and power. It turns into a serpent, teaching that power comes with the danger of corruption. God instructs Moses to grab it by its tail rather than its neck. Grabbing a serpent by the neck suggests overpowering it, whereas grabbing it by the tail indicates that Moses must trust God and constantly be on guard not to be bitten. Moses' placing his hand in his bosom suggests that a leader must never get lulled into complacency. If a leader keeps his or her hands out of the fray, that too is destructive, symbolized by the *tzara'at*. Thus, God's presentation of signs to Moses addressed his fears of credibility, but also taught Moses additional lessons about leadership.

Hayyim Angel, Review Essay: "A Modern *Midrash Moshe*: Methodological Considerations." Review of *Tsir va-Tson*, by Rabbi Mosheh Lichtenstein, *Tradition* 41:4 (Winter 2008), pp. 73–86; reprinted in Angel, *Revealed Texts, Hidden Meanings: Finding the Religious Significance in Tanakh* (Jersey City, NJ: Ktav-Sephardic Publication Foundation, 2009), pp. 48–64.

Rabbi Moshe Shamah, "At the Burning Bush," *Intersession Reader* (New York: Tebah, 2009), pp. 14–36.

—

Vaera

MOSES' SPIRITUAL DEVELOPMENT

After his first encounter with Moses, Pharaoh took away the Israelites' straw for brickmaking, and the Israelites were outraged. Moses returned to God, flustered that the

Israelites were suffering even more. God reaffirmed the promise of redemption, but the Israelites would not listen, since they were short of spirit and overwhelmed by their hard work (6:9). Moses asks God how Pharaoh ever would listen if even the Israelites would not listen to him. All eyes turn to God to relieve this tense moment (6:10–13). Instead, the Torah interrupts with a lengthy genealogy of Reuben, Simeon, and Levi down to Moses (6:14–26). Why interrupt the suspenseful narrative now? A look at the broader context is necessary.

Despite having been raised in the Egyptian palace, Moses identified with the Israelites from his youth (2:11). Moses must have been stunned and traumatized when his fellow Israelites scolded him after killing an Egyptian taskmaster on their behalf (Abarbanel).

Many years later, after a lengthy back-and-forth with God at the burning bush, Moses finally agrees to return to Egypt. No sooner does he embark toward Egypt that God attacks him (4:24–26). Moses needed to learn that he was not returning merely to rescue an oppressed people; he had to completely rejoin covenantal Israel to lead them. Therefore, God forced him to have his son circumcised prior to the return.

God's plan worked. The Israelite foremen resent Moses and Aaron as a result of Pharaoh's deprivation of straw. Instead of fleeing Egypt again, Moses runs to God and protests on the people's behalf. Moses had transformed, identifying fully with his people and defending them before God.

This is the moment to introduce Moses' pedigree. Moses had been physically and ideologically removed from his brethren. Now, he has rejoined his people to the point where he was willing to take their side. The weight of his family's history now comes to back him up as he stands for his people. The family tree is an essential component of the story of Moses' return to the covenantal people. At this point, Moses was ready to lead his people out of Egypt.

Rabbi Yonatan Grossman, "The Two Consecrations of Moses," Yeshivat Har Etzion Virtual Beit Midrash, Vaera 5759, at www.vbm-torah.org/parsha.59/14vaera.htm.

THE EGYPTIAN MAGICIANS

*R*abbi Jonathan Sacks notes that the Egyptian magicians believed that they could control nature and the gods through their magic. A civilization that believes that it can manipulate the gods certainly believes that it can control human beings. The magicians responded to the first two plagues as though they were magic, and produced blood and frogs (even though that made things worse for Egypt). When they could not replicate lice, they immediately concluded, "This is the finger of God" (Exodus 8:15).

Rabbi Sacks explains that the magicians' reaction is the first reference to "the god of the gaps," whereby a "miracle" is something for which we do not have a scientific explanation. This attitude leads to the false conclusion that religion and science clash. The more we can explain scientifically, the less God is relevant. The Torah repudiates this approach. God is involved in history, whether or not He needs to violate the laws of nature.

Rambam similarly rules that we do not believe in the prophets because they produced supernatural miracles or signs, but rather because of their righteousness and faithfulness to the Torah (*Hilkhot Yesodei ha-Torah* 7:7). Science is not opposed to God, but rather is God's created order through which we can stand in awe of God.

The Egyptians built huge structures, but it took a tiny louse to teach them that power over nature is not an end in itself, but solely the means to an ethical ends. The magicians could not control human destiny. Rabbi Sacks quotes Mircea Eliade, who states that faith means absolute emancipation from any kind of natural law, and therefore the highest freedom is to intervene in history. This requires God. To think of history as an arena of change is scary, but the alternative is to despair that things always will remain the same and that history will necessarily repeat itself.

Rabbi Jonathan Sacks, *Covenant and Conversation: A Weekly Reading of the Jewish Bible, Exodus* (New Milford, CT: Maggid Books, 2010), pp. 54–57.

Bo

THE TEN PLAGUES

*A*lthough we praise God for redeeming the Israelites with ten plagues, these plagues were not necessarily supernatural events. One theory, first proposed by a Dutch scholar named Greta Hort in 1957, describes how at least the first nine plagues could be explained according to the laws of nature.

The Nile River is fed by melting snow and summer rains from Ethiopia carrying sediment from tropical red earth. During the plagues, an abnormally heavy rainfall brought in far more sediment than usual. The higher rise of the river brought more bacteria from mountain lakes, killing fish and producing a stench. While the Nile was filled with sediment, digging around it would enable the Egyptians to obtain potable water (see Exodus 7:24). Eventually, the Nile would wash the sediment out to the sea, which explains why Pharaoh was so unconcerned and why the plague ended by itself. An ancient Egyptian text dated at latest to 2050 BCE, centuries before the exodus, describes a similar phenomenon: "Why really, the River [Nile] is blood. If one drinks of it, one rejects (it) as human and thirsts for water."

Because of the stench from the dead fish, frogs left the river earlier than usual. The dead fish would have been the source of infection carried by insects, so the frogs would die en masse. After the first two plagues, lice or mosquitoes would have multiplied astronomically.

Stable flies are vicious blood sucking insects that multiply in tropical or subtropical conditions. Israelites lived in Goshen which has a Mediterranean climate. *Arov* (swarms) is the first plague where the Torah that explicitly says that the Israelites were not affected.

Contaminated by rotting frogs, the soil became a breeding ground for disease, probably anthrax. Again, Goshen would be unaffected. Anthrax was transmitted to cattle by grazing in contaminated fields, and to humans by stable flies. Skin ulcerations and malignant pustules characterize anthrax. Since the swarms affected only Upper Egypt, these plagues would not have affected the Israelites in Goshen.

Thunderstorms originating in Upper Egypt and moving northward may be trapped in the narrow Nile valley and not affect Goshen in the northeastern part of the Nile Delta. Locusts also could follow that pattern.

The plague of darkness likely was a *hamsin*, a scorching wind that blows in each spring, raising a thick layer of dust. It may persist for several days and blacken the sky. It would have been worse than usual because of the locust plague. Based on the way a *hamsin* travels, Goshen could escape unscathed.

The Torah does not make sharp distinctions between the natural and the supernatural, since all ultimately emanates from God. Many religious people may look to the plagues as a source of mystery, and may become discouraged with Hort's theory. The fact remains that we can explain these phenomena within the laws of nature. As the Torah constantly teaches, we recognize God's majesty in nature. Many who are not religiously inclined may dismiss the plagues as natural phenomena, but they miss the Torah's focus on how nature itself should bring us to a recognition of God, the Creator of nature.

Greta Hort, "The Plagues of Egypt," ZAW 69 (1957), pp. 84–103; 70 (1958), pp. 48–59.

Nahum Sarna, *Exploring Exodus* (New York: Schocken Books, 1986–1996), pp. 68–73.

DECEPTION DURING THE EXODUS

*T*here are several examples of Israel's using deception before they leave Egypt. (1) Moses and Aaron repeatedly ask Pharaoh for a three-day leave, when in fact they intend to leave permanently (5:3; cf. 3:18). (2) The Israelites are instructed to "borrow" the Egyptians' vessels as they leave Egypt (3:21–22; 11:2; 12:35–36). (3) God tells Moses to take a circuitous route so that the Egyptians would think that the Israelites were lost and pursue them (14:2–4).

How do we explain God's ordering Israel to use deception? Several commentators, including medieval figures Rabbis Yitzhak Arama and Yitzhak Abarbanel, as well as the twentieth-century scholar Nehama Leibowitz, adopted an apologetic approach. The request for a three-day leave was a genuine request meant to serve as a test for Pharaoh. If he would refuse even this minor request, his hard-heartedness would be revealed to all. If he would have listened, the Israelites would indeed have returned to Egypt after several days, and Moses would then continue to negotiate slowly for their freedom.

Although we can appreciate the ethical motivations behind this interpretation, it is apologetic. Moses continues to ask for a three-day leave (see 5:1, 5:3, 7:16, 7:26, 8:4, 10:8–11, 10:24–26, 12:31–32). After proving this point once, he would not need to keep doing it. The "borrowing" of the Egyptian possessions, not to mention the ongoing narrative, demonstrates that they were planning on leaving for good.

Other commentators therefore adopt an unapologetic reading. Its leading proponents include medieval commentators Ibn Ezra and Ran (end *derashah* #11), and it is championed by the contemporary scholar Rabbi Elhanan Samet.

God told the Israelites to ask for a three-day leave so that the Egyptians would give them vessels. Had they known the Israelites would not return, they would not have given them. Israel deserved these valuables as wages for their slavery (cf. *Sanhedrin* 91a). Additionally, their taking wealth would lure the Egyptians to the Red Sea. The purpose of this ruse was to drown Pharaoh and his army. They deserved to be punished for their enslavement and murder of the Israelites.

Negotiations between Moses and Pharaoh were not diplomatic. They were one aspect of the war between them. In a war, deception is permissible, since its purpose is to bring about the enemy's downfall. It is similar to the use of an ambush.

All agree that the Egyptian enslavement and murder of the Israelites was immoral. Our commentators interpret the ethical dimensions of how to best respond given those extreme circumstances. In this instance, the weight of the Torah's evidence appears to be with Ibn Ezra, Ran, and Rabbi Samet.

Nehama Leibowitz, *Studies in Shemot (Exodus)*, translated and adapted by Aryeh Newman (Jerusalem: Eliner Library), pp. 183–192.

Rabbi Elhanan Samet, *Iyyunim be-Parashot ha-Shavua* (first series) vol. 1 (Hebrew) ed. Ayal Fishler (Ma'aleh Adumim: Ma'aliyot Press, 2002), pp. 178–191.

Rabbi Elhanan Samet, *Iyyunim be-Parashot ha-Shavua* (second series) vol. 1 (Hebrew) ed. Ayal Fishler (Ma'aleh Adumim: Ma'aliyot Press, 2004), pp. 263–285.

Beshallah

Israel's Slave Mentality

*G*od splits the Red Sea, leading to Israel's breaking out in spontaneous song dedicated to the glory of God. God gives the people "bread from heaven" and provides water for the nation. Despite those miracles, God does not emerge victorious. God did not lead Israel via the short route through the land of Philistines, lest they see war and return to Egypt (Exodus 13:17). Instead, the Israelites go to the Red Sea and panic as they see Egyptian chariots. They wander through a wilderness where they do not find water or food, and they repeatedly suggest that they should return to Egypt. One year later, when Moses sends spies, the people want to return to Egypt since they do not think that they will defeat the powerful Canaanites. In other words, they saw the prospect of war and wanted to return to Egypt—exactly what God was trying to avoid by not bringing them to Israel via the short route! What is the Torah trying to teach with this mixed message?

Medieval commentaries such as Ibn Ezra and Abarbanel propose that the generation leaving Egypt had a "slave mentality." They had become accustomed to their sorry lot and felt a certain security in Egypt. The Israelites leaving Egypt had their spirits defeated. *Nothing*, not plagues, not a sea splitting, not Sinai, could change them. They go from singing the

Song at the Sea to a wave of complaints, and from the Revelation at Sinai to a Golden Calf.

The Israelites wanted to return to the security of slavery, not thinking that by doing so they would be condemning their children to the same life. Their view was shortsighted and self-centered. Because they were so caught up in their slave mentality, they were unable to look beyond the immediate present or beyond themselves.

God prevented this outcome by leading them via the long route so that they would not be able to return even though they constantly would want to. Then their children would be born free and grow into a nation that could enter Israel.

In this vein, Rabbenu Bahya (on Exodus 3:18) turns the focus around on Moses' request for a three-day leave. Rather than a ruse to fool the Egyptians, it was primarily for the sake of the Israelites. They were slaves, and an abrupt change in the human condition is nearly impossible. Therefore God told Moses to ask for three days since that was something *Israel* could accept.

JOSEPH'S BONES

"And Moses took with him the bones of Joseph, who had exacted an oath from the children of Israel, saying, 'God will be sure to take notice of you: then you shall carry up my bones from here with you'" (Exodus 13:19).

Midrashim use the biblical text as a springboard to advance their educational goals, and often were not intended as literal. The Sages ask: (1) Where was Joseph's coffin kept in Egypt? (2) How did Moses obtain it? These questions belong primarily to the realm of *derash*, as the biblical text provides insufficient information to ascertain answers at the level of *peshat*.

One midrashic tradition expounds on these questions as follows:

When God went down to Egypt and the time for the redemption of Israel had come . . . Moses was going around the city, and for three days and three nights was laboring to find Joseph's coffin, for the Israelites could not leave

Egypt without Joseph. Why? Because he so bound them by oath before his death, as it is said, "And Joseph took an oath of the children of Israel saying, etc." (Genesis 50:25). . . . Moses placed himself by the bank of the river and called out: "Joseph, Joseph, you know how you have adjured Israel [with the words], God will surely remember you; give honor to the God of Israel and do not hold up the redemption of Israel; you have good deeds to your credit. Intercede then with your Creator and come up from the depths." Whereupon immediately Joseph's coffin began to break through the waters and to rise from the depths like a stick. (*Deuteronomy Rabbah* 11:7)

This midrash portrays Moses as encouraging Joseph to rise from the depths since Israel could not be redeemed unless he came with them.

A related tradition appears in Tractate *Sotah*, but with a different slant:

Moses went and stood on the bank of the Nile and exclaimed: "Joseph, Joseph! The time has arrived which the Holy One, blessed be He, swore, 'I will deliver you,' and the oath you imposed upon the Israelites has reached [the time of fulfillment]; if you come, well and good; otherwise, behold, we are free of your oath." Immediately Joseph's coffin floated [on the surface of the water]. (*Sotah* 13a)

In this version, Moses threatened Joseph. If Joseph refused to rise, then Israel would leave Egypt without him—and Joseph would remain unredeemed.

Understanding these sources conceptually, *Deuteronomy Rabbah* teaches that Israel requires a deep connection to its ancestors to attain redemption—Israel needs Joseph. In contrast, *Sotah* teaches that the legacy of Israel's ancestors depends on whether later generations faithfully preserve their traditions—Joseph needs Israel. These lessons complement one another, teaching Israel's intergenerational dependence on one another to carry out the eternal vision of the Torah.

Hayyim Angel, "Joseph's Bones: *Peshat, Derash*, and in Between," *Intersession Reader 2013* (New York: Tebah, 2013), pp. 83–94.

DIFFERENT FAITH TYPOLOGIES AT THE SEA

*A*fter Moses led the men in the Song at the Sea, Miriam led the women: "Then Miriam the prophetess, Aaron's sister, took a timbrel in her hand, and all the women went out after her in dance with timbrels. And Miriam chanted for them: Sing to the Lord, for He has triumphed gloriously; horse and driver He has hurled into the sea" (Exodus 15:20–21).

Although on the surface it appears that the men and women sang in parallel, one midrash observes that there was an important difference between the two groups. Only the women used timbrels: "From where did they have timbrels? From here we learn that the righteous always confidently believe that God will perform miracles for them. Before they left Egypt, they prepared timbrels" (*Pirkei D'Rabbi Eliezer* 41).

This midrash detects something special in the faith of these women. While still in Egypt, they believed in God's promises of redemption, and therefore prepared instruments for their future celebration. In contrast, the men did not prepare anything in advance. In this way of thinking, the men and women recited identical words of praise to God, but their tones were different. The women expressed the sentiment, "So *this* is how God was going to save us!" The men, on the other hand, were shocked that there was any salvation at all.

This reading parallels another midrash wherein Amram (the father of Miriam, Aaron, and Moses) led the Israelite men to separate from their wives after Pharaoh decreed the drowning of the baby Israelite boys (*Sotah* 12a). In this talmudic passage, Miriam challenged her father: It is true that having no children will spare the future drowning of the boys. However, your decision to have no children is even worse—we will no longer have any boys *or* girls! Amram looked at the immediate situation, whereas Miriam had a broader perspective. In this midrash, Amram realized that his daughter was correct, so he and the other men returned to their wives. At that point Moses was born.

These midrashim develop two typologies of faith. One represents a deep confidence that justice will prevail. Another represents uncertainty toward the future. While the midrashim prefer Miriam's approach, halakhah in fact requires that we have faith in redemption but also must not rely on God's supernatural intervention (*en somekhin al ha-nes*; see, for example, *Pesahim* 8b; *Kiddushin* 39b; *Bava Kamma* 60b; *Hullin* 142a). By combining the traits of the two typologies, we can always hope for a better future while simultaneously taking full responsibility for our actions and actively building that better future.

———

THE TESTS OF THE REVELATION

*A*t one level, the overwhelming moment of the Revelation at Sinai changed history forever. At a different level, God revealed a number of laws to Israel prior to Sinai, creating a feeling of gradual buildup.

God gave seven laws to Noah following the flood (Genesis, chapter 9). God commanded circumcision to Abraham (Genesis, chapter 17). Jacob's wrestling match with an angel led to a prohibition of eating the sciatic nerve of a kosher animal (Genesis, chapter 32). Prior to the exodus, God commanded some 20 laws pertaining to Passover (Exodus, chapter 12). After the splitting of the Red Sea, God revealed laws at Marah: "There He made for them a fixed rule, and there He put them to the test" (Exodus 15:25).

One of the most interesting examples of this phenomenon is rabbinic interpretation of the "fixed rule" revealed at Marah. According to some Sages (*Sanhedrin* 56b; *Horiyot* 8b), God revealed 10 commandments at Marah: the seven Noahide laws, and three others: to establish a legal system (*mishpatim*); the Shabbat; and honoring parents. This list moves strikingly close to *the* Ten Commandments revealed at Sinai.

Steven Wilf observes that at Marah, God "put them to the test" (Exodus 15:25). God essentially revealed 10 commandments without any fanfare. Can people live with Torah law in their everyday lives when God's presence is not hovering over them as it did at Sinai? Can they build an ideal society together?

One may add that the Torah also presents Sinai as a test: "Moses answered the people, 'Be not afraid; for God has come only in order to test

———— 80 ————

you, and in order that the fear of Him may be ever with you, so that you do not go astray'" (Exodus 20:17). Revelation is a different test—whether people are prepared to accept a direct encounter with God.

These dual tests describe two central aspects of religious experience. Marah teaches that we must learn to bring God into our daily lives without encountering God's direct Presence. Sinai teaches that we must seek the great experiences in addition to the day-to-day routine of religious life.

The Torah's laws were revealed gradually without any fanfare, often linked to narratives. The one great moment at Sinai, then, gave eternal covenantal authority to these earlier traditions.

Steven Wilf, *The Law Before the Law* (Lanham: Lexington Books, 2008).

AN AMAZING COMMENT OF RABBI JOSEPH BEKHOR SHOR

*R*abbi Joseph b. Isaac Bekhor Shor (twelfth-century Northern France) was a Tosafist who became one of the outstanding Tanakh commentators of the Northern French School championed by Rashi. In Parashat Beshallah, Bekhor Shor proposes an innovative approach to several Torah narratives.

God miraculously provides the nation with manna, meat, and water (Exodus, chapters 16–17). Yet there are also narratives in Numbers that recount God's providing these physical needs (Numbers, chapters 11, 20). Based on the strong similarities between the accounts, Bekhor Shor posits that in fact these stories occurred only once and are told in two places with different emphases (see his comments on Exodus 16:13; Numbers 20:8). Chapters 16 and 17 in Exodus catalogue the food provisions as a thematic exposition of God's looking after Israel during their 40 years of wandering. Numbers, in contrast, narrates these events with greater detail in their proper chronological sequence among the other desert episodes.

To bolster his novel hypothesis, Bekhor Shor marshals several textual arguments. (1) If God already had provided meat for the entire nation in

Exodus, chapter 16, why would Moses still question God's ability to do so in Numbers, "Could enough flocks and herds be slaughtered to suffice them?" (Numbers 11:22)? (2) In Exodus, God provided water through the agency of Moses' striking a rock, and "the place was named Massah and Meribah" (Exodus 17:7). The Numbers account, where God provided water through the agency of Moses' striking a rock, similarly concludes, "Those are the Waters of Meribah" (Numbers 20:13). (3) The Exodus water episode occurred in the wilderness of Sin (with a *samekh*), and the Numbers account similarly was located in the wilderness of Tzin (albeit with a *tzaddi*).

Bekhor Shor parallels these episodes with the narratives in Exodus-Numbers that are retold in Deuteronomy. Each book relates different facets of the same events in accordance with its respective religious and educational objectives.

In practice, most commentators reject Bekhor Shor's interpretation. They maintain that the parallel accounts diverge too significantly and therefore must be relating different events. Regardless, this novel suggestion encourages us to reread these narratives meticulously to ascertain the similarities and differences in their messages. It also underscores the difficulties we might encounter reading the respective texts in the conventional way, forcing us to refine our understanding. Finally, this innovative approach to viewing Torah narratives broadens our horizons. It inspires us to constantly revisit and rethink these familiar yet infinitely complex stories to attain a deeper level of insight every time we encounter them.

Hayyim Angel, "An Amazing Comment of Rabbi Yosef Bekhor Shor," *Enayim LeTorah*, Beshallah 5767–2007.

THE WAR AGAINST AMALEK

When Amalek attacks, Moses ascends a mountain to overlook the Israelite camp. When he raises his hands, Israel succeeds. When he lowers his hands, Israel retreats. Why should the position of Moses' hands affect the results of a battle?

Rabbi Elhanan Samet explains that Parashat Beshallah begins with a battle against Pharaoh and ends with a battle against Amalek. Although only a few weeks separated these events, they are different in nature. In the battle against Pharaoh, the Israelites panic. Moses leads the events and assures them that God will fight on their behalf. The victory is a result of God's direct intervention. Against Amalek, in contrast, nobody panics. The Israelites fight their own naturalistic war, led by Joshua.

The exodus is bound up with overt divine intervention, with the nation assuming a passive role. The war against Amalek, on the other hand, is the first stage of the war to conquer Canaan. These wars are fought with armies and military strategy.

Despite these fundamental differences, the two battles also have a common element. In both instances, Moses' hand, grasping the staff of God, has a direct effect on the outcome of the battle. No one watching Moses lift his staff attributes the splitting of the sea to Moses. Everyone understands that Moses is acting as God's agent, and his arm symbolizes God's arm.

Is God's hand active also in a natural war? Certainly, but in such a war God's hand works in hidden ways and is not clearly visible. The measure of God's involvement in a natural battle depends on the extent to which the nation at war is worthy of divine assistance. When God is among them, they will be victorious; when God is not among them, then the natural balance of forces will decide the outcome of the battle.

Moses turns his own hand with the staff into the symbol of God's arm active within the natural reality through hidden miracles. This natural war turns into an educational opportunity to mold the religious consciousness of this generation, already used to supernatural intervention. The nation will learn not only that God's hand operates also within the natural reality—through hidden miracles—but that the nature of this activity depends directly on the nation's behavior.

The events on the battlefield and mountain are the result of the nation's actions at that very place, in their sin of Masah U-Merivah. They tested God and asked, Is God in our midst or not? The weakening of their faith causes a weakening of Moses' hands, which is really a symbol of the weakening of the help from God.

A strengthening of action of God's hand among Israel is result of reinforcement from below. The more the nation seeks God's presence, the more worthy they will be of it.

Rabbi Elhanan Samet, *Iyyunim be-Parashot ha-Shavua* (second series) vol. 1 (Hebrew), ed. Ayal Fishler (Ma'alei Adumim: Ma'aliyot, 2004), pp. 286–306.

—

Yitro

JETHRO'S COMPLEX CHARACTER

*T*he story of Jethro appears between the battle against Amalek and the Revelation at Sinai. Jethro was a pagan priest before joining Moses and the Israelites (some midrashim maintain that he converted) who encouraged Moses to establish a court system.

Surprisingly, Jethro abruptly leaves and returns to Midian at the end of the narrative. Why not remain with his family and the God who so impressed him? This question becomes more interesting when we study the Book of Judges. Evidently, some of Jethro's descendants did move to Israel. They are referred to as Kenites and were a tent-dwelling community that lived apart from mainstream Israel (see Judges 1:16; 4:11).

In Judges, chapter 4, Jael was married to Heber the Kenite during Deborah's battle against Sisera and the Canaanites. Sisera had fled to the tent of Heber and Jael because the Canaanites had a treaty with the Kenites. However, Jael allied herself with Israel, rather than with her husband's people, and killed Sisera.

Similarly, when King Saul attacks the Amalekite stronghold in I Samuel, chapter 15, he finds Kenites living nearby. He asks that they leave because of Israel's warm relations with them. However, the Kenites are living in the vicinity of Israel's archenemy, Amalek. In both stories, the descendents of Jethro are friendly both to Israel and to Israel's greatest enemies.

This conflict regarding the Kenites is manifest in midrashim about Jethro as well. One midrash (*Exodus Rabbah* 27) grapples with Jethro's relationship with Amalek. One Sage contrasts them: Amalek and Jethro both heard that Israel came out of Egypt. Amalek attacked, whereas Jethro joined the nation. There is a different opinion that Jethro and Amalek advised Pharaoh to enslave the Israelites. After Jethro heard that God would punish Amalek, he distanced himself from Amalek and came to Israel on friendly terms.

In light of the above, one can make the case for a literary presentation of three philosophies in Exodus, chapters 17–19. Amalek and Israel are two extremes, and Jethro represents the person who wavers between these two, never committing to either side and befriending nations and ideologies that are diametrically opposed. Jethro can be impressed by God, but ultimately remains noncommittal and returns to his pagan home. Jethro appreciates Israel's values, but does not have the resolve to commit to its ideology.

—

THE EDUCATIONAL EXPERIENCE OF MOSES' SONS

*O*ne of the mysteries in Scripture is the almost total silence about Moses' sons, Gershom and Eliezer. Professor Adrian Ziderman suggests that Gershom and Eliezer did not inherit leadership from Moses because they were unsuitable. How is it that Moses failed to instill in his own sons a feeling toward Torah and mitzvot?

Jethro arrives in the Sinai desert together with Moses' wife Zipporah and their two sons (Exodus, chapter 18). But we had been told that Moses took them with him when he left Midian for Egypt (Exodus, chapter 4)! What convinced Moses to send Zipporah and their sons back to Midian?

Basing himself on the *Mekhilta*, Rashi states that Aaron convinced Moses to send his family back to Midian: "We feel sorrow for those already enslaved and you want to add to their number?" It was senseless to bring more Israelites to suffer.

In a different midrash, Jethro offers advice at the time that Moses seeks leave from Jethro to return to Egypt with his wife and sons. "Jethro said 'Those that are already in Egypt seek to leave and you are taking them there?' Moses replied: 'In the future, they are due to leave and stand at

Mount Sinai to hear from the mouth of God—I am The Lord your God—and my sons will not hear this with the others?'" (*Exodus Rabbah* 4:4).

Professor Ziderman understands this midrash as an expression of Jethro's technical concerns. It would be inefficient for Moses to take his family to Egypt only to bring them back again to Mount Sinai. It would be more sensible for Moses to meet up with his family in the desert. In contrast to Jethro's view, Aaron argued that if they traveled to Egypt, Moses' family would suffer the miseries of slavery.

The advice of Jethro, based on logistics, is firmly rejected by Moses. His sons should not miss the most climactic events of the Jewish historical experience—the exodus and Sinai—simply to save travel time. When Aaron describes slavery, however, Moses sends his sons back to Midian so that they would avoid the pain and hardship of enslavement.

As a result of this decision, Moses' sons certainly missed experiencing the exodus. According to Rabbi Elazar Hamodai (in the *Mekhilta*) and Ibn Ezra, Gershom and Eliezer also did not witness the Revelation at Sinai. Even if they were more comfortable in Midian, they could not relate to our nation's religious basis and ultimately faded from history. Although Moses protected his family by returning them to Midian, this decision deprived his sons of irreplacable educational opportunities.

Adrian Ziderman, "On Bringing Up Children," Bar-Ilan University, Yithro 5760/2000, at http://www.biu.ac.il/JH/Parasha/eng/ytro/zid.html.

Jethro's Advice

*I*n his book, *The Nursing Father: Moses as Political Leader*, Professor Aaron Wildavsky observes that God seldom helped Moses lead. Had God constantly guided Moses as a leader, we would be unable to turn to Moses as a role model, since we do not have God to directly guide us. Moses' leadership is a process that evolves through the Torah. Leaders must be participants in their own education.

One of the formative moments in Moses' development as a leader is when his father-in-law Jethro advises him to set up a system of judges (Exodus, chapter 18). The Torah teaches how everyone—even Moses—has much to learn from others (*Or HaHayyim*).

How could it be that Moses never thought of setting up lower judges? Rabbi Samuel David Luzzatto suggests that devoted leaders want to work directly with their people. In the long run, however, Jethro was correct—this approach can wear leaders out.

Within Wildavsky's framework, we might suggest an alternative reason why Moses chose to lead by himself. Until then, he might have defaulted to Pharaoh's system, since that is all he knew. Jethro's advice changed Moses forever. Over time, Moses understood that sharing responsibility was a central aspect of ideal Torah leadership. By Numbers, chapter 11, Moses demands leadership help from God: "I cannot carry all this people by myself, for it is too much for me. If You would deal thus with me, kill me rather, I beg You, and let me see no more of my wretchedness!" (Numbers 11:14–15).

God responds with the appointment of 70 prophets to assist Moses. Two renegades, Eldad and Medad, are reported prophesying in camp. "Joshua son of Nun, Moses' attendant from his youth, spoke up and said, 'My lord Moses, restrain them!' But Moses said to him, 'Are you wrought up on my account? Would that all the Lord's people were prophets, that the Lord put His spirit upon them!' Moses then reentered the camp together with the elders of Israel" (Numbers 11:28–30).

Joshua was concerned over Moses' power and honor. Moses teaches his disciple that Israel's leadership is not about honor or power. It is about sharing ideas and growing together with the community. The ideal society is when everyone is a prophet—sharing a religious vision.

Joshua internalized this lesson well, working together with communal elders and people throughout his tenure as Moses' successor. Wildavsky observes that by distributing leadership, Moses ensured that tradition would be carried on. In this way, Moses left an eternal legacy as a teacher and leader.

Aaron Wildavsky, *The Nursing Father: Moses as Political Leader* (University, Alabama: University of Alabama Press, 1984).

APPROACHING GOD AT SINAI

*D*uring the awesome experience of Revelation, God was concerned that the Israelites would approach the burning mountain. God therefore repeatedly instructed Moses to create a barrier so that the people would stand back.

Rabbi Samson Raphael Hirsch explains that God wanted to teach the people that the Torah's premises emanate from God, rather than from human input. In religious behavior, it is difficult to separate egotism from true religious feeling. Some use religion to exert power over others, to feel superior, to stand in judgment. God therefore stressed the boundary between the divine and human realms.

Additionally, one might suggest that some people may take spiritually dangerous shortcuts to try to get close to God. This approach causes more harm than good. The Talmud (*Hagigah* 14b) describes four Sages who entered the mystical realm of "*pardes.*" Ben Azzai died from the experience; Ben Zoma went insane; Elisha ben Abuyah became a heretic; and only Rabbi Akiva emerged spiritually enhanced. From this vantage point, God was concerned that during the singular experience at Sinai, the people needed to maintain their distance. Spirituality comes in developmental stages; what is good for one person can be damaging for another.

For all the concern about the people coming too close, however, the Torah then relates the response of the people. Not only were the people terrified, but Moses had to bring them to the mountain (19:16–18). Moreover, when the nation perceived the sounds and sights of Sinai, "they fell back and stood at a distance" (20:15). They tell Moses that they do not want so direct a relationship with God. Moses should receive prophetic transmission, and they would listen. They feared that they would die with this close a relationship to God. Moses responds that they should not worry. This whole experience was a test (20:17). God wanted to gauge the spiritual thirst of the people. Although a select few may try to come too close, many more will retreat from God.

Spirituality requires behavior appropriate for one's level. One who runs away demonstrates either a conscious or subconscious reluctance to commit. The optimal position is exactly what God planned for. One should determine one's own level and then push up against the boundaries. This balance leads to healthy religious progress and growth.

———

THE TEN COMMANDMENTS (PART ONE)

*A*ccording to a medieval work on the commandments, *Sefer ha-Hinnukh*, there are 13 commandments in the "Ten Commandments." The reason for this anomaly is that "Ten Commandments" is a poor translation of the Torah's term, *aseret ha-devarim* (Exodus 34:28; Deuteronomy 4:13; 10:4), now referred to as *aseret ha-dibberot* following talmudic nomenclature (e.g., *Berakhot* 12a; *Shabbat* 86b).

Abarbanel and Umberto Cassuto observe that the term *devarim-dibberot* should be translated "statements" rather than "commandments." Some statements contain no commandment, such as the introduction to the covenant, "I am the Lord your God." Other statements may contain more than one commandment, such as the prohibitions against idolatry and graven images. Most statements contain one commandment apiece.

Regarding the structure of the commandments, Ibn Ezra posits that commandments can be divided into actions, speech, and thought. The first five statements—often understood as encapsulating our relationship with God—move from thought (belief in God, rejection of idolatry), to speech (not taking God's Name in vain), to actions (Shabbat, honoring parents). In contrast, the second five statements—governing our relationships with other people—move in the opposite direction. First there are actions (prohibitions against murder, adultery, and theft), then speech (not bearing false witness), then thought (not coveting).

Ibn Ezra concludes that for our relationships with God, thoughts are paramount and actions are secondary. The reverse is true in our interpersonal relationships. For example, prayer without proper intention is not so meaningful. In contrast, it is preferable to give more charity with less sympathy than to give less charity with more sympathy. Of course the ideal is to excel in both; however, the Torah indicates the most important aspect of interpersonal relationships is in doing for others.

The Ten Statements differ from ancient codes of law in meaningful ways (see Umberto Cassuto's commentary on Exodus). The Sinaitic Revelation represents the first time that a transcendental Deity created a relationship with human beings, and the first time that a people made a covenant with their God. This was the first time there was a prohibition against creating physical representations of God. Although a seven-day week existed prior to the Torah, the Torah's exalted concept of Shabbat was unprecedented. The Torah was also the first legal code where an individual's responsibility to God was equal to his or her responsibility to other human beings.

Finally, the Ten Statements' prohibition of coveting the possessions of another is unique. In this legal system, inappropriate desire is a sin in itself, rather than merely a safeguard against some greater evil. Rabbi Samson Raphael Hirsch pointed to this commandment as evidence of the divine origin of the Torah. No human court could enforce such a prohibition, whereas the all-knowing God can.

Through the use of ancient literary forms and covenant making procedures, God spoke to Israel to create a singular relationship that has transformed humanity's relationship with God and with one another forever. We can appreciate the eternal meaning of the Ten Statements even more by understanding it against its ancient historical context.

THE TEN COMMANDMENTS (PART TWO)

The "Ten Commandments" consisted of 10 statements on two tablets. How many statements were on each tablet? One rabbinic view is that the first five statements were on the first tablet, and the latter five on the second. The rationale of this view is that the first five govern the relationship between people and God. The second five govern interpersonal relationships. On a practical level, this view was adopted by most Jews worldwide. Enter almost any synagogue and the depiction of the Ten Statements above the Ark will depict five on one tablet and five on the other.

However, the division of the statements between those governing relationships between God and people vs. people and people is only 90 percent accurate. The fifth statement instructs us to honor our parents. As important as our parents are—even being considered partners with God in our creation (*Kiddushin* 30b)—parents are still people, and therefore that law pertains to interpersonal relationships.

Tellingly, the distribution of the Ten Statements on two tablets is debated in rabbinic tradition (*Mekhilta D'Rabbi Ishmael De-Ba-Hodesh* 8; *Exodus Rabbah* 47:6). The view of five and five is a minority opinion. The majority view is that all 10 statements were written on each tablet. If the majority view is correct, what purpose would duplicate copies serve?

Professor Meshullam Margaliot of Bar-Ilan University employs our knowledge of ancient Near Eastern practices to shed light on the nature of the two tablets. The Torah speaks in a manner that people can understand. Although the Sinaitic covenant is unique in the annals of human history, Israel needed to understand the nature of their covenant with God from within their historical context.

In the ancient Near East, treaties and other contracts were issued in duplicate with each party keeping one copy. For example, there was a pact between Ramses II in Egypt and the Hittite King Hattusilis III around 1270 BCE. The Egyptian copy has been found in Egypt, and the Hittite copy was found in the Hittite capital, located in what is now Eastern Turkey. The contents of both treaties were identical. Similarly, the Ten Statements are a covenant between God and the people of Israel. There would be two identical copies: one for God, and one for the people.

Another common practice is that when a treaty was made between equal partners, each party kept its copy in the palace of the king. When the partners were unequal, the vassal would place his copy in the temple of his god. This strengthened the vassal's level of obligation to the greater king, and the most solemn religious sanctity was ascribed to the treaty.

Following this logic, Israel would have placed their copy in the Temple of their God, since God is superior and they were vassals. As the dominant party of the treaty, God would keep His copy in His palace. In the end, then, both identical tablets found their way into the Ark of the Covenant but for different reasons. God's copy was kept in His symbolic throne room or palace, whereas Israel's copy was placed in the holiest part of their Temple.

Meshullam Margaliot, "What Was Written on the Two Tablets?" Bar-Ilan, Ki Thisa, 5758, at http://www.biu.ac.il/JH/Parasha/eng/kitisa/mar.html.

Mishpatim

THE LAWS OF THE TORAH
IN THEIR ANCIENT CONTEXT

We now have access to over 500,000 legal documents from the ancient world. These treasures allow for a nuanced understanding of the Torah's laws, both in terms of what they have in common with their surrounding societies, and what makes the Torah unique.

Mesopotamian legal collections stand independently as codes. The Torah's laws are intertwined with narrative. The history of Israel is portrayed in terms of the people's faithfulness or lack thereof to the Torah and its laws.

In Mesopotamian codes, the king is an agent of a higher power. Humans and the gods are part of the same continuum, created from the same matter. People were created as slaves to provide for the gods' needs. In the Torah, God is above creation and gives laws directly to the people. Violation of any law is a rebellion against God. No Israelite king may establish laws, not even Moses. Keeping the commandments provides well-being for society but also is counted as righteousness toward God.

Mesopotamian legal collections deal with civil law, and these laws are primarily utilitarian. The Torah blends all types of laws: civil, religious, cultic, ethical. *All* derive from God. Observance of the laws creates holiness.

As a direct consequence of the low value of humans and the utilitarian emphasis of Mesopotamian laws, certain property crimes were capital offenses, and people often had a monetary value. In the case of murder, the family of the murdered person could accept monetary compensation. In the Torah, human life is absolute, whereas no property is. No monetary crime has a capital punishment associated with it, and no ransom may be accepted in case of a human killing another human (Numbers 35:31).

The same contrast is found in the laws of adultery. In Mesopotamian law, a man could pardon his wife and the adulterer since his wife was viewed as his possession. In the Torah, adultery is a crime against God. The adulterer has not only committed a social wrong, and a woman is not the possession of her husband.

Finally, Mesopotamian laws were a specialty reserved for experts. The Torah is for all Jews, beginning with its public revelation and ratification at Sinai. The Torah and its laws are among the most basic components of Jewish education.

Although there are several parallels between the Torah and earlier ancient Near Eastern legal codes, the Torah presents laws that shape a greater vision. It teaches that God revealed all laws; it teaches the centrality human dignity, which provides the basis for human morality; and it is accessible to all people.

Barry Eichler, "Study of Bible in Light of Our Knowledge of the Ancient Near East," in *Modern Scholarship in the Study of Torah*, ed. Shalom Carmy (New Jersey: Jason Aronson Inc., 1996), pp. 81–100.

Moshe Greenberg, "Some Postulates of Biblical Criminal Law," and "The Biblical Concept of Asylum," in Greenberg, *Studies in the Bible and Jewish Thought* (Philadelphia: JPS, 1995), pp. 25–50.

Rabbi Chaim Navon, *Genesis and Jewish Thought*, translated by David Strauss (Jersey City, NJ: Ktav, 2008), pp. 59–77.

Nahum Sarna, *Exploring Exodus* (New York: Schocken Books, 1986–1996), pp. 158–189.

Rabbi Moshe Shamah, *Recalling the Covenant: A Contemporary Commentary on the Five Books of the Torah* (Hoboken, NJ: Ktav, 2011), pp. 356–363; 385–398; 953–962.

WHAT DOES GOD LOOK LIKE?

he Torah describes the awesome experience at Mount Sinai. The Israelite camp was divided into three groups. Most remained distant from the mountain; the elders were allowed closer; Moses ascended into the realm of the mountain. How did each perceive the revelation?

"Now the Presence of the Lord appeared in the sight of the Israelites as a consuming fire on the top of the mountain" (Exodus 24:17). Where did this perception come from? Prior to Mount Sinai, their experience of God was one of plagues, destruction, and death. God was simply too awesome for most people to confront, and the Israelites retreated from the mountain in terror. In contrast, an attractive feature of the Golden Calf was its accessibility.

"Then Moses and Aaron, Nadab and Abihu, and seventy elders of Israel ascended; and they saw the God of Israel: under His feet there was the likeness of a brick of sapphire, like the very sky for purity" (Exodus 24:9–10). A sapphire is beautiful, precious, clear—a reminder of the heavens. But the sapphire was in the form of a brick—the symbol of slavery. The elders apprehended the beauty of God, but were profoundly affected by the brutal oppression. Where was God while the Israelites suffered with their brickmaking? They could partially ascend the mountain, but they, too, remained at a distance.

And Moses? In his initiation vision of the divine, he too saw fire, but he walked closer to inspect the bush. Upon closer reflection, Moses realized that the flame was not consuming the bush. As Moses grew in his relationship with God, "The Lord would speak to Moses face to face, as one man speaks to his friend" (Exodus 33:11). Moses could ascend to the pinnacle of the mountain.

Today, we still have this spectrum of religious experience. Many find the path to God too daunting or inaccessible. These individuals either stand at a distance, or else they look for an easier and more accessible alternative to spirituality that does not involve commitment to the Torah.

Those who grapple with God and develop a relationship with Him emulate the elders. God is lofty and beautiful, but still difficult to fathom.

These inviduals understandably are held back by the troubles of the world, and by their own personal experiences and limitations.

Just as God created us in His image, so too we shape God in *our* image. It is difficult to perceive God beyond our own realm of experience. Yet, Moses was able to transcend himself, to ascend the fiery mountain and perceive God as a "Friend." The Torah challenges us not to ignore the bricks or the flames, but to look beyond them as did Moses.

What does God look like? When one can answer this question, one has developed a profound sense of self, and a deeper relationship with God.

THE CHARACTER OF HUR

From the beginning of Moses' tenure as Israel's leader, three people stood by his side: his brother Aaron, his disciple Joshua, and Hur. Who was Hur? From the Torah's scant evidence, Ibn Ezra aptly remarks that "we do not know who he is."

First, let us consider the explicit references to Hur in the Torah. During Israel's battle against Amalek, Moses ordered Joshua to lead the troops. Moses, Aaron, and Hur ascended the hill, and Aaron and Hur supported Moses' tiring arms (Exodus 17:10–12). Hur clearly is to be counted among the highest echelons of the nation's leadership at the time of the exodus.

This impression is confirmed as Moses ascended Mount Sinai to receive the Torah. Again, his three associates occupied important positions. Joshua waited for his master at the base of the mountain while Moses delegated the leadership to Aaron and Hur (Exodus 24:13–14).

It is surprising, then, that when the people despaired of Moses' return from Sinai they clamored only to Aaron and built the Golden Calf (Exodus 32:1). Where was Hur? We never hear of him again. We are left to the world of midrash, which capitalizes on any information it can glean from Tanakh.

"[During the episode of the Golden Calf,] Hur arose and rebuked them: 'You brainless fools! Have you forgotten the miracles God performed for you?' Whereupon they rose against him and killed him. They then came to Aaron…and said to him: 'We will do to you what we have done to this man.' When Aaron saw the state of affairs, he was afraid" (*Exodus Rabbah* 41:7).

This midrash casts Hur as a religious martyr. His sudden disappearance in the text lends itself to this interpretation. This reading also helps explain Aaron's willingness to build the Calf, and provides *someone* in the camp who opposed the Calf while Moses was atop the mountain.

The next layer of Hur's midrashic portrait derives from the construction of the Tabernacle. God designated Bezalel as the chief artisan in the construction: "See, I have singled out by name Bezalel son of Uri son of Hur, of the tribe of Judah" (Exodus 31:2). Why would the Torah trace Bezalel back to his grandfather Hur? One midrash states that since Hur martyred himself during the Golden Calf episode, God rewarded him by choosing his grandson Bezalel as the chief artisan (*Exodus Rabbah* 48:3). My sister Ronda Angel Arking observes that this connection is especially cogent given that Hur opposed the artistic rendering of a source of golden worship. His grandson Bezalel then created artistic golden (and other precious) objects that were used in the process of true worship.

Other midrashim depict Hur as the son of the heroic spy Caleb and Miriam (*Sotah* 11b). Both of his midrashic parents put their lives on the line for God and their people. As a bonus, these associations would make Hur into Moses' nephew. The two individuals supporting Moses' tired arms in the battle against Amalek would be Moses' brother and his sister's son.

The various midrashim we have considered expand Hur into a religious hero and martyr, son of the elite of the desert generation, and grandfather of the leading artisan of the Tabernacle. Hur thereby is brought to life through these midrashic expansions.

Hayyim Angel, "Chur and Pharaoh's Daughter: Midrashic Readings of Silent Heroes," in *Mitokh Ha-Ohel: Essays on the Weekly Parashah from the Rabbis and Professors of Yeshiva University*, ed. Daniel Z. Feldman & Stuart W. Halpern (New York: Yeshiva University Press, 2010), pp. 205–213; reprinted in Angel, *Creating Space Between Peshat and Derash: A Collection of Studies on Tanakh* (Jersey City, NJ: Ktav-Sephardic Publication Foundation, 2011), pp. 35–43.

Terumah

THE TABERNACLE

*W*hen dedicating the First Temple, King Solomon expressed concern. If God is everywhere, how can He be contained in a specific place (I Kings 8:27)? Abarbanel explains that the Temple symbolically taught that God's Presence is manifest in this world.

However, the Torah's descriptions of God's Presence sound more than merely symbolic. God's Presence is perceptible in a way that people can sense, such as in the pillar of fire and the cloud of glory. Rabbi Marc D. Angel explained that this manifestation is analogous to focusing the sun's rays with a magnifying glass. The sun does not change at all, but we experience a higher concentration of rays. Similarly, God's Presence is felt more directly in the Temple than elsewhere.

Some midrashim and later commentators argue that God commanded Israel to build the Tabernacle (and later the Temple) to address human limitations. Israel's building of the Golden Calf demonstrated that they were unable to handle a purely abstract relationship with God (*Exodus Rabbah* 33:3; Rashi). In a similar vein, Rambam (*Guide for the Perplexed* III:32) explains that the Tabernacle and the sacrificial service were steps in weaning the people away from paganism, but the goal was for people eventually to be able to worship God without any physical intermediaries.

In contrast, Ramban (on Exodus 25:2) explains that the Tabernacle was an ideal, symbolizing the daily re-enactment of the Revelation at Sinai. Both Sinai and the Tabernacle had a tripartite division of holiness: (1) The mountain's summit is analogous to the Temple's Holy of Holies, accessible only to Moses or the High Priest. (2) The middle of the mountain is analogous to the Temple's Holy section, accessible only to the elders or the priests. (3) The base of mountain is analogous to the Temple courtyard, where all people could gather to experience God's revelation and service.

In addition to Ramban's association with the Revelation at Sinai, several midrashim ascertain connections between the Temple and the Garden of Eden. Ideally, Adam and Eve were supposed to follow God's commands and remain in the Garden. Instead, they sinned and were expelled, and God guarded the Tree of Life with Cherubim. Later on, the Torah replaced the magical Tree of Life with the Ark of the Covenant. Cherubim were placed above it, to guard it. This is the only other reference to Cherubim in the Torah, and the Book of Proverbs refers to Torah and Wisdom as the Tree of Life: "She is a tree of life for those who grasp her" (Proverbs 3:18) (*Midrash HaGadol* Genesis 3:24).

The Temple houses God's Presence, but the point of the Torah's teachings is for people to bring God's Presence into their midst by living a life of holiness. The Israelite camp, and ultimately all humanity, must extend itself to becoming a throne for God's Presence.

Rabbi Jonathan Sacks (*To Heal a Fractured World*, 2005, pp. 192–193) observes that the Torah takes 34 verses to describe the creation of universe. It affords between 500 and 600 verses to describe the building of the Tabernacle. Of course God can construct a home for people. The ultimate question is whether people will construct a home for God.

THE SYMBOLISM OF THE ARK

*R*abbi Elhanan Samet offers a nuanced portrayal of the Ark's significance. First is the command for a wooden box covered in gold to hold the Tablets. There are wooden poles also covered in gold to carry the Ark. This description is followed by a command for the Ark's cover to be fashioned out of pure gold with the Cherubim formed out of that gold.

The parallels in the two commandments create the analogy of poles : Ark :: Cherubim : Ark cover. The two poles parallel the two Cherubim. The poles are made of the same materials as the Ark (gold-covered wood), and the Cherubim are made of the same material as the Ark cover (pure gold).

Following the Torah's description, talmudic law rules that removing the poles from the Ark is a sin (*Yoma* 72a). Rabbi Samet explains that this prohibition is linked to the commandment of bearing the Ark on the shoulders of the Levites. This law demonstrates our perpetual subservience to the word of God.

The angelic world is represented by pure gold, symbolized by the Ark cover and Cherubim. The Ark and its poles represent humanity, and they are comprised of wood covered with pure gold symbolizing an integrated whole between body and soul.

Rambam (*Hilkhot Kelei ha-Mikdash* 2:12) rules that the people who carried the Ark had to face one another. Their formation parallels the Cherubim, which also faced one another.

The Ark represents the mutual covenant between God and Israel. The human side is to bear the burden of the Torah. The poles must be kept attached to the Ark since we must always bear the covenant. The divine side is that God communicates to Israel from between the Cherubim.

Additionally, the Cherubim were fashioned out of the gold of the Ark cover. This symbolizes that the angelic world has no free will and is essentially linked to the divine. In contrast, the *law* requires that the poles never be removed, but they physically could be removed. This relationship illustrates the need to accept God's covenant with our free will.

Rabbi Elhanan Samet, *Iyyunim be-Parashot ha-Shavua* (first series) vol. 1 (Hebrew) ed. Ayal Fishler (Ma'aleh Adumim: Ma'aliyot Press, 2002), pp. 224–236.

Tetzavveh

PRIESTHOOD IN THE TORAH

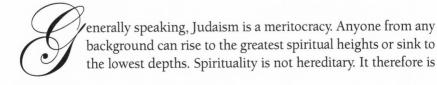

enerally speaking, Judaism is a meritocracy. Anyone from any background can rise to the greatest spiritual heights or sink to the lowest depths. Spirituality is not hereditary. It therefore is somewhat surprising that God chose Aaron and his descendents for a hereditary priesthood.

Rabbi Joseph Bekhor Shor suggests a practical reason for a hereditary priesthood. If one could earn the position, the system would inevitably fail. Perhaps not enough people would want to become priests. Alternatively, perhaps there would be too much competition. The Torah therefore prescribed a professional spiritual caste to avoid those pitfalls.

Rabbi Eitan Mayer suggests a different approach. Priests carried out Temple functions. They blessed Israel, represented Israel before God, and were responsible to teach and judge the people. Breaking those functions into two broad categories, the priest sometimes served as a bridge from God to the people: teaching, judging, and blessing. On other occasions, the priest was the bridge from the people to God: running the Temple service, and representing Israel before God.

Rabbi Mayer explains that the laws of the priesthood are included among the laws of the Tabernacle to teach that priests are like vessels. While in service, their personal identity is eclipsed by their position. A bridge must stand still to function.

Priests were anointed with oil like the other Tabernacle utensils (Exodus 30:25–33; 29:7; 29:21; 40:9–16). The priests were sprinkled with blood, parallel to the sprinkling of the altar (Exodus 29:12, 16, 20–21). During their installation, they remained passive while Moses performed the rituals on them. While in the service of God on behalf of the nation, they needed to follow an exact prescribed ritual without any creative input. From this vantage point, there needed to be a hereditary spiritual caste. The priest was a conductor, rather than an independent functionary. Even becoming a priest was a passive process of simply being born a priest.

During the Revelation at Sinai, God challenged Israel to be a nation of priests (Exodus 19:6), using our free will to rise to great heights. A priest must be worthy of his position; the challenge of every Jew is to voluntarily act like a priest, serving God and representing the community.

Rabbi Eitan Mayer, *Parsha Themes Tetzaveh*, at http://www.parshathemes.blogspot.co.il.

THE *TZITZ* AND THE *HOSHEN*

*I*n an oral presentation (Yeshivat Chovevei Torah Bible Study Days, 2004), Rabbi Mosheh Lichtenstein of Yeshivat Har Etzion explored the symbolism of two of the High Priest's garments: the *tzitz* (frontlet) on his forehead and the *hoshen* (breastplate) over his heart.

The *tzitz* was made of pure gold. It was placed over the High Priest's forehead, representing his intellect. On it was inscribed, "Holy to the Lord." The *hoshen* was made of fabric that was folded in half to form a pouch, symbolizing flexibility. The *hoshen* was placed over the priest's heart, the seat of emotion. The names of the 12 tribes were engraved on the gemstones on the *hoshen*, representing the nation.

The *tzitz* was a monochromatic gold, representing God and absolute truth. The *hoshen* contained 12 colorful gemstones, representing human diversity. The High Priest wore both, illustrating the duality of the relationship when standing before God. God is eternal, whereas we are diverse and subjective.

We may apply Rabbi Lichtenstein's analysis to synagogue life. The physical sacred space creates an objective realm where the most ideal standards are upheld. At the same time, synagogues are comprised of people who bring their colorful diversity into the fray. The leadership must demonstrate the flexibility of the *hoshen* in welcoming and embracing a diversity of congregants, while upholding the objective sacred traditions of the Torah when standing before God.

The balance represented by the *tzitz* and *hoshen* requires integrity and thoughtfulness. Some synagogues compromise ideal standards in favor of popular demand. Others are too rigid and sacrifice human diversity. It takes a dedicated community to constantly grow and improve within the framework of complete faithfulness to tradition.

Our minds proclaim, "Holy to the Lord!" This is sacred ground and our tradition is pure gold—permanent, never tarnishing, precious. Our hearts bring flexibility, colorful diversity, and passion into building our community.

Ki Tissa

RASHBAM ON MOSES' SHATTERING THE TABLETS

*D*escending Mount Sinai, Moses finds the nation dancing around the Golden Calf. Moses had entrusted the people under the leadership of his older brother Aaron. Instead, Aaron built the Golden Calf right at the heart of the camp. At that moment, Moses was abandoned.

Shockingly, Moses shattered the tablets, the most sacred objects ever transmitted to humanity. Most interpreters view this gesture as reflecting Moses' blazing anger. One lone voice argues otherwise. Rashbam posits that Moses was tired and dropped them as a result of his energy ebbing.

Professor Nehama Leibowitz dismisses this interpretation: "Rashbam, a literalist par excellence, veers far from the plain sense here. There is no clue in the text for his interpretation…." Professor Elazar Touito of Bar-Ilan University responded to Nehama's comment. Rashbam was engaged in anti-Christian polemic. Medieval Christians argued that Moses' shattering of the tablets meant that God's covenant with Israel was null and void. To deflate this argument, Rashbam offered an opinion that is not what the Torah means. Moses dropped the tablets by accident.

Professors Leibowitz and Touito agree that Rashbam's comment cannot possibly be what the Torah is saying. But perhaps Rashbam's insight has more textual and conceptual merit. Moses worked tirelessly on behalf of his people. His astounding energy derived from his faith and commitment to building community and vision. When Moses saw the people dancing around the Golden Calf, he was so demoralized that he temporarily lost his super-human energy, overwhelmed by the burden that had been there all along.

The positive side of Rashbam's analysis is that a faithful community can generate remarkable energy in all who participate.

Nehama Leibowitz, *Studies in Shemot (Exodus)*, translated and adapted by Aryeh Newman (Jerusalem: Eliner Library), pp. 605–606.

Elazar Touitou, "Between 'The Plain Sense of the Text' and 'The Spirit of the Text': Nehama Leibowitz's Relationship with Rashbam's Commentary on the Torah," (Hebrew), in *Pirkei Nehama: Nehama Leibowitz Memorial Volume*, ed. Moses Ahrend, Ruth Ben-Meir & Gavriel H. Cohn (Jerusalem: Eliner Library, 2001), pp. 221–240.

———

MOSES IN THE MIDDLE AND AT THE FRINGE OF THE CAMP

Following the Golden Calf episode, Moses distanced himself from the people by moving to the outer fringe of the camp (Exodus 33:7–11). Those who wanted to seek God needed to take personal responsibility to seek out Moses' guidance. The downside of Moses locating himself at the fringe of the camp is that most people likely did not seek him out.

Once Moses returned to Tabernacle, he stood again at the center of the camp. The whole nation once again had access to him. The positive aspect of this return to the center is that people should have access to their leader and teacher. The negative aspect is that many of those people brought Moses grief.

Moses did have one ideal moment when he stood in the center of the camp. During the Revelation at Sinai, the entire nation shared his commitment. Moses' boundless energy during that narrative is evident.

After the mass atonement from the Golden Calf and the construction of Tabernacle, Moses evidently expected everything to revert to the way it had been pre-Calf. Moses tried to enter the Tabernacle during its dedication as he had ascended Mount Sinai. However, God did not allow Moses to enter (Exodus 40:33–38).

God needed to teach Moses something vital about his leadership. After the Golden Calf, Israel no longer enjoyed the harmony that had existed at the revelation of the Torah. Two models of leadership present themselves in an imperfect world. Moses could dwell at the fringes of the camp and deal only with those who truly seek God. Or, he could station himself at the center of the camp where he would lead everyone—risking attack from those who did not share his vision and idealism.

Moses heroically stands at the center of camp through the insults and mutinies of the nation, his siblings, the spies, and Korah (Numbers, chapters 11–17). He remains with the people, but they wear him down.

When the people complained again for water in the 40th year, Moses finally retreated: "Moses and Aaron came away from the congregation to the entrance of the Tent of Meeting, and fell on their faces" (Numbers 20:6). Ibn Ezra explains that Moses and Aaron went to the Tabernacle "in the image of those fleeing." At this moment of weakness, Moses craved for a return to the Tent of Meeting at the fringe of the camp, surrounded by loyal friends and supporters. Fleeing to the Tabernacle was a failure in his leadership, and God informed Moses that he no longer would lead the people into the Land.

Moses' position at the center brought him much grief and ultimately contributed to his downfall. In the process, however, Moses guided a nation from Egyptian slavery to the border of the Promised Land. He trained them away from their slave mentality to become a free people with the potential to become the nation of God. He was the teacher of his generation, and all subsequent generations.

Vayakhel-Pekudei

THE GENESIS-EXODUS CONTINUUM

One of the basic axioms of Jewish tradition is that the divinely revealed Torah does not waste words. Why would Exodus open with information we know almost verbatim from the lengthier genealogy in Genesis 46? Ramban addresses this difficulty: "This is the very same verse that He [i.e., God in the Torah] repeats here. Even though they are two separate books, the narrative is connected with subjects which follow one another successively" (Ramban on Exodus 1:1, Chavel trans.). Ramban's response yields the essential argument that although there are indeed five books in the Torah, Genesis and Exodus are intimately linked and form one larger unit.

Ramban's argument has potentially significant ramifications. If Genesis and Exodus are considered as a single unit, the Book of Exodus may be viewed as the culmination of creation. There are several literary associations between the two books that draw them together. We will look at a few poignant examples from Exodus and briefly consider how we may ascertain a deeper layer of meaning when reading them in light of their parallels in Genesis.

The Israelites Fill the Land

The Israelites carry out the purpose of creation at the beginning of Exodus by being fruitful, multiplying, and filling the land (Exodus 1:7). Although the "land" in this verse refers specifically to Egypt, the formulation echoes the blessing to humanity in creation (Genesis 1:28). With Israel's role understood in this manner, Pharaoh's enslavement of Israel interferes with God's very creation, rather than only the people of Israel. As a result of Pharaoh's impeding divine blessings, God unleashes the forces of creation against him and his nation through the plagues, just as He had done against all humanity in Noah's time with the flood.

Moses

Moses' mother sees that her baby is "good" and therefore chooses to save him (Exodus 2:2). To what does Moses' "goodness" refer? One talmudic passage captures the literary import of this verse by drawing a parallel to the creation narrative, where God looks at His creation, and sees that it was good: "'And when she saw that he was good' (*va-tere oto ki tov hu*)...When Moses was born, the whole house was filled with light. It is written here, 'And when she saw that he was good,' and elsewhere it is written (Genesis 1:4): 'And God saw that the light was good' (*va-yar*

Elokim et ha-or ki tov)" (*Sotah* 12a). The birth of Moses, then, represents the beginning of a new world order to redeem it from the Pharaoh, who is threatening creation.

The Garden of Eden and the Tabernacle

One midrash considers the building of the Tabernacle to be the final act of creation, thereby linking it directly to Genesis: "What was the world like at the time of creation? It was like a chair on two legs which cannot stand erect but wobbles, and when they make for it a third leg it becomes steady and stands firm. In the same way, as soon as the Tabernacle was constructed ... the world was immediately set on a firm foundation and stood erect" (*Numbers Rabbah* 12:12). God's very creation is incomplete and unstable and requires the partnership of humanity to bring it stability.

The Tabernacle forms a perfect culmination to Genesis through several striking textual parallels to the creation account:

> And God saw all that He had made and found it very good (*va-yar Elokim et kol asher asah ve-hinnei tov me'od*). . . . The heaven and the earth were finished (*va-yekhulu ha-shamayim ve-ha-aretz*), and all their array. On the seventh day God finished the work that He had been doing (*va-yekhal Elokim ba-yom ha-shevi'i melakhto asher asah*) . . . God blessed (*va-yevarekh Elokim*) the seventh day and declared it holy, because on it God ceased from all the work of creation that He had done. (Genesis 1:31–2:3)

> Thus was completed all the work (*va-tekhel kol avodat*). . . . (Exodus 39:32)

> And when Moses saw that they had performed all the work—as the Lord had commanded, so they had done—Moses blessed them (*va-yar Moshe et kol ha-melakhah ve-hinnei asu otah ka'asher tzivvah Hashem ken asu, va-yevarekh otam Moshe*). (Exodus 39:43)

> When Moses had finished the work . . . (*va-yekhal Moshe et ha-melakhah*). (Exodus 40:33)

To summarize, "to see" (*r-'-h*), "to complete" (*y-k-l*), "all He/they had made" (*et kol asher asah*), "blessed" (*b-r-k*), "work" (*melakhah*), and several other idioms appear in both. While God "worked" in the creation, the Tabernacle is built through the "work" of Moses and the Israelites.

The laws of Shabbat are intimately linked to the building of the Tabernacle. God created the universe, and He ceased creative work on Shabbat. We emulate God in our Shabbat observance by our cessation of creative labor. In addition, the commandment to observe Shabbat flanks the laws of the Tabernacle on both sides. It concludes the descriptions of what needs to be built (Exodus 31:12–17) and then is reiterated immediately preceding the actual building (Exodus 35:1–3). Following these biblical precedents of connecting Shabbat and the Tabernacle, the prohibited categories of work on Shabbat enumerated in the Talmud are derived specifically from the categories of creative labor used in the construction of the Tabernacle (e.g., *Shabbat* 31b, 49b, 73b).

As a further link between the creation narratives and the Tabernacle, God Surrounded the Tree of of Life in Eden with sword wielding cherubim to protect it from Adam and Eve (Genesis 3:23–24). In the Tabernacle, the supernatural Tree of Life in Eden is replaced. Instead of a magical fruit that grants eternal life, we are given the Torah as a means of connecting to eternality. The Book of Proverbs links the Garden of Eden and Torah-wisdom by referring to the latter as a tree of life: "She is a tree of life (*etz hayyim hi*) to those who grasp her, and whoever holds on to her is happy" (Proverbs 3:18; cf. *Midrash ha-Gadol Bereshit* 3:24). In the Tabernacle, cherubim are placed above the Ark, to guard our "Tree of Life." The references to the cherubim in the Tabernacle are their only occurrences in the Torah outside the Eden narrative.

By viewing Genesis-Exodus as one greater unit, the Tabernacle belongs to all humanity and is the culmination of creation and an Eden replacement. Israel is the kingdom of priests to safeguard the Tabernacle and teach the world: "Now then, if you will obey Me faithfully and keep My covenant, you shall be My treasured possession among all the peoples. Indeed, all the earth is Mine, but you shall be to Me a kingdom of priests and a holy nation" (Exodus 19:5–6).

Israel's procreating and filling the world and Moses' being "good" further emphasize that Israel was positioned to fulfill the purpose of creation in the Book of Exodus. However, they were doing so as representatives of all humanity, and they would find their ultimate purpose in being a kingdom of priests that brings God's Presence to all people. In this spirit, Netziv (Rabbi Naftali Tzvi Yehudah Berlin, nineteenth-century Lithuania, introduction to Exodus) similarly stresses that Exodus completes the creation narrative from Genesis. Israel's receiving of the Torah was designed to transform Israel into a light unto the nations (Isaiah 42:6), thereby fulfilling the purpose of creation through that religious model.

To summarize, Genesis and Exodus reflect complex realities. On the one hand, there is a clear separation between the two books. On the other hand, the two books are intimately related. The beginning of Genesis parallels the beginning of Exodus and also the end of Exodus, joining them into a broader unit. Ramban's reflections on a simple redundancy have the potential to add layers of meaning toward a global interpretation of Genesis-Exodus. Ultimately, the two books taken together should inspire us to fulfill our purpose in creation—to be a light unto the nations and bring God's Presence to all humanity, created in God's Image.

Hayyim Angel, "The Genesis-Exodus Continuum: What Happens When They Are Viewed as a Larger Unit," *Intersession Reader* (New York: Tebah, 2009), pp. 43–52; reprinted in Angel, *Revealed Texts, Hidden Meanings: Finding the Religious Significance in Tanakh* (Jersey City, NJ: Ktav-Sephardic Publication Foundation, 2009), pp. 65–74.

Vayikra

ויקרא

Leviticus

Vayikra-Tzav

THE LITTLE ALEPH AT THE BEGINNING OF THE BOOK

The first word in Leviticus, *va-yikra*, ends with a small *aleph*. There is a technical scribal reason for this small *aleph*. The word that follows *va-yikra*, *el*, begins with the letter *aleph*, and ancient scribes often wrote one *aleph* to serve as both the ending of one word and the beginning of the following word.

Midrashic imagination adds color to the small *aleph*. The word *va-yikra* refers to deliberate calling from God to Moses. The deficient spelling—*va-yiker*—means "God chanced upon." The Torah uses this term in the Balaam narrative (Numbers, chapters 22–24). The deficient spelling of *va-yikra* as *va-yiker* thus downgrades Moses' prophetic revelation to the lesser level of God's chancing upon him (*Leviticus Rabbah* 1:13).

Rabbi Shlomo Riskin develops this idea further. Moses did not want to write that he was receiving a higher level of revelation. He therefore omitted the *aleph* to suggest that God chanced upon him. He was humble and therefore gave himself less credit than what he rightly deserved.

Another imaginative midrash continues this line of thought. If Moses did not write that *aleph* that means he saved up a little ink. What did he do with this ink? God took it and lovingly placed it on Moses' forehead, and this ink caused Moses' face to radiate (Exodus 34:29). Moses needed to wear a mask after that, as his glow was too overwhelming for the people.

Most people are less than they think they are. Rather than deceiving only themselves, they try to impress us, exaggerating their performance hoping to fool everyone. They wear masks to obscure their true selves, hiding behind inauthentic personas.

There are rare individuals who are more than they appear. They present less of themselves than who they truly are. Moses' concealed depths of spirituality and intellect were so great that he physically radiated. He needed a mask to shield his face from the people. His mask was not to fool any-one about who he was, but rather to temper his overwhelming greatness.

Rabbi Shlomo Riskin, *Torah Lights: Vayikra* (Jerusalem: Urim, 2009), pp. 9–11.

———

RAMBAM AND RAMBAN ON SACRIFICES

*S*ymbolically, the Tabernacle is the place where heaven meets earth. It created the opportunity to relive the most exalted moment in human history, namely, the Revelation at Sinai (Ramban). It represents humanity united in the service of God, and our desire to come ever closer to that perfect world.

Rambam (*Guide for the Perplexed* III:32) offered a far less romanticized picture. The Israelites grew up in pagan Egypt. God prescribed the Temple and its rituals to wean Israel away from paganism. Gradually, this system could be replaced with forms of worship such as prayer and other philo-sophical reflections that do not require physical intermediaries.

Ramban (on Leviticus 1:9) was appalled by Rambam's theory. He wrote: "Behold, these [Rambam's] words are worthless; they make a big breach, raise big questions, and they make the table of God polluted." The Temple was an ideal, as were the rituals performed there.

Writing in nineteenth-century Germany, Rabbi Samson Raphael Hirsch confronted a different problem. Many Jews were assimilating and citing Rambam as a precedent for their assimilation. They claimed that the commandments were given in a certain ancient context, but we no longer require those commandments in modern times since we no longer need to be weaned away from ancient forms of paganism. Ramban fundamentally disagreed with Rambam, whereas Rabbi Hirsch was concerned with the misapplication of Rambam's methodology on a practical level to many other commandments.

Elsewhere in his writings, Rambam speaks more favorably about sac-rifices, and notes that we cannot fully understand the reasoning behind the commandments (*Hil. Me'ilah* 8:8). He also codifies the laws of the Temple in his *Mishneh Torah* even though these laws had not been practiced for centuries. He obviously believed them relevant for the future when the Temple will be rebuilt.

Perhaps Rambam was trying to protect the honor of the Torah. Many in his time thought that Torah ritual sounded primitive. Rambam retorted that God knew that people cannot transform from a world of paganism and superstition to a sophisticated philosophical Rambam-style religiosity overnight, so God set out a long-term educational agenda. From this point of view, Rambam agreed that these practices *were* primitive, and justified the wisdom in the Torah's prescription of those practices within its historical setting.

Rambam also may have downplayed the Temple because many Jews placed too much emphasis on ritual details and not enough emphasis on the transcendent. Rambam wanted Jews to bear maximal responsibility for their spiritual well-being. They should not depend on ritual expiation.

Finally, since there is no Temple today, many commandments currently are out of practice. One could argue that this state of affairs should make us long for Temple and feel perpetually inadequate (Ramban). Or, one could argue that we need to channel our spiritual energies forward. Let us develop spiritually now and make the most of what we have (Rambam).

Hayyim Angel, "Rambam's Continued Impact on Underlying Issues in *Tanakh* Study," in *The Legacy of Maimonides: Religion, Reason and Community*, ed. Yamin Levy & Shalom Carmy (Brooklyn: Yashar Books, 2006), pp. 148–164; reprinted in Angel, *Through an Opaque Lens* (New York: Sephardic Publication Foundation, 2006), pp. 35–55.

THE ETHICAL DIMENSION OF SACRIFICES

The Hebrew word generally translated as "sacrifice," *korban*, does not actually mean "sacrifice," which implies giving something for nothing in return. It has a meaning closer to "that which is brought near, that which is presented." *Korbanot* were vehicles for getting closer to God (Rabbi Samson Raphael Hirsch on Leviticus 1:2).

Additionally, there was a strong ethical dimension lying beneath the surface of many offerings. Jacob Milgrom (*Anchor Bible 3: Leviticus*, p. 51) observes that the Torah is concerned that the poor also should have access to the altar. Birds, a lower-cost option, are acceptable for the burnt offering, *olah* (Leviticus 1:14–17). A midrash (*Leviticus Rabbah* 3:5) also assumes that the Torah permitted birds for this reason (see further in 5:7–10; 12:8; 14:21–22). The same philosophy lies behind the meal offering, *minhah* (chapter 2, 5:11–13; cf. *Leviticus Rabbah*; *Menahot* 104b). Both types of *korban* were inexpensive, and would ensure that nobody would feel excluded from coming closer to God.

In Leviticus, chapter 19, there are many ethical laws. In the middle of the chapter, we find legislation against *piggul*, or the bringing of a *korban* with the intention of eating it outside of the proper location in the Temple or its allotted time frame. The punishment for *piggul* is severe: "And he who eats of it shall bear his guilt, for he has profaned what is sacred to the Lord; that person shall be cut off from his kin" (19:8). In addition, the *korban* is invalid and must be replaced with another.

These laws relate specifically to the *shelamim* ("peace offering"). It had to be eaten in Jerusalem and before sunset of the day after bringing it. Curiously, if one has the proper intentions when bringing the offering, but then eats outside of the designated place or time, the punishment is less severe.

Rabbi Menachem Leibtag explains the rationale behind this law: The *shelamim* generally is too large for the person bringing it to eat by himself, so he must share the offering with others in Jerusalem. Therefore, the thought of eating it outside of the designated area reflects the owner's profound selfishness. If, at the height of one's spiritual experience, one thinks only of him or herself, God becomes "disgusted" (the literal meaning of *piggul*). When trying to create a bond with God, it *must* be accompanied by strong interpersonal values as well. Otherwise, the purpose of *korban* is undermined from within.

Rabbi Menachem Leibtag, Tanach Study Center, Kedoshim, at http://www.tanach.org/vayikra/kdosh/kdoshs1.htm.

Shemini

THE UNDERLYING MEANING OF SACRIFICE

*T*he term for a vegetable offering in the Torah is *minhah*, when the one offering the sacrifice leaves it before God. In the narrative of Cain and Abel, which represents the primeval act of sacrifice, both offerings are called *minhah*. A *minhah* is different from a *mattanah*, a gift. With a *minhah*, an inferior gives to a superior, leaving it with the hope that God will accept it. A gift applies only when one gives to his or her peers.

While the *minhah* teaches humility before God, there also is the potential for trauma if one presents to God and God rejects the offering—as He did with Cain. This trauma was so powerful that it led Cain to murder his brother. Moshe Halbertal explains that the human desire to give is so profound that when thwarted it can lead to destructive behavior. The exclusion from giving—a profoundly human act—is a deeper source of violence than deprivation from not receiving.

The Torah's laws address this anxiety of rejection. God prescribes detailed rituals, which guarantee that offerings will be accepted. But although the Torah solved the problem of rejection anxiety, it created a new hazard in any change in this prescribed ritual. Nadab and Abihu died because they breached God's protocol (Leviticus 10:1–3). The laws of Yom Kippur are directly linked to deaths of Nadab and Abihu (Leviticus 16:1), stressing that the only way to guarantee safety and intimacy with God is through precisely following God's prescribed ritual.

The underlying message of sacrifices was a message of love. Love is different from lust and contract, which are about the fulfillment of one's needs through the other. The paradox of the Torah is that God wishes to be loved by us, but that type of relationship is almost impossible. We are absolutely dependent on God. Therefore, we are extremely likely to create an instrumental relationship with God, where we serve God in order to receive our sustenance in return.

What could we possibly offer that proves our true love of God? Halbertal explains that this paradox lies at the root of the Akedah, where God demanded a gift outside of the realm of exchange, since nothing could replace Isaac, whose value to Abraham was absolute. As soon as Abraham showed willingness, he proved his absolute love.

While rejecting child-sacrifice, God taught Abraham that true love of God requires the willingness to sacrifice anything for God without hope of getting something in return. The ram Abraham offered in place of Isaac represented the element of replacement inherent in all animal sacrifice. Underlying all sacrifice is the idea is that we love God to the point where we are ready to sacrifice ourselves, and the animal is substitution. Thus, sacrifice appears like a part of a gift cycle where we offer an animal or flour with the hopes of receiving more, but the Torah teaches that they are symbolic of the gift that cannot be reciprocated.

Moshe Halbertal, *On Sacrifice* (Princeton, NJ: Princeton University Press, 2012).

KASHRUT

*S*everal commentators attempt to explain the rationale behind the laws of kashrut. Rashbam (on Leviticus 11:3) and Rambam (*Guide for the Perplexed* III:48) suggest that it is more healthful to eat only kosher foods. However, observing the laws of kashrut does not necessarily lead to a healthful diet, and many people who do not observe the laws of kashrut are perfectly healthy.

Ramban and Abarbanel adopt the doctrine of "you are what you eat." The Torah prohibits eating predators and thereby trains us to be gentle. However, this rationale is incomplete since we also are prohibited from eating several gentle animals. Rabbi Yitzhak Arama therefore concludes that this commandment teaches obedience to God, as we cannot ascertain God's reasons for determining which animals are permitted or prohibited.

One may posit a broader framework to these laws. The first direct commandment to humanity was for people to eat all the fruits of the Garden of Eden except for the Tree of Knowledge (Genesis 2:15–17). There is no rationale given for this prohibition, which pertains to permitted and prohibited foods.

When Noah disembarks from the Ark, God issues a new set of commandments. The first post-flood law governs eating: "You must not, however, eat flesh with its life-blood in it" (Genesis 9:4). Halakhah understood this as a prohibition against eating limbs taken from living animals. There is an ethical component to this prohibition.

Jacob Milgrom (*Anchor Bible 3: Leviticus*, pp. 704–742) cogently argues that the laws of kashrut for Israel extended the Noahide laws. The Torah prohibits eating various animals. Predators are excluded, giving credence to Ramban's interpretation. Much of the commandment cannot be explained with reason. The lack of a full explanation teaches God-consciousness, as per Rabbi Arama.

The Noahide prohibition against eating life-blood was extended to Israelites who have further restrictions on draining blood. Soaking and salting meat are essential aspects of kashrut. The slitting of an animal's throat always has meant the laws of *shehitah* (*Hullin* 27a). Although the Torah does not explain its details, the Talmud provides regulations with the clear intent of minimizing pain to the animal.

Similar reasoning applies to the prohibition against cooking a kid in its mother's milk. Ibn Ezra and Rashbam explain that the prohibition teaches compassion, related to the prohibitions against slaughtering an animal and its offspring on the same day (Deuteronomy 22:28), sacrificing an animal in the first week of its life (Deuteronomy 22:27), and keeping the mother bird present while taking her young (Deuteronomy 22:6–7).

Kashrut limits the animals we may eat, prohibits the eating of blood, prescribes *shehitah*, and creates a network of other laws that teach compassion. Rather than viewing the laws of kashrut purely as divine commandments with no rationale, they reinforce our compassion and ethical behavior and simultaneously teach God-consciousness every time we eat.

Rabbi Elhanan Samet, *Iyyunim be-Parashot ha-Shavua* (second series) vol. 2, ed. Ayal Fishler (Ma'alei Adumim: Ma'aliyot, 2004), pp. 37–58.

Tazria-Metzora

RITUAL IMPURITY

*R*itual impurities arose from coming into contact with certain types of dead animals; childbirth; the skin affliction *tzara'at*; seminal and menstrual discharges; and coming into contact with a human corpse. "Impurity" is a ritual state that prohibits one from entering the Temple precincts or coming into contact with sacred foods, such as sacrifices or tithes.

Rabbi Yehudah Halevi (*Kuzari* II:58–62) explains that impurities generally relate to death. Even the ultimate life-giving process, childbirth, also rendered a woman ritually impure. Some have proposed that life came out of her, or perhaps the impurity stems from an unusually high loss of blood during childbirth. Given that God and the Temple represent eternal life, one who came into contact with some form of death would undergo a rehabilitation period and purification process before being permitted to return to the Temple.

Jacob Milgrom observes that the Torah and rabbis did not want menstruating women to leave the camp to special menstruation huts. There was nothing dangerous or negative about menstrual blood. The Torah's practice stood in sharp contrast to those of surrounding nations (*Anchor Bible 3: Leviticus*, pp. 948–953).

A different question arises regarding the laws of childbirth. A mother who gives birth to a boy is ritually impure for seven days, and a mother who gives birth to a girl is ritually impure for 14 days. Why the difference?

Some ancients thought that male and female embryos took different amounts of time to develop. Rabbi Yishmael (Mishnah *Niddah* 3:7) believed that the male embryo formed in 41 days, whereas a female embryo took 81 days to form. Aristotle thought similarly: 40 days for a boy, three months for a girl. Hippocrates estimated boys at 30 days and girls at 42 days.

Alternatively, Rabbi Simeon bar Yohai (*Niddah* 31b) argued that a mother should be ritually impure for 14 days both for boys and for girls. However, boys are circumcised on the eighth day, so the Torah returns the mother to a ritually pure state so that husband and wife can touch one another affectionately by the time of the celebration (Bekhor Shor, Hoffmann, Boleh).

Rabbi Samson Raphael Hirsch suggests that after the birth of a girl, a mother has brought into the world another female who also will hopefully grow up and give birth one day. This recognition makes the mother want more time to think about the wonder of life and life-giving. Baruch Levine (JPS, p. 250) also suggests this possibility.

Of course, we cannot know with certainty why God prescribed the laws as written, but our commentators offer illuminating possibilities.

Shlomo Spiro, "On Rationalizing Biblical *Tum'a*," *Tradition* 43:1 (Spring 2010), pp. 23–37.

—

TZARA'AT

*T*he skin affliction *tzara'at* has not been extant for some 2,000 years. Although we do not know the exact nature of the biblical disease, we can explore its meaning.

Most commentators explain that *tzara'at* was a spiritual affliction rather than a contagious physiological ailment (Rambam, comm. Mishnah *Nega'im* 12:5; Ramban, Sforno). The Torah also never explains how to cure the disease. It teaches only how to diagnose the condition, and then prescribes rituals for reentry to the community after healing.

Considering biblical instances of *tzara'at*, it generally appears to result from sin (*Arakhin* 16b). There is a similar purification ritual as one who comes into contact with a dead person.

The *metzora* (one afflicted by *tzara'at*) tears his clothing, loosens his hair, and "covers his lip" thereby hiding from the rest of the world. These are also signs of mourning. Furthermore, the *metzora* is not allowed to live within the city limits and is banished from society during the course of the ailment. As he walks, he cries out *tamei! tamei!* (impure! impure!) (13:45). The Talmud (*Mo'ed Katan* 5a) explains that this cry is to keep people away from him. This is the only law in the Torah where a person receives this extreme treatment.

When God afflicted Miriam with *tzara'at*, Aaron begged Moses, "O my lord, account not to us the sin which we committed in our folly. Let her not be as one dead, who emerges from his mother's womb with half his flesh eaten away" (Numbers 12:11–12). Someone with *tzara'at* looks dead. His skin peels profusely and spontaneously like a stillborn. Not only does the *metzora* mourn, but he is considered dead. He mourns for himself.

The isolation of the *metzora* serves as a punishment but also affords the chance for introspection. *Tzara'at* symbolically offers the unique chance for an individual to die, but then to repent and become alive again.

Rabbi Eitan Mayer, Tazria-Metzora, at http://www.parshathemes.blogspot.co.il.

THE PURIFICATION OF THE METZORA

*P*arashat Metzora focuses on the purification process for the healed *metzora*. Jacob Milgrom (*Anchor Bible 3: Leviticus*, p. 837) observes that the person must be fully healed before this ceremony. The Torah has transformed an exorcistic healing rite to the realm of ritual purification. Healing comes from God, and the priest takes care of the Temple.

The former *metzora* takes two birds. One is brought as a sacrifice to God, and the other is set free. This ceremony resembles the taking of two goats on Yom Kippur (Leviticus, chapter 16). There is a bifurcation in these two dual-sacrifices. Sacrifices symbolically replace the person bringing them, and make those who offer them whole again. *Tzara'at* represents a situation so severe that one needs to symbolically amputate part of oneself. The remaining part is then purified and dedicated to God. The same concept underlies the Yom Kippur ceremony to atone for the sins of the nation.

The next aspect of the purification of the *metzora* involves sprinkling blood mixed with cedar, hyssop, and scarlet wool. This potion resembles that mixed with the ashes of the Red Cow (Numbers, chapter 19). Just as the ashes of the Red Cow purify someone who had come into contact with a human corpse, this mixture purifies the *metzora* who was ritually considered as dead.

Following the purification, blood is sprinkled on the extremities of the healed *metzora*: his ears, fingers, and toes (Leviticus 14:14–17). This process resembles the installation of the priests for Temple service (Leviticus, chapter 9).

The opposite of *tumah* (impurity) is *taharah* (purity). However, the ultimate goal of the purification process is not simply to eliminate *tumah*, but rather to elevate the individual to the level of *kedushah*, holiness. For this reason the healed *metzora* follows the Red Cow ritual to eliminate *tumah* but then follows the procedure of the installation of the priesthood to attain *kedushah*. The Torah teaches that one living through a crisis should seize the opportunity and end in a better place than before the crisis.

To summarize, the *metzora* went through a three-step process: symbolic amputation of sin; purification from having come into contact with a corpse (=himself); and elevation to the level of *kedushah*. Going through a traumatic experience leads to self-mourning and introspection, isolation. The desire to move ahead requires letting the negativity fly away. If we follow this process properly we end in a better place than before we began. The Torah sets out a process of healing whose relevance endures beyond the existence of this disease and the Temple.

Rabbi Eitan Mayer, Tazria-Metzora, at http://www.parshathemes. blogspot.co.il.

Aharei Mot

DYNAMIC LOVE OF GOD

*P*arashat Aharei Mot connects the laws of Yom Kippur pertaining to the High Priest's entry into the Holy of Holies with the deaths of Nadab and Abihu. During the dedication of the Tabernacle, Aaron's sons spontaneously offered incense and lost their lives as a result.

Rabbi Yoel Bin-Nun offers an analysis of this association. There is an immense distinction between the two sections of the Tabernacle: the Holy, and Holy of Holies. The priests performed services in the Holy section year-round. They kindled the menorah, offered incense, and arranged the showbread. The Holy represented the realm of humanity, where people reach out to God.

The Holy of Holies, by contrast, contained the Ark, the Ten Commandments and Torah, the manna, and Aaron's staff. Everything in that section came from God to the people. The Holy of Holies symbolized God's domain reaching out to humanity. The Tabernacle (and later the Temple) epitomized the encounter between God and humanity, carefully preserving the boundaries between the two realms by placing a separating curtain between them.

These areas were not static, however. On the day the Tabernacle was consecrated, God's Presence descended onto both sections. For that one day, the Holy became an extension of the Holy of Holies, and people were not allowed to enter. Yom Kippur represents a move in the opposite direction, when the High Priest traversed the curtain in the Tabernacle, entering the Holy of Holies.

Rabbi Bin-Nun explains that Nadab and Abihu blurred the realm of the human with the divine. On a day when God wanted the entire Tabernacle to be filled with His Presence, Aaron's sons violated the separation between the two domains.

Although Nadab and Abihu had committed an atrocious theological crime, their death posed a new challenge: People might conclude that God was unapproachable. Yom Kippur addresses that concern. On that day, God "retreats" from the Holy of Holies, allowing the High Priest, the representative of all humanity, to enter the realm of the divine for a brief moment. People are invited to enter a dimension they normally cannot, in order to deepen their connection with God.

In the Song of Songs, the two lovers likewise oscillate between pursuit and retreat. There exists a constant and deepening desire in their amorous pursuit. Our Sages understood this magnificent poem as symbolic of the love that exists between God and religious individuals: "Rabbi Akiva said . . . [all the ages of] the whole world are not worth the day on which the Song of Songs was given to Israel. For all of the writings are Holy, but the Song of Songs is the Holy of Holies" (Mishnah *Yadayim* 3:5).

Rabbi Yoel Bin-Nun. "The Eighth Day and Yom Kippur" (Hebrew), *Megadim* 8 (1989), pp. 9–34.

———

Kedoshim

THE MEANING OF HOLINESS

*I*n an article in *Converations* 9 (Institute for Jewish Ideas and Ideals), Professor Steven Kepnes explores different interpretations of the Torah's concept of holiness. Leviticus, chapter 19 begins and ends with God. People attain holiness by looking outward, not inward. Actions have a social context, rather than meditation in isolation. In the Torah's view, we become holy when we focus on others and belong to a community of God.

Rashi defines holiness as refraining from that which is prohibited. Ramban objects and insists that holiness also encompasses a positive dimension. It is possible to refrain from the prohibited and still be an obnoxious, unrefined person. The Torah and its commandments are intended to refine us, and that collective outcome is what it means to be holy.

The nineteenth-century Rabbis Yisrael Salanter and Moshe Sofer adopted a different definition. Holiness is defined by one's honesty in business and ethical conduct. Holiness is not about what we refer to as spirituality, but rather about living an upright life in the most mundane settings.

In that same issue of *Conversations*, Rabbi Marc D. Angel quotes Alan Watts, whose definition of spirituality resembles that of Rabbis Salanter and Sofer: "The most spiritual people are the most human. They are natural and easy in manner, they give themselves no airs: they interest themselves in ordinary everyday matters, and are not forever talking and thinking about religion. For them, there is no difference between spirituality and usual life" (*The Supreme Identity*, 1972, p. 128).

At a different level, a life of holiness involves our attempting to emulate God. The Talmud describes this endeavor:

What does this text mean: "You shall walk after the Lord your God" (Deuteronomy 13:5)?... [The meaning is] to walk after the attributes of the Holy One, blessed be He. As He clothes the naked...so do you also clothe the naked. The Holy One, blessed be He, visited the sick...so do you also visit the sick. The Holy One, blessed be He, comforted mourners...so do you also comfort mourners. The Holy one, blessed be He, buried the dead . . . so do you also bury the dead. (*Sotah* 14a)

Just as [God] is gracious and compassionate, so you be gracious and compassionate. (*Shabbat* 133b)

The Hasidic Rabbi Menahem Mendel of Kotsk observed that the Torah's injunction to be holy is not only a commandment but is also a promise that any person can be holy. Holiness is not reserved for an elite few but rather is availble to all who pursue it. All of the aforementioned elements are facets of a life of holiness. Instead of creating a vague, ethereal sense, the Torah challenges all people to pursue this noble path in all walks of life.

Steven Kepnes, "Holiness: The Unique Form of Jewish Spirituality," *Conversations* 9 (Winter 2011), pp. 30–44.

PLACING A STUMBLING BLOCK
BEFORE THE BLIND

"*Y*ou shall not insult the deaf, or place a stumbling block before the blind" (Leviticus 19:14). Although these commandments seem straightforward enough, halakhah understands the prohibition against placing a stumbling block before the blind metaphorically; that is, the Torah prohibits giving misleading advice or extending a prohibited item to someone else. If someone literally places a stumbling block in front of a blind person, it is obviously sinful and otherwise depraved, but it is unclear if it violates this specific prohibition.

Nowhere in talmudic or midrashic literature is there mention of the literal prohibition. It always is understood metaphorically. Rambam, Semag, Hinnukh, and many others follow this lead and assume that the Torah's prohibition is exclusively metaphorical. Several more recent rabbinic authorities contend that halakhah extends the literal law, which is obviously included in the prohibition (*Meshekh Hokhmah, Torah Temimah, Minhat Hinnukh*). If these latter authorities are correct, though, it is odd that the Sages and earlier codifiers do not include the literal reading under this prohibition.

Although the rabbinic evidence supports the position that the verse is to be understood exclusively as metaphorical, we must ask: How can there be a metaphorical reading of a *legal* text? We cannot have a legal system where there are many ways to interpret basic laws. Are there good reasons to have a metaphorical reading of the text here?

Rabbi Elhanan Samet suggests that the Torah knows the ethical level of its audience. Most prohibitions in the interpersonal arena are easily understood. One might steal to acquire possessions, for example. But what motivation is there for placing a physical obstacle in front of a blind person? This is pure, malicious sadism with no gain for the sinner. The Torah would not waste time to expressly prohibit this behavior, since it was so out of the range of its audience. Rabbi Abraham Isaac Kook similarly suggested that this is why the Torah never expressly prohibits cannibalism. It is so obviously forbidden that there was no need to write this.

Therefore, the Sages adopted a metaphorical interpretation of this verse. One might be tempted to give bad advice to another if one stands to gain. One might extend prohibited food to a friend because one's feelings of friendship might prevail over one's halakhic sense.

If this analysis is correct, though, why would the Torah not just write out this metaphorical understanding literally? Rabbi Samet argues that giving bad advice or extending prohibited food to a friend are both easy to rationalize. Giving bad advice is at worst indirect harm. Extending forbidden food to a friend is "helping" the person who wants to violate the law. Therefore, the Torah uses forceful poetic language to discourage people from such rationalizations. If you do this, it is as though you are placing a stumbling block in front of a blind person! In this reading, the Torah creates a fundamental connection between law, poetry, and ethics in order to elevate us morally and religiously.

Rabbi Elhanan Samet, *Iyyunim be-Parashot ha-Shavua* (first series) vol. 2 (Hebrew) ed. Ayal Fishler (Ma'aleh Adumim: Ma'aliyot Press, 2002), pp. 78–93.

———

LOVE YOUR NEIGHBOR AS YOURSELF

"You shall not take vengeance or bear a grudge against your countrymen. Love your neighbor as yourself: I am the Lord" (Leviticus 19:18). This verse is one of the most celebrated in the Torah. However, the precise meaning of this verse has been hotly debated.

Ramban explains that this commandment is an ideal aspiration rather than something possible to fulfill in entirety. Alternatively, Rambam (*Hilkhot De'ot* 6:3) interprets this commandment in the realm of actions. One should praise one's neighbor and care for his property as one would care for himself. Elsewhere (*Hilkhot Avelut* 14:1), Rambam includes ethical commandments such as visiting the sick and comforting the mourner under the general dictum of loving one's neighbor. Rabbi Moshe Shamah notes that in the ancient Near East, the term *love* often had the connotation of "to be loyal to," or "to be devoted to." From this perspective, the commandment is action-based rather than emotion-based.

Midrashim and medieval commentators generally assume that this verse refers to fellow Jews. In the eighteenth century, Naftali Hertz Wessely (*Biur*, 1782) insisted that the verse commands Israelites to love all humans as themselves. His view became accepted to the point where some completely ignored the existence of the predominant earlier Jewish opinion. For example, in his commentary on the Torah, Dr. Joseph H. Hertz blames "anti-Semites" for insisting that the Torah refers only to fellow Israelites (pp. 563–564).

However, a later verse in the same passage commands that Israelites must love strangers as themselves (19:34). That verse suggests that "Love your neighbor as yourself" refers to fellow Israelites. The collective force of chapter 19, however, commands that Israel love all people, Israelites and non-Israelites.

Harold Fisch explains that it is incredibly difficult to love all *Israelites* as we love ourselves. Certainly, then, to extend that commandment to all humanity is unrealistic. Other forms of human relations exist besides love. The Torah can, however, command upright ethical behavior for all humanity, and we can expect that behavior to be reciprocated. We love members of our family, and have a deep moral obligation toward all people who themselves act morally.

Jacob Milgrom (*Anchor Bible 3A: Leviticus*, p. 1656) explains that on the psychological plane, the commandment is a statement of fact. The extent of how much one is capable of loving others is the extent that one loves oneself. This ideal state can be approached when one recognizes that all people are created in the image of God. Fulfillment of this ideal is a goal of a lifetime.

Professor Yeshayahu Leibowitz stresses that the commandment to love our neighbor is a divine commandment, and the verse ends, "I am God." The duty of love toward our neighbor does not stem from humanistic responsibility to our neighbor but rather from responsibility to God (*Judaism, Human Values, and the Jewish State*, pp. 6–7, 19).

Reinhard Neudecker, "'And You Shall Love Your Neighbor as Yourself—I Am the Lord' (Lev 19,18) in Jewish Interpretation," *Biblica* 73 (1992), pp. 496–517.

Rabbi Moshe Shamah, *Recalling the Covenant: A Contemporary Commentary on the Five Books of the Torah* (Jersey City, NJ: Ktav, 2011), p. 632.

Ernst Simon, "The Neighbor (*Re'a*) Whom We Shall Love," (and response of Harold Fisch) in *Modern Jewish Ethics: Theory and Practice*, ed. Marvin Fox (Ohio: Ohio State University Press, 1975), pp. 29–61.

—

Emor

THE DAY AFTER SHABBAT

*R*abbi Jonathan Sacks addresses two classical questions pertaining to Shavuot: (1) Why doesn't the Torah link Shavuot with the Revelation at Sinai? The Torah's description of Shavuot revolves around the *omer* offering of barley, and then counting seven weeks from Pesah to Shavuot. (2) When was the *omer* offering brought? This latter point was the subject of a fierce debate in the Second Temple period.

The Torah commands to bring the *omer* offering on "the day after the Sabbath" (Leviticus 23:11). In the Second Temple period, there were two predominant factions, the Sadducees and Pharisees. The Sadducees were generally more affluent than the Pharisees, and were connected to the priestly establishment and Temple. They viewed Jewish identity in terms of State and Temple, whereas the Pharisees measured Jewish identity by one's personal piety and observance of the Torah. The Pharisees—generally regarded as the forerunners of rabbinic tradition—gave equal weight to the Written and Oral Law, whereas the Sadducees exclusively accepted the authority of the Written Torah.

This fundamental divide became central in the debate over when to observe Shavuot. The Sadducees understood "Sabbath" in this verse as meaning "Saturday," so the following day is Sunday. On the basis of this verse, they rigged their calendar so that the first day of Pesah always fell on Shabbat, and Shavuot therefore fell on a Sunday seven weeks later. In contrast, the Pharisees interpreted "Sabbath" in this verse to mean "the first day of Pesah." They insisted that the *omer* be brought on the second day of Pesah, regardless of the day of the week. To this day, we begin counting the *omer* on the second day of Pesah, following Pharisaic-Rabbinic tradition.

There are major implications to this debate. The Sadducees denied the Oral Law, and therefore read only the surface of the Torah. For them, Shavuot was simply an agricultural holiday determined by the barley harvest on Pesah. God had farmers in mind by giving them a long weekend— Shabbat and then a Sunday off. The Torah was a religion of the people in Israel, linked directly to land, priesthood, sacrifices, and the Temple.

Adhering to Oral tradition, the Pharisees looked beneath the surface of the Torah to its subtext. There is a deep connection between the exodus and the Revelation at Sinai. Shavuot is not only an agricultural holiday, but rather it has eternal historical significance that transcends the Land of Israel.

After the Romans destroyed the Temple, the Sadducees became obsolete. Their whole religion was linked to the Temple/priesthood and land/farmers—and that world was gone. Had the Sadducees won this argument during the Second Temple Period, Judaism would have disappeared after the destruction of the Second Temple. Thankfully, the Pharisees prevailed, and Judaism thrives as a result of their insistence that the Torah applies eternally to Jews wherever they may live.

Rabbi Jonathan Sacks, *Faith in the Future: The Ecology of Hope and the Restoration of Family, Community, and Faith* (Macon, GA: Mercer University Press, 1997), pp. 145–148.

Behar-Behukkotai

CITY-DWELLER, FARMER, SHEPHERD

*R*abbi Samson Raphael Hirsch (on Genesis 4:1) discusses the difference between farmers and shepherds. An agrarian lifestyle calls for the expenditure of bodily strength, pride of possession, and accomplishment. Since landowners cannot easily move despite unfavorable weather, most great cultural advances have been stimulated by creative agrarians. Genesis 4:20–22 credits the farmer Cain's descendants with the development of new techniques in animal husbandry, music, and metallurgy.

On the other hand, farm labor can work a person down to the level of a beast of burden. Similarly, an agrarian society can create conditions of subjugation and lead to the worship of the forces of nature that give life and death to the farmer. The Sabbath, sabbatical year, and other agricultural laws of the Torah protect Israel from succumbing to the negative elements of an agrarian lifestyle. By teaching that the world belongs to God, the Torah prevents Israelites from feeling absolute ownership over their land or others.

In contrast, the leisure time enjoyed by shepherds provides the potential to open avenues toward spiritual growth. Additionally, shepherds care for and guide creatures, thereby developing essential qualities for compassionate leadership. The Patriarchs, Moses, David, and other great biblical figures were shepherds.

City living is a third type of lifestyle. The Torah is not opposed to city living per se, but it is wary of the spiritual dangers of the false sense of permanence and secularization inherent in being removed from a direct dependence on nature. The Torah's real estate laws codify this distinction. Sales of fields were never permanent, since the land belongs to God (Leviticus 25:23). In walled cities, however, sales became permanent after the first year of the sale (Leviticus 25:29–30).

Two later prophets used this analysis when addressing corruption in Jerusalem. The seventh-century B.C.E. prophet Zephaniah proposed the idyllic humble lifestyle of shepherds as the antidote to the negative aspects of cities he witnessed in his time. The cities had become hotbeds of arrogance and corruption by the wealthy classes in Jerusalem and in other nations. He envisioned the downfall of these cities and their being replaced by shepherds.

Zephaniah's approach may be contrasted with the eighth-century B.C.E. prophet Isaiah's alternative model of Jerusalem as the ideal city: "In the days to come, the Mount of the Lord's House shall stand firm above the mountains and tower above the hills; and all the nations shall gaze on it with joy. And the many peoples shall go and say: 'Come, let us go up to the Mount of the Lord, to the House of the God of Jacob; that He may instruct us in His ways, and that we may walk in His paths.' For instruction shall come forth from Zion, the word of the Lord from Jerusalem" (Isaiah 2:2–3).

In Isaiah's vision, Jerusalem will become a metropolitan center to which the world will congregate to serve God. The Temple and the religious-moral code it represents will unite humanity. In this regard, cities can become powerful forces for the good when run properly from a religious perspective.

Hayyim Angel, "Zephaniah's Usage of the Genesis Narratives," in Angel, *Revealed Texts, Hidden Meanings: Finding the Religious Significance in Tanakh* (Jersey City, NJ: Ktav-Sephardic Publication Foundation, 2009), pp. 162–170.

A DUAL-READING OF CHAPTERS 25–26

"*I*f you follow My laws and faithfully observe My commandments, I will grant your rains in their season, so that the earth shall yield its produce and the trees of the field their fruit..." (Leviticus 26:3–4). If Israel upholds the covenant, they will receive many blessings. If they are unfaithful, they will receive a litany of curses.

To what do "My laws" and "My commandments" refer? Rashi assumes that this is a blanket statement that refers to all the laws of the Torah.

Although Rashi's interpretation makes sense in a vacuum, it becomes more difficult when we consider the surrounding context. The Torah links the curses to the exile for non-observance of the Sabbatical year: "Then shall the land make up for its sabbath years throughout the time that it is desolate and you are in the land of your enemies; then shall the land rest and make up for its sabbath years" (Leviticus 26:34). If the blessings and curses refer to the entire Torah, why should there be an emphasis on non-observance of these specific agricultural laws?

This question becomes compounded from the broader context in chapter 25, which legislates the Sabbatical year. Verses 18 and 19 in chapter 25 describe these laws as "*hukkotai u-mishpatai.*" It appears that these are the referent in 26:3, which uses the same words (see Rashi, Ramban, Hizkuni, Sforno on 25:18–19).

These questions led Rashbam to conclude that chapters 25–26 are linked through a literary inclusio. The passage begins and ends with the expression "on Mount Sinai." *Hukkotai u-mishpatai* refer specifically to the laws of the Sabbatical and Jubilee years. Given the emphasis on the land being restored for the years the Sabbatical year was not observed, Rashbam's view accounts for the evidence better than Rashi's view.

However, why would the covenant rest exclusively on observance of the Sabbatical and Jubilee years? We may adopt a view that combines Rashi and Rashbam. On the local level, Rashbam appears correct. The references to the Sabbatical year in 26:34, 43; the reference to *hukkotai u-mishpatai* in 25:18–19; and the literary inclusio with "on Mount Sinai" in 25:1 and 26:46, support the notion that the blessings and curses are contingent specifically on the observance of these laws.

The question then arises: Why is the passage in Leviticus, chapters 25–26 positioned toward the end of Leviticus, instead of in Exodus with the rest of the Sinai revelation? One may answer that the literary positioning at this juncture forces the reader to think that the blessings and curses refer to the entire Torah up until this point. This global view supports Rashi's reading. Thus Rashi and Rashbam highlight different dimensions of meaning to the literary unit of chapters 25–26 and how it fits into the Exodus-Leviticus continuum.

SANCTIFYING ONESELF

*T*he final chapter of Leviticus (27) appears to be a strange epilogue to the book. After the climactic blessings and curses in chapter 26, chapter 27 then focuses on one who wishes to sanctify him or herself to the Temple. Such individuals then would contribute money equal to their slave market value.

Rather than viewing it as an intrusion, one may argue that this chapter epitomizes the entire Book of Leviticus. Its emphasis is on how to sanctify oneself and the nation and to serve God. There are four sections in the Book of Leviticus:

(1) Sacrifices in chapters 1–7

(2) Dedication of the Tabernacle and the Yom Kippur service in chapters 8–10, 16

(3) The laws of ritual purity and impurity that govern who may and may not enter the Temple precincts in chapters 11–15

(4) Taking the Tabernacle-centric service and applying holiness to every aspect of personal life in chapters 17–27.

The commandments teach us to dedicate our lives to God. Leviticus, chapter 27 represents the ultimate impulse of the religious individual. We do not want to use an animal substitute as a sacrifice, but rather we go to sanctify ourselves.

The Book of Leviticus lies at the heart of the Torah. Its final two chapters present two models of a relationship with God. Chapter 26 presents the Torah as a mutual covenant. God and Israel made an agreement at Sinai, and we must fulfill our side of the covenant as obligation. In contrast, the dedication of oneself in chapter 27 stems from voluntary love. I love You, God. Here I am—not to sacrifice myself, but to dedicate my life completely to You.

There are three commandments to love in the Torah. We must love our neighbor as ourselves (Leviticus 19:18). We must love the resident alien as ourselves (Leviticus 19:34). We must love God with all of our heart, soul, and might (Deuteronomy 6:5). Holiness, what the Torah strives for, is rooted in these loves and our ability and desire to do so. Rather than being an appendix unconnected to the body of the Book of Leviticus, this final chapter epitomizes the book's purpose.

Rabbi Yehudah Shaviv, "The Location of the Laws of *Arakhin* in the Torah and Its Significance" (Hebrew), *Megadim* 6 (1988), pp. 12–16.

Bemidbar
במדבר
Numbers

Bemidbar

THE PURPOSE OF THE CENSUSES

The censuses at the beginning of the desert journey (Numbers, chapter 1) and in the 40th year of the journey (Numbers, chapter 26) frame the Book of Numbers. Commentators explore various aspects of meaning in these censuses.

At one level, the censuses serve military and inheritance purposes. Rashbam (on 1:50) adds that the Levites were not counted in the general censuses because they would not serve in the military. Ramban (on 1:45) agrees that there is a military component to the censuses, but does not think that the Torah would devote so much space on the details just for military purposes. Rather, the lengthy accounts are a celebratory means of demonstrating God's love for Israel. He had redeemed the nation, and the promise to the Patriarchs and Matriarchs of many descendants had been achieved.

Adopting a more negative perspective, Rashi notes that regarding the second census, God wanted to count the Israelites after a series of plagues, as a loving shepherd counts his flock after it was attacked. Rashi's interpretation speaks to the important statistical point that Israel experienced a zero population growth in the desert. In the first year in the wilderness, they numbered 603,550 males aged 20 to 60, and in the 40th year they numbered 601,730 adult males.

Rabbenu Bahya suggests that the detailed accounts ascribe importance to each person and family by addressing them separately. Even with a large nation, every individual is significant and has something to contribute.

On a broader level, the emphasis on the people shifts focus from the Tabernacle to the nation. Even though the Tabernacle was positioned in the center of the camp, its significance is manifest only when people surround it and serve God. Ramban (on 1:1) likens the Tabernacle to a palace, which is not the same when not surrounded by the king's guards. This shift already began in second half of Leviticus. Chapters 1–16 focus on the Tabernacle and how to use it, whereas chapters 17–27 focus on personal holiness. At the beginning of the Book of Numbers, the focus shifts to the entire nation and its encampments, surrounding the Tabernacle.

At one level, the Book of Numbers represents the history of Israelites developing from slaves into a strong nation. At a deeper level, it represents a transition of holiness from the Tabernacle onto the people themselves.

—

Naso

SOTAH

The trial of the Sotah, the suspected adulteress, is one of the most unusual laws in the Torah. Ramban notes that it is the only case where God must serve as judge, since it is unlikely to have human witnesses in the case of adultery.

Some scholars liken this trial to other trials by ordeal common in the ancient Near East. However, the Sotah trial was different from ordeals. The most common form of ordeal used in the ancient Near East involved hot iron: The suspect would hold an iron pole upon his hands, or would tread on it barefoot. If the burn had begun to heal nicely a few days later, the suspect was declared innocent. The test of the Sotah differs. She is not tested with something inherently harmful, but rather by drinking water containing dust and ink. An ordeal by something that causes harm, such as a red-hot iron, also creates fear in the heart of the subject, potentially causing him to confess to a crime even if he is not guilty.

We now turn to the talmudic understanding of Sotah. The husband may bring his wife for a Sotah trial only if he saw her associating with a certain man, and then warned her in the presence of witnesses not to seclude herself with him (see *Sotah* 2a; 5b; Rambam *Hil. Sotah* 1:1–2). Despite these warnings, the accused woman was then seen secluding herself with that or another man. The husband has genuine reason for suspicion, but no other legal recourse, since the courts cannot handle a situation with no witnesses.

The husband can divorce his wife and pay her Ketubah. The issue, however, is that he does not want to pay the Ketubah, since he believes that his wife is in the wrong. Alternatively, the husband may be interested in saving the marriage, but has no security in the relationship since he suspects her of cheating. If the woman confesses, she leaves her husband without her Ketubah (*Sotah* 24a), and she also would be prohibited to marry her suspected lover (*Sotah* 27b). She drinks the water only if she does not confess.

If the suspected adulteress emerges from the procedure, her husband can regain confidence in the relationship. Only this procedure can allow for faith to be entrusted once again, for the woman to return to her husband, and for their "*shelom bayit*" to be restored.

Rabbi Elhanan Samet, *Iyyunim be-Parashot ha-Shavua* (second series) vol. 2 (Hebrew) ed. Ayal Fishler (Ma'aleh Adumim: Ma'aliyot Press, 2004), pp. 158–174.

THE HIGH PRIEST AND THE NAZIRITE

The High Priest stands at the center of the camp. He teaches Torah and upholds religious ritual standards. Special laws govern his behavior, including the prohibition against wine or other intoxicating beverages while in service and the prohibition against coming into contact with human corpses (Leviticus, chapter 21).

The High Priest must follow the identical ritual on a daily basis. Aaron's sons Nadab and Abihu paid the price for priestly spontaneity, losing their lives on the day the Tabernacle was dedicated after offering incense that was not commanded. (Leviticus 10:1–3). The High Priest's special garments help define his role. Without these special garments, he essentially is not considered a priest (*Sanhedrin* 83a, *Zevahim* 17b). The position is honored, not the person.

The laws governing the nazirite (Numbers, chapter 6) are modeled after those of the High Priest. A nazirite may not come into contact with a human corpse and must avoid all grape products. The Torah gives anyone, man or woman, the opportunity to temporarily emulate the High Priest (Abarbanel). The position of High Priest represents one of the pinnacles of religious life, attaining a special closeness with God. The nazirite vow is intended to offer every man and woman the opportunity to experience this additional closeness.

Unlike the priesthood, *nezirut* is not genetic. *Nezirut* can be accepted permanently throughout one's lifetime as in the case of Samson, but generally is a temporary state—typically 30 days. The main difference between the priest and the nazirite is that the nazirite must let his or her hair grow for the term of the vow. In contrast, the Talmud (*Ta'anit* 17a) rules that priests must get haircuts every 30 days, and the High Priest every Friday. They must always be well-groomed for the Temple service. The word *nazir* has a dual-meaning: It is related to the word *neder*, vow. *Nezer* also means "crown," referring to his/her hair. The High Priest was anointed with oil, called his *nezer*, crown (Leviticus 21:12).

More fundamentally, the High Priest represents and upholds the rules, dignity, and the Temple order. Everything about this position is mandatory. The act of becoming a nazirite, however, is spontaneous religiosity—exactly that which is anathema to the priesthood.

There are hazards of each position. By standing at the center of the camp, the priest risks being overly diplomatic at the expense of standards. Aaron became too accommodating with the Golden Calf. A priest also might become arrogant, wrongly believing that his position places him above others. The Torah stresses that the position, and not the person, is what deserves the honor—it is for the glory of God. A priest also risks an overemphasis on minutiae.

The nazirite confronts different challenges. Since the role is voluntary and temporary, one may not take the position seriously enough since the vow would end after 30 days. The Sages of the Talmud lament that in their time, some people would make wagers over *nezirut*. A separate challenge for sincere nazirites is that they might become alienated from the community.

The High Priest and nazirite represent two means of attaining special closeness to God. Although certain laws govern both of them, the High Priesthood is the ultimate institutionalized position, whereas the nazirite vow is spontaneous and voluntary. The Torah wants us to amalgamate these dimensions in spiritual life and leadership, in order to follow the rules but also to have fresh creativity and spontaneity. As different as the two positions might appear, they are unlikely sides of the same coin in our desire to attain increased religious experience.

—

Beha'alotekha

FROM CHAPTERS 1–10 TO CHAPTER 11

*T*he Book of Numbers opens with 10 chapters that paint a picture of Israel's majestic camp. At the conclusion of these chapters, Moses is confident that the people are ready to enter the Promised Land:

> Moses said to Hobab son of Reuel the Midianite, Moses' father-in-law, "We are setting out for the place of which the Lord has said, 'I will give it to you.' Come with us and we will be generous with you; for the Lord has promised to be generous to Israel." "I will not go," he replied to him, "but will return to my native land." He said, "Please do not leave us, inasmuch as you know where we should camp in the wilderness and can be our guide. So if you come with us, we will extend to you the same bounty that the Lord grants us." (Numbers 10:28–32)

Did Hobab go or not? Since his only spoken response is "I will not go," it sounds like he did not go. If Hobab is another name for Jethro, we know that Jethro went home (Exodus 18:27). However, in Judges 1:16 and 4:11, we find that some of Hobab's descendants lived in the Land of Israel. Perhaps Jethro went home but then subsequently returned and came to Israel (Ramban). Perhaps Hobab is not Jethro but rather Jethro's son—and he accompanied the Israelites to the land while Jethro remained in Midian (Ibn Ezra).

After the Hobab exchange, the Torah describes how the Ark led the way and then interjects a war song involving the Ark: "When the Ark was to set out, Moses would say: Advance, O Lord! May Your enemies be scattered, and may Your foes flee before You! And when it halted, he would say: return, O Lord, You who are Israel's myriads of thousands!" (10:35–36).

These two verses are surrounded by upside down *nuns*. Professor Saul Lieberman writes that upside down *nuns* were ancient scribal notes that indicated that something is in the wrong place or quoted from another source (*Hellenism in Jewish Palestine*, pp. 38–43). Although this is their only occurrence in the Torah, they appear in Psalm 107 as well.

Rabbi Shimon (in *Shabbat* 116a) states that these two verses are out of place, and were inserted to separate the disasters in chapters 10 and 11. After Moses expressed optimism to Hobab regarding the anticipated entry of the land in chapter 10, chapter 11 begins the litany of complaints that leads to 40 years of wandering and additional suffering. Rabbi Shimon explains that in chapter 10, the people left Sinai with immature gusto, like children running from school (see Ramban). In his reading, the Israelites were not adequately transformed by the Revelation, and therefore happily left the holy site.

This dramatic shift from the 10 positive chapters to the complaints and rebellions makes it sound like there are "two books" in Numbers. The Book of Joshua essentially picks up where these *nuns* leave off, as Joshua finally leads the next generation into the Promised Land.

THE CUSHITE WOMAN

"*M*iriam and Aaron spoke against Moses because of the Cushite woman he had married: 'He married a Cushite woman!' They said, 'Has the Lord spoken only through Moses? Has He not spoken through us as well?' The Lord heard it" (Numbers 12:1–2).

The remainder of this narrative focuses on God's angry response to Miriam and Aaron for speaking against Moses. God demonstrates that Moses' level of prophecy was superior to anyone else's. There is no further mention of the Cushite woman or what upset Miriam and Aaron about Moses' marriage to her.

Is there a relationship between the two complaints? Rashi adopts a midrashic reading that links the two complaints by radically reinterpreting several words. First, the midrashim identify this anonymous Cushite woman with Zipporah. Since Zipporah was Midianite, midrashim reinterpret "Cushite" to mean "beautiful" as opposed to "from Cush/Ethiopia."

In this reading, one may ask: If Miriam and Aaron were concerned about Moses' marriage to Zipporah, why did they wait until now to say anything? The midrash responds that while *lakah* generally means "married," here it means "left" or "divorced"—the exact opposite of the word's general meaning. Moses felt that since he always was "on call" to receive prophecy, it was appropriate to separate from Zipporah. Miriam and Aaron took umbrage on behalf of Zipporah. We *also* are prophets, yet we and have not left our spouses! Why does Moses think he is different?

Although this reading creates a powerful link between the two complaints, it depends on reinterpretations that stray far from the plain meaning of the text. Rashbam, R. Joseph ibn Caspi, and others therefore insist that Miriam and Aaron were upset that Moses had married a second wife, from Cush. Perhaps they objected to polygamy (Ibn Caspi). Although polygamy was permitted in the Torah, it never was considered ideal because of the inevitable family tensions it caused. Alternatively, Shadal suggests that when a leader of a nation finds a wife from outside the people, it looks bad. Was there no Israelite woman good enough for him?

Rabbi Mordechai Breuer adds an additional dimension to this line of interpretation. Numbers chapters 11–12 contain intertwined complaints, with one physical and one spiritual element. Chapter 11 deals with the people's complaints concerning meat and leadership. Chapter 12 deals with Miriam and Aaron's complaints about Moses' marriage and prophecy. The two stories focus on the interrelationship between the physical and spiritual. The people complained for meat, whereas Moses complained that there were not enough people of spirit leading the nation. Miriam argued that Moses' desire for a woman demonstrated that he was no greater a prophet than she and Aaron.

Both narratives teach that it is wrong to separate the two realms. Moses' desire for a woman was sanctified by his spiritual level. God taught Miriam and Aaron that there was no contradiction between his superior prophecy and being married. Similarly, there is nothing wrong with wanting meat, but there is a problem when this demand is not accompanied by people of spirit properly guiding the nation in their religious life and attitude.

Rabbi Mordechai Breuer, *Pirkei Mikraot* (Alon Shevut: Tevunot, 2009), pp. 263–278.

——

MOSES' LEADERSHIP (PART ONE)

*A*lthough Moses' leadership occupies much of the Torah's narrative from his birth until his death, there are others who help him in different capacities. Aaron, Miriam, Hur, and Joshua are at the upper echelon; and there also were elders, judges, and other unnamed helpers.

We get the first sense of Moses' need for help when Jethro offers him leadership advice. Jethro saw that Moses was judging the nation from morning until night. He therefore commented to his son-in-law, "The thing you are doing is not right; you will surely wear yourself out, and these people as well. For the task is too heavy for you; you cannot do it alone" (Exodus 18:17–18).

At one level, Jethro was correct. As long as Moses spent all day judging people, he could not focus on any other issues. However, Jethro did not understand that transferring judgeship to others did not mean that Moses would work less. It just meant that Moses would be able to devote every waking moment to other aspects of communal leadership. Notwithstanding, this managerial move was beneficial in the short term. Moses was energized by the opportunity to move the people ahead to the Promised Land.

In the first 10 chapters of Numbers, Moses organizes the camp, and excitement dominates the narrative. Then come the complaints. First some people complain at the outskirts of the camp. Moses does not even hear these grumblings. Then other people demand meat. This complaint gains popular support and reaches Moses. There is no sign of help from

Moses' underlings. Moses must confront a complaining nation all alone. Moses feels overwhelmed and turns to God, offering his resignation.

Jethro's advice came back to haunt Moses. Moses had been occupied with other components of leadership, counting on his underlings to deflect troubles such as these. When the crises arose, however, these leaders were nowhere to be found. Moses had to do his new job, and also pick up where the others were falling short. Moses complains that his job has become impossible: "I cannot carry all this people by myself, for it is too much for me" (Numbers 11:14). Even after God provided Moses with 70 leaders, it is unclear from the remaining desert narratives whether they provided any meaningful assistance during the national crises that followed.

At this point, Moses expected support from those closest to him— his brother and sister. They were prophets sharing his vision and leadership. Incredibly, Miriam and Aaron level a personal attack. God immediately intervened to defend Moses, but Moses did not need to hear that he was right. He needed to know that he could count on Miriam and Aaron. Throughout the desert saga, Moses continued to show them unwavering support: praying for Miriam's cure, and defending Aaron's honor during the Korah rebellion. But Moses no longer was the same leader after this failure in support from those closest to him, as we will see in the next essay.

Shelah

Moses' Leadership (Part Two)

There are several contrasts between Moses' behavior during the Golden Calf episode and during the episode of the Spies. The most striking contrast is that during the Spies episode, Moses convinces God to spare the people's lives but does not attempt to obtain complete forgiveness. Moses had gone all out during the Calf episode. It is surprising that he chooses not to during the Spies episode.

Rabbi Eitan Mayer explains that this change has to do with a downward progression in Moses' leadership. After the Calf, Moses was audacious and daring in defending his people. At that time, Moses' energy was high, and the people were relative newcomers to freedom and to monotheism. Moses was confident that the people had the potential to make the jump from their current weaknesses to the lofty goals they had been called upon to meet. He perceived the Calf as a terrible, but temporary, lapse.

By the time of the Spies, the situation was different. Moses had lost his bold edge, beaten down by the people's repeated demonstrations of pettiness. It started with riffraff at the fringes of the camp, but then those closest to him—Miriam and Aaron—also lashed out against him. Moses no longer believed in the people as he had while at Sinai. He had not yet written them off, but doubts were beginning to nag at him. Over a generation, as the people continued the same patterns, Moses became so frustrated with them that he eventually struck the rock when they requested water at Mei Meribah (chapter 20). Moses' actions during that episode led to God's preventing him from entering the Land of Israel.

Moses no longer could lead the people effectively because he had lost his faith in them. He never understood why their dedication did not equal his, why they could not trust God as he did. During the Spies episode, Moses does not defend the people beyond saving their lives because he had lost a great deal of faith in their potential to meet the spiritual rigors of this mission.

While the primary message of the Spies narrative revolves around faith in God, it also contains a message about leadership. Leaders need to believe in their people in order to lead them effectively, and people need to support their leaders and be worthy of their leaders' confidence to benefit from their leadership.

Rabbi Eitan Mayer, Parsha Themes Shelah, at http://www.parshathemes.blogspot.co.il.

THE LAWS IN CHAPTER 15

*F*ollowing the Spies episode in chapters 13–14, there is a collection of laws and a brief narrative in chapter 15. They pertain to sacrifices, the separation of *hallah* (dough given to the priest), sin and atonement, and *tzitzit* (the fringes placed at the corners of one's garment). There also is a brief narrative where a man gathering sticks on Shabbat is sentenced to execution. Although at first glance, these verses seem unrelated, Rabbi Samson Raphael Hirsch elaborates on the links within this chapter and the Spies episode.

The first laws prescribe various sacrificial rituals that apply only after the Israelites enter the land (15:1–6, see verse 2). In addition, these laws reflect national prosperity. Those laws are followed in 15:17–21 by the laws of *hallah*, the separation of a portion of dough for the priest when baking bread. These laws also mention entry to the land, and reflect private prosperity. Coming in the wake of the Spies episode, these laws encourage the Israelites that the next generation would eventually enter the land and enjoy prosperity.

The next law describes the scenario when national leaders mislead the public to sin (15:22–26). This law connects to the Spies, as the nation's leaders led the people to lose faith in God. Ibn Ezra adds that there also is an element of forgiveness in these verses, leading to further encouragement in the wake of the Spies narrative. The subsequent law describes atonement for the sins of the individual (15:27–31), connecting to the Spies episode with a focus on the people rather than their leaders.

These laws are followed by a brief narrative of a man who gathered sticks on Shabbat and was executed (15:32–36). Although the story is jarring, it teaches that the same nation that had mutinied with the Spies turned around and was almost entirely faithful to the Torah.

Chapter 15 culminates with the commandment for *tzitzit*, the fringes placed at the corners of one's garment. They teach constant God-consciousness and protect against wrongful desires. The Torah also employs the language from the Spies narrative: "That shall be your fringe; look at it and recall all the commandments of the Lord and observe them, so that you do not follow (*ve-lo taturu*) your heart and eyes in your lustful urge (*asher attem zonim aharehem*). Thus you shall be reminded to observe all My commandments and to be holy to your God" (15:39–40). The Spies went *la-tur* (to scout) the land, and their sin is referred to as infidelity (*zenut*) in 14:33, thus heightening the connection between the laws of *tzitzit* and the rejection of rebellions against God, such as that of the Spies.

The laws and brief narrative contained in chapter 15 thus offer a corrective to the damage of the Spies. They assure Israel that after their period of wandering they will enter the land and prosper. They prescribe how leaders and individuals can atone for their sins. They stress faithfulness to Shabbat and to God's covenant. *Tzitzit* is the antidote to the lapse of faith during the Spies episode. Constant God-consciousness is the positive approach to faith rather than needing only to atone for sin.

⁓

Korah

OVERVIEW OF THE PARASHAH

*R*amban observes that Korah's rebellion occurs immediately after the Spies episode. The people were in a state of despair once they realized that they would not enter the Land of Israel. Two separate rebellions broke out. Korah and his 250 followers attacked Aaron and were interested in being priests. They approached Moses at the center of the camp. Simultaneously, Dathan and Abiram attacked Moses' leadership from their tents.

Following Ramban's reading of the primary narrative in Numbers chapter 16, Korah was with the 250 at the center of the camp. While Dathan and Abiram remained in their tents in the Reuben encampment. Given this arrangement, one may conclude that the fire from heaven killed Korah and his 250 followers, whereas Dathan and Abiram were swallowed by the pinpoint earthquake. This reading of Numbers chapter 16 is supported by later retellings of the rebellion: ". . . what He did to Dathan and Abiram, sons of Eliab son of Reuben, when the earth opened her mouth and swallowed them . . ." (Deuteronomy 11:6). "The earth opened up and swallowed Dathan, closed over the party of Abiram. A fire blazed among their party, a flame that consumed the wicked" (Psalm 106:16–18). In both accounts, only Dathan and Abiram are swallowed by the earth.

However, one other retelling of the story suggests that Korah was swallowed up with the earthquake: ". . . Dathan and Abiram…the earth opened its mouth and swallowed them up with Korah—when that band died, when the fire consumed the 250 men . . . " (Numbers 26:9–10).

Ibn Ezra and Ramban are sufficiently convinced by their reading of Numbers chapter 16 that Korah was among those killed by the fire from heaven. Therefore they repunctuate the verse against the traditional cantillation marks in 26:9–10: ". . . Dathan and Abiram . . . the earth opened its mouth and swallowed them up. Korah and that band died when the fire consumed the 250 men."

After God stopped the rebellions of Korah, Dathan, and Abiram, the people still rallied against Moses and Aaron. The almond branch's blossoming proved that the Tribe of Levi was chosen from among the other tribes. Perhaps On son of Peleth from the Tribe of Reuben headed this rebellion. He may have wanted his firstborn tribe to reclaim the spiritual leadership of the nation (see Numbers 16:1).

After all these rebellions ended, the people offer one last expression of fear. God is dangerous, so how do we approach Him? (17:27–28). It is striking that the people get the last word in this episode. These also are the final words recorded from the first generation leaving Egypt.

As an antidote to the people's challenge, chapter 18 contains laws for priests and Levites who must guard the boundaries of the Temple. By following God's laws and respecting boundaries, people may approach God.

Chapter 19 then follows with the laws of the Red Cow, containing the purification rituals after coming into contact with a human corpse. Rabbi Haim David Halevi explains that this chapter, which pertains to human death, is the Torah's subtle way of suggesting that the first generation died out. By the time we get to the Mei Meribah narrative in chapter 20, we have arrived at the 40th year since the exodus, with the new generation prepared to enter the Land.

THE "GRAY AREA" WITHIN KORAH'S REBELLION

*R*abbi Yehoshua Engelman observes that one of the qualities of good literature is complexity. Even in stories that seem to have clear "good guy–bad guy" delineations, the Bible sometimes hints that these lines are not intended to be clear-cut. The surface reading of Korah's rebellion is of Korah as the bad guy, jealous of Moses' power.

The *Mei Ha-Shiloah* (mid-nineteenth-century Hasidic commentary) argues that the story of Korah presents two sides that battled, and one side losing does not imply its being entirely mistaken.

The event was handled badly. Moses wanted a public confrontation. He initiated the contest by fire (16:16–17), and suggested that the earth open its mouth to swallow the rebels and their families (16:29–30). The dramatic results were ineffective. Rather than being persuaded, the people afterward accused Moses and Aaron saying, "You have killed the Lord's people" (17:6–8).

No rule, not even that of Moses, is above criticism merely by virtue of its being ordained by God. The Talmud censures Moses for these words to Korah: "He [Moses] used the term 'You have enough' (*rav lakhem*)—and the same words were used by God when refusing him entry into the land 'You have enough' (*rav lakh*) (Deuteronomy 3:26)" (*Sotah* 13b).

This rabbinic criticism of Moses could be interpreted as saying: How can one say to someone seeking closeness to God, "You have enough?" Saying "You have enough" is not only saying that Korah is mistaken in his belief that all people can be greater and that they should aspire to more, but that there can be, in regard to closeness to God, "enough." Questioning others' motives for desiring holiness is a travesty, whereas the seeking itself is holy.

The Talmud's suggestion that Moses' setting boundaries to Korah is what ultimately denies his own entry to the Promised Land is portraying how, tragically, the boundaries with which we protect ourselves will always limit our own expansion and growth. While Korah himself sought power, his message resonated deeply with the people.

The Seer of Lublin (early nineteenth-century Hasidic master) said, "Were I alive at the time, I would have supported Korah." When meeting Moses, people could not but be awestruck (Exodus 33:10); however, when meeting Korah, people saw their own sanctity, realized how God inhered in them, too. Korah had that rare ability to reflect to people their own holiness. Although Korah was wicked, his message contained elements that deeply resonated with the people and their religious quest.

Rabbi Yehoshua Engelman, "Hasidic-Psychological Readings: Revelation and Korah," in *Where the Yeshiva Meets the University: Traditional and Academic Approaches to Tanakh Study*, ed. Hayyim Angel, *Conversations* 15 (Winter 2013), pp. 200–208.

Hukkat

THE RED COW

The Red Cow ritual is unusual even by biblical standards. The Israelites were to take a perfectly red cow (it was actually reddish-brown; what made it so unusual is that it was *purely* that color), and burn it outside the camp as a sacrifice. They then mixed its ashes with hyssop, crimson yarn, cedar, and water. This potion became a purifying agent sprinkled on one who had come into contact with a human corpse.

Rabbi Elhanan Samet addresses the classical paradox of the Red Cow. The ashes that purify the one who came into contact with a human corpse also render the key participants in the ceremony as ritually impure. The priest (or multiple priests), the one who burns the cow, and the gatherer of the ashes (who halakhically does not need to be a priest) all become ritually impure.

Rabbi Samet argues that the paradox is an illusion. We can gain further insight by comparing it with related laws in the Torah. The Red Cow ceremony is similar to the purification of the *metzora* (Leviticus, chapter 14). That ceremony cannot take place in the Temple precincts since the healed *metzora* is ritually impure until he or she goes through this ceremony. In the Temple, the only sacrifice fully burned is the *olah*, burnt offering. The *hattat* (purification offering) was partially burned and partially eaten by the priests. However, the Red Cow is called a *hattat* but entirely burned outside of the Temple precincts.

On Yom Kippur, the sent away goat also was brought outside of the Temple, and also rendered the person bringing it outside ritually impure. The *hattat* on Yom Kippur also rendered the priestly participants impure. The Red Cow was not unique in making its participants ritually impure.

Rambam rules that one touching the sent goat or the ashes of the Red Cow does not become ritually impure. Only those directly participating in the ceremony do. This law demonstrates that the objects themselves do not transmit ritual impurity. The impurity of the participants stems from a different cause from simply touching the ashes.

The common denominator of the Red Cow, *metzora*, and Yom Kippur ceremony is that they are sacrificial ceremonies linked to the Temple but that take place outside the Temple precincts. Rabbi Samet suggests that the Torah teaches that there are occasions when such ceremonies are necessary to take place outside of the Temple, but there is a price to pay by bringing them there since generally all sacrifices must be brought in the Temple.

So there is no paradox. Contact with the ashes purifies the person who had come into contact with a corpse. The impurity of several participants emanates not from mere contact with the ashes, but rather in their participation in a necessary ceremony that brought a sacrifice connected to the Temple outside of the Temple precincts.

Rabbi Elhanan Samet, "The Passage of the Cow" (Hebrew), at http://www.etzion.org.il/vbm/archive.php.

ANOTHER LOOK AT MEI MERIBAH

*I*nterpreters have struggled with the nature of Moses' sin at Meribah for millennia. In a recent article, Uzi Paz suggested a holistic reading of the passage that contributes new insights to the age-old discussion.

Paz argues that Moses and Aaron misunderstood the people's true complaint. The people were not attacking their leaders, but rather complaining against God. Although they verbalized their grumblings against Moses and Aaron—"the people quarreled with Moses" (Numbers 20:3), the conclusion of the narrative clarifies their intentions: "Those are the Waters of Meribah—meaning that the Israelites quarreled with the Lord" (20:13).

The people had learned that when they complain against God directly, they get smitten, and therefore verbalized their complaint only against Moses and Aaron, "Why have you brought the Lord's congregation into this wilderness for us and our beasts to die there? Why did you make us leave Egypt to bring us to this wretched place?" (20:4–5). They referred to themselves as "the Lord's congregation," highlighting that they were not rebelling against God. Moses and Aaron were so frightened of the complaining mob that they retreated from the camp.

To respond to the people, God told Moses and Aaron to take Aaron's rod from the Korah rebellion. The use of the blossom-covered rod made clear that the people were rebelling against God: "The Lord said to Moses, 'Put Aaron's staff back before the Pact, to be kept as a lesson to rebels, so that their mutterings against Me may cease, lest they die'" (Numbers 17:25).

Since the people were complaining against God but using Moses and Aaron as their cover, God told Moses to speak to the rock—when in fact he was criticizing the people. It did not matter what Moses would say to the rock, which is why God did not specify what Moses should say.

Moses and Aaron sinned by not mentioning God as the source of the water, since they believed that they needed to demonstrate their own competence as leaders: "Moses and Aaron assembled the congregation in front of the rock; and he said to them, 'Listen, you rebels, shall we get water for you out of this rock?'" (20:10).

Since Moses and Aaron did not sanctify God's name, God responded by turning the people's complaint into the punishment. The people had protested that Moses and Aaron brought them out of Egypt to suffer in the desert (20:4–5). God responded, "therefore you shall not bring this congregation into the land that I have given them" (20:12).

Moses and Aaron failed to teach that God always supplies the needs of the people. However, the narrative stresses that God's name still was sanctified: "Those are the Waters of Meribah…through which He affirmed His sanctity" (20:13). God successfully conveyed the message to the people that He supplies their needs. By the following chapter, the people did not complain for more water, but rather sang the song of the well out of gratitude (21:17–20). The people now were ready to enter the land.

Uzi Paz, "The Sin of Moses and Aaron at Mei Meribah: A Close Reading of Numbers 20:1–13" (Hebrew), *Megadim* 53 (2012), pp. 75–89.

THE BRONZE SERPENT

*S*oon to enter the Land of Israel, the Israelites complained about the manna. God sent fiery serpents and then healed the snakebite victims through a bronze serpent (Numbers 21:4–9). The Mishnah (*Rosh HaShanah* 3:8) stresses that God, and not the bronze serpent, healed the people. The bronze serpent was merely a means of directing people's thoughts toward the heavens. Additionally, keeping the bronze serpent would serve as a reminder of God's beneficence so that the people could be grateful.

For a while, the bronze serpent fulfilled its original purpose to remind people of the miracle and strengthen faith in God. When later in history the serpent became an object of worship, it fell into the same category as the other signs of idolatry that the righteous King Hezekiah abolished (II Kings 18:4).

According to Rabbi Samson Raphael Hirsch, the Israelites' sin lay in their not recognizing the miracles that had been accompanying them throughout their wandering in the wilderness. The serpents' coming was not divine intervention. To the contrary, God's previous *protection* from these serpents was the miracle. When the Israelites failed to appreciate God's help, God allowed nature to take its course.

One midrash suggests that the serpents may be associated with the primordial serpent in the Garden of Eden. Life in the Garden of Eden resembled that of the Israelites in the wilderness. In both places those involved were under God's close supervision. Nevertheless, in both cases, human beings were ungrateful and sinned.

> Since the serpent was the first to speak evil and was cursed, and they [the generation of the desert] did not learn from him, the Holy One, blessed be He, said: Let the serpent, who was the first to speak evil, come and exact the punishment from those who spoke evil. . . .
>
> Although the serpent may eat all the delicacies of the world, they turn to dust in his mouth and his entrails . . . whereas [the Israelites] ate the manna that takes on many flavors. . . . Therefore let the serpent, that eats many varieties yet they all have one taste in his mouth and he does not complain to his Maker, let him come and exact punishment from those who eat a single food yet enjoy in it many flavors. (*Tanhuma Hukkat* 45)

Yair Barkai, "The Copper Serpent," Bar-Ilan University, Hukkat 5764/2004, at http://www.biu.ac.il/JH/Parasha/eng/chukath/bar1.html.

Leah Himmelfarb, "The *Seraph* Serpents," Bar-Ilan University, Hukkat 5760/2000, at http://www.biu.ac.il/JH/Parasha/eng/chukath/him.html.

Balak

BALAAM: THE LEARNING PROPHET

*W*hen the Moabite king Balak's first delegation requested Balaam's services, God ordered the prophet not to go, since Israel is a blessed nation. Balak then sent senior officials to lure Balaam, to whom Balaam responded, "Though Balak were to give me his house full of silver and gold, I could not do anything, big or little, contrary to the command of the Lord my God" (Numbers 22:18). Balaam's self-sacrificing declaration confirmed his unequivocal allegiance to the word of God—or so it appears.

Although Balaam had received explicit instructions not to curse Israel, he still returned to God, evidently hoping that God's new message would be different from the original. Astonishingly, God *did* acquiesce; on condition that Balaam speak only that which God would tell him. Rashi and other commentators explain that God realized that Balaam was set on cursing Israel, so He enabled him to pursue that path.

Verse 22, though, states that God was outraged at Balaam's decision despite having given him permission. It appears that Balaam was culpable for requesting a second prophecy; after all, God's initial refusal and rationale were unambiguous (Rashi, Ibn Ezra). Evidently, Balaam wanted to curse Israel, perhaps out of hatred for Israel, or possibly to receive royal compensation and honor. Although God conceded Balaam's request, the prophet should have had the good religious sense to remain faithful to his original prophecy. Therefore, God was angry with the prophet and sent an angel to obstruct his journey.

To denigrate Balaam, God revealed to the donkey what the prophet himself could not see. God then opened the mouth of the donkey, furthering the rebellious prophet's humiliation. God ultimately would convince the prophet that fighting against God's will is futile. In his second blessing of Israel, Balaam had internalized this message: "God is not man to be capricious, or mortal to change His mind" (Numbers 23:19).

Balaam's first two blessings came as a result of God's dictating them. By his third oracle, Balaam recognized God's will and blessed Israel spontaneously: "Now Balaam, seeing that it pleased the Lord to bless Israel, did not, as on previous occasions, go in search of omens, but turned his face toward the wilderness. As Balaam looked up and saw Israel encamped tribe by tribe, the spirit of God came upon him" (Numbers 24:1–2). He reached a higher level of prophecy by recognizing and internalizing God's will (Ramban).

When reading chapters 22–24 in a vacuum, it appears that Balaam underwent a complete spiritual transformation. However, we learn in chapter 31 that Balaam was behind the Midianite plot to send women to prostitute themselves with the Israelites and lead them astray to their gods in chapter 25. The broader narrative teaches that while Balaam's magical curses posed no threat to Israel, intermarriage and assimilation threatened Israelite identity at the core.

Hayyim Angel, "When God's Will Can and Cannot Be Altered: The Relationship between the Balaam Narrative and 1 Kings 13," *Jewish Bible Quarterly* 33:1 (2005), pp. 31–39; reprinted in Angel, *Through an Opaque Lens* (New York: Sephardic Publication Foundation, 2006), pp. 215–225.

BALAAM AND ISRAEL'S SELF-CONFIDENCE

*A*midst a series of rebellions, the focus of our narrative shifts to a mountaintop, where Balak and Balaam are looking at the people of Israel from a distance. Balak sent delegates to Mesopotamia for the world-renowned Balaam to curse Israel. Balaam is outclassed by his donkey, and then God puts blessings into Balaam's mouth.

Although this story unfolds without directly impacting the Israelite saga, it is a welcome break from the constant sins and punishments of the Israelites. Why did the Torah include this story?

In part, this story was an antidote to Israel's woes. The people may have felt hopeless as they continued to wander in the desert. Moses recently had despaired of the people's ability to improve, striking a rock in disgust (Numbers, chapter 20).

Balaam reminded the people of their potential. When the Israelites learned of Balaam's praises after a steady stream of rebellions and rebukes, they must have felt energized with new positive thinking. Rabbenu Bahya adds that Balaam's blessings gave them more confidence than had an Israelite blessed them since one is more likely to listen to the compliments of an outsider (cf. *Deuteronomy Rabbah* 3:6).

Ironically, while Balaam was admiring Israel from afar, the Israelites were about to commit the sin of Baal Peor, involving prostitution and idolatry (Numbers, chapter 25). One midrash blames Balaam's blessings for Israel's becoming overconfident, allowing them to slip (*Ecclesiastes Rabbah* 7:12).

Many communities open their daily liturgy with Balaam's blessing: "How fair are your tents, O Jacob, your dwellings, O Israel!" (24:5). This prayer reminds us of proper communal perspective. After recognizing our collective potential, we can attempt to strive toward those ideals. At the same time, we must never become overconfident, as there always is work to be done.

—

Pinehas

ZEALOTRY

Moses stood up in the gate of the camp and said, "Whoever is for the Lord, come here!" And all the Levites rallied to him. He said to them, "Thus says the Lord, the God of Israel: Each of you put sword on thigh, go back and forth from gate to gate throughout the camp, and slay brother, neighbor, and kin." (Exodus 32:26–27)

*I*n the aftermath of the Golden Calf, Moses tells the Tribe of Levi that God has commanded these killings. However, there is no textual record that God ordered a massacre of the perpetrators of the sins of idolatry and immorality. Rashi quotes a *Mekhilta* that says that God did not specifically command Moses in this instance. Rather, Moses was applying a Torah law from elsewhere: "Whoever sacrifices to a god other than the Lord alone shall be proscribed" (Exodus 22:19).

Ramban adopts a different approach that is endorsed by several later commentators. God explicitly commanded Moses to do this. The Torah depends on our figuring that out from Moses' statement that God had commanded him.

A third view is found in *Tanna Devei Eliyahu* chapter 4. Moses realized that if he did not attribute the command to God, nobody would listen to him. Therefore, he told the people that God had commanded the massacre, even though God had not.

A different midrash takes a daring approach in addressing human zealotry in the Torah. Even though God praised the zealotry of Phinehas (Numbers 25:6–13), one midrash finds a way to criticize Phinehas. It suggests that the sages at that time wanted to excommunicate Phinehas, until God came to testify on his behalf (J.T. *Sanhedrin* 9:7, 27b). The Babylonian Talmud places this criticism in the mouth of the ministering angels (*Sanhedrin* 82a).

The Sages address a world without prophecy, where we cannot verify God's will. They must concede that Moses and the Levites, as well as Phinehas, were correct, since God approved of their actions. However, no person can be *that* confident that he/she is absolutely pure in motive. Therefore, the Sages accept God's judgment in principle but note that these people received God's explicit approval. In a post-prophetic age, there is no room for such zealous conduct.

THE DAUGHTERS OF ZELOPHEHAD

*R*abbi Elhanan Samet asks: It legitimate to view the struggle of the five daughters of Zelophehad to inherit their father's land as an example of an ancient, proto-feminist struggle for equality? At first glance, the answer appears to be positive. In a world where the laws of inheritance allowed only men to inherit, these five women demanded rights. God answers, "The plea of Zelophehad's daughters is just" (Numbers 27:7).

We have to first examine the argument of the daughters of Zelophehad. After they explain the background, they come to the main point: "Let not our father's name be lost to his clan just because he had no son! Give us a holding among our father's kinsmen!" (27:4). The name of a man is a central concept in Tanakh. It means that which continues a man's existence after his death. How does the Israelite man in Tanakh perpetuate his name? There are two ways that are necessarily combined: (1) by having children and (2) by passing over to his children his ancestral portion in the land.

Zelophehad's daughters counter that their father did have children, and those daughters are capable of continuing the familial line by marrying and having children of their own. The daughters of Zelophehad were not motivated by their own rights, nor was equality of inheritance rights for women what lay at the root of their demands. In fact, their argument is deeply rooted in a patriarchal social structure.

Nonetheless, at the root of their argument, and in its acceptance by God, lies a basic principle connected to the inherent equality of the sexes. The daughters of Zelophehad point out an injustice, that because of the laws of inheritance whereby only males inherit, their father's name will be eliminated from within his family. They argue that the principle of preserving a man's name should take precedence over the laws of inheritance.

On a basic human level, a man who has children, whether male or female, understands that he has in fact achieved continuity. This continuity is a fact stronger than any social order that gives precedence to one sex or the other.

The statement of the daughters of Zelophehad sharpens the contradiction between the arrangements of the patriarchal society and that which is prior to any social arrangement—the basic human equality of humankind as created in the Image of God. In this case, the precedence of that equality over social arrangement becomes clear.

Rabbi Elhanan Samet, *Iyyunim be-Parashot ha-Shavua* (first series) vol. 2 (Hebrew) ed. Ayal Fishler (Ma'aleh Adumim: Ma'aliyot Press, 2002), pp. 248–261.

Mattot

DEFERRED KNOWLEDGE
IN THE BAAL PEOR NARRATIVE

he Baal Peor narrative reflects Israel's last great sin in the wilderness. The sudden lapse into prostitution and idolatry led to a catastrophic plague, leaving some 24,000 Israelites dead.

There are layers of deferred knowledge in this story. In Parashat Balak (25:1–9), we learn about the prostitution and idolatry, God's judgment against the leaders, and Phinehas' killing two perpetrators, which stopped the plague.

In Parashat Pinehas, we learn the identity of these two perpetrators: Zimri, chieftain of a Simeonite ancestral house, and Cozbi daughter of Zur; a tribal head of an ancestral house in Midian (25:14–15). This new information increases our appreciation of the decisive action of Phinehas. He took on leaders while most of the camp cried but did nothing.

This knowledge also explains God's command of a war of revenge against Midian, since they sent their princesses: This was state-sponsored prostitution and idolatry with the intent of bringing about Israel's spiritual downfall.

There is additional deferred knowledge in chapter 31. During the battle against Midian, the Israelites killed the Midianite kings, including Zur, the father of Cozbi, and Balaam (31:8). Even more surprisingly, we learn only here that Balaam had given the advice to send these women (31:15–16).

Rabbi Elhanan Samet explains that Balaam had attempted to curse Israel while overlooking Peor (23:18), but failed. However, his counsel to bring about Israel's spiritual demise at Peor was effective. The narrative teaches that attempting to curse Israel achieves nothing. Undermining Israel spiritually is the most effective strategy to defeat Israel. The story of Peor is a prelude to Israel's living in the land, threatened with intermarriage and acculturation.

Nehama Leibowitz adds that the Torah deferred this knowledge about Balaam for a different reason. The Israelites had to take personal responsibility for their actions, rather than attempting to transfer blame to Balaam and the Midianites. Had the Torah mentioned Balaam's counsel at the beginning of the narrative, readers would conclude that the Torah places the primary blame on him. By deferring that knowledge, Israel's sudden lapse into prostitution and idolatry lies at the center of the narrative, rightly placing the primary responsibility on their shoulders.

Nehama Leibowitz, *Studies in Bamidbar (Numbers)* translated and adapted by Aryeh Newman (Jerusalem: Eliner Library), pp. 375–378.

Rabbi Elhanan Samet, *Iyyunim be-Parashot ha-Shavua* (second series) vol. 2 (Hebrew) ed. Ayal Fishler (Ma'aleh Adumim: Ma'aliyot Press, 2004), pp. 256–277.

———

MOSES' INTERVENTION AGAINST REUBEN AND GAD

*A*fter the Tribes of Reuben and Gad request land on the East Bank of the Jordan River, Moses responds with a lengthy and harsh monologue (Numbers 32:6–15). He likens these tribes to the spies. The two tribes counter by offering to leave their wives and children to settle the East Bank while the men lead the Israelite forces in their war of conquest of Israel. Moses accepts their proposal.

Abarbanel views Moses' response as a misunderstanding of a legitimate request by Reuben and Gad. These tribes had intended to send troops with the rest of the nation from the beginning, but Moses thought that they had no intention of assisting. In contrast, Rabbi Yitzhak Arama (*Akedat Yitzhak*, chapter 85) insists that Moses correctly assessed their desire to remain on the East Bank. Moses' heroic intervention caused them to return with a modified proposal whereby they would send troops to assist the rest of the nation. According to Rabbi Arama, Moses took up the challenge of this renewed danger of national disintegration—a danger that again threatened the imminent inheritance of the land.

Rabbi Elhanan Samet considers Rabbi Arama's reading more likely. After first presenting the geographic and economic conditions relevant to their petition, Reuben and Gad proceed to request: "'It would be a favor to us,' they continued, 'if this land were given to your servants as a holding; do not move us across the Jordan'" (32:5). The key to understanding the request lies in these final words: "do not move us across the Jordan." The straightforward reading suggests that they refer here to their bodies, not their permanent residence. It appears that they had no desire to cross the Jordan at all, not even to help the rest of the nation. Thus, Rabbi Yitzhak Arama's approach appears preferable.

Moses formulates his response in a way that most effectively express-es his somewhat startling message. The "innocent" request of Reuben and Gad threatens to bring about a catastrophe similar to that which resulted from the mission of the spies 38 years earlier. Moses never accuses Reuben and Gad of lack of trust in God or of unwarranted fear from the nations of Canaan. He rather takes the tribes of Reuben and Gad to task for their inappropriate attitude toward the land that God had given them. Anyone who spurns the land that God has given them is considered dis-loyal to God.

Even according to this interpretation we must note that ultimately our story also points to the difference between the generation of those who left Egypt and the generation destined to inherit the land. The tribes in ques-tion are quick to deny any such similarity with the spies, and without any difficulty they place themselves at the head of the fighting forces for the conquest of the land. History does not need to repeat itself; courageous religious-moral leadership can make a difference.

Rabbi Elhanan Samet, *Iyyunim be-Parashot ha-Shavua* (first series) vol. 2 (Hebrew) ed. Ayal Fishler (Ma'aleh Adumim: Ma'aliyot Press, 2002), pp. 262–277.

Masei

THE SIGNIFICANCE OF THE JOURNEY LIST: A SYMPTOM OF THE STRUGGLE BETWEEN JACOB AND ESAU

*A*fter Jacob's encounter with Laban, his subsequent reunion with Esau, and his return to Canaan, the Torah lists the descendants of Esau (Genesis, chapter 36). Several midrashim and later commentators wonder why the Torah includes this list. Some observe that several of these marriages were incestuous; this chapter demonstrates how immoral Esau's family had become (see *Tanhuma Vayeshev*; *Genesis Rabbah* 82; Rashi; Abarbanel).

Sforno (on Genesis 36:31) asserts that none of the kings of Edom were native members of Esau's family. Ramban adds that there were no dynasties among these kings, demonstrating political instability and unworthiness.

Following midrashic lines, Rashi (on Genesis 37:1) explains the contrast between the lackluster account of Esau's descendants followed immediately by a lengthy account of Jacob's family history: "It may be compared to a pearl that fell into the sand; one searches in the sand and sifts it in a sieve until he finds the pearl; and after he has found it he throws away the pebbles from his hand and retains the pearl." According to Rashi, even though the Torah records Esau's generations, their significance is eclipsed by the longer record of the family that would achieve lasting greatness—that of Jacob.

Beyond these reasons why Esau's lineage is recorded, this passage casts light on a broader issue that epitomizes the relationship between Jacob and Esau throughout Tanakh. Why, for example, does Numbers, chapter 33 enumerate such a detailed list of Israel's wanderings in the wilderness?

In his *Sefat Emet* (*Masei*, 5653), Rabbi Yehudah Aryeh Leib Alter of Ger suggests that this passage reflects the relationship between Jacob and Esau. Even when he initially suffers, Jacob ultimately will succeed. In contrast, Esau's gains are illusory and ultimately end in emptiness. The lengthy listing of Israel's travails in the desert are a symptom of a trend that runs through the Torah.

Esau was born fully developed (Genesis 25:25). He was named Esau, meaning "complete, fully formed" (Rashi, Rashbam). In contrast, Jacob tagged along and was named for his clinging to his brother's heel. Esau immediately wins his father's love, whereas Jacob must wait years before being appreciated by Isaac. Esau wants food now and therefore trades a long-term birthright for immediate satisfaction from lentil stew. When Jacob returns from Laban, he is the father of 11 sons and one daughter. Esau is the chieftain over at least 400 men. Esau receives his inheritance in Seir immediately, whereas Jacob's descendents go to Egypt where they were eventually enslaved.

Esau's nation produced eight kings before Israel left Egypt and wandered through the desert (Genesis, chapter 36, cf. Ibn Ezra). Israel instead had to wander from place to place.

Esau represents the quick-fix, instant gain, whereas Jacob represents a longer road to success. Whereas Esau always gets a jump start, Jacob ultimately prevails and endures.

Hayyim Angel, "*Elleh Toledot*: A Study of the Genealogies in the Book of Genesis," in *Haham Gaon Memorial Volume*, ed. Marc D. Angel (Brooklyn: Sefer Hermon Press, 1997), pp. 163–182; reprinted in Angel, *Through an Opaque Lens* (New York: Sephardic Publication Foundation, 2006), pp. 111–126.

TRIBAL INHERITANCE IN LIGHT OF THE DAUGHTERS OF ZELOPHEHAD

*I*n Numbers, chapter 27, the daughters of Zelophehad successfully petitioned Moses to preserve their father's name by enabling them to act as heirs given the absence of brothers. God approved and enacted new legislation confirming that a father has a future title on his ancestral plot with daughters as well as with sons.

In Numbers, chapter 36, however, the elders of the Tribe of Manasseh approached Moses with a new concern. If the daughters of Zelophehad were to marry men from outside their tribe, then their overall tribal inheritance would be diminished. God agreed and introduced further legislation: "Every daughter among the Israelite tribes who inherits a share must marry someone from a clan of her father's tribe, in order that every Israelite may keep his ancestral share. Thus no inheritance shall pass over from one tribe to another, but the Israelite tribes shall remain bound each to its portion" (Numbers 36:8–9). Moses instructed the daughters of Zelophehad to marry within their tribe, and they obeyed.

Rabbi Elhanan Samet observes that although the legislation sounds like it was ongoing for all the time Israel lived in their land, a Mishnah (*Ta'anit* 26b) states that the fifteenth of Av was one of the happiest days of the year. In addition to the marriage festival described in the Mishnah, the Talmud offers a second reason for the joyous nature of that day: " Rav Judah said in the name of Samuel: It is the day on which permission was granted to the tribes to intermarry. From where may this be adduced? Scripture says, 'This is what the Lord has commanded concerning the daughters of Zelophehad, etc.' (Numbers 36:6) [meaning] *this* shall hold good for this generation only" (*Ta'anit* 30b). In other words, the legislation in Numbers 36 applied exclusively to the generation entering the land.

Ramban explains that once Joshua distributed the land to the tribes in the subsequent generation, those tribal boundaries became permanent. The daughters of Zelophehad lived prior to the distribution, and therefore the Tribe of Manasseh was concerned that they would lose territory from the outset.

The abolition of this legislation was a national cause for joy. Why? It affected only a tiny percentage of the population, namely, daughters who inherited their fathers' ancestral plots because there were no brothers. Rabbi Elhanan Samet explains that this law symbolically affected the entire nation, as it created psychological barriers between tribes. Once the tribes understood that anyone from each tribe could marry someone from any other tribe, the entire nation could view itself as one entity. This was a cause for genuine joy.

Rabbi Elhanan Samet, *Iyyunim be-Parashot ha-Shavua* (second series) vol. 2 (Hebrew) ed. Ayal Fishler (Ma'aleh Adumim: Ma'aliyot Press, 2004), pp. 299–312.

Devarim
דברים
Deuteronomy

Devarim

INTRODUCTION TO THE
BOOK OF DEUTERONOMY

The Book of Deuteronomy is called "Devarim" based on its first major word. *Devarim* means "words" or "things." The name Deuteronomy comes from the Hebrew *mishneh Torah* (literally, "a second Torah," *Sifrei* 160, based on Deuteronomy 17:18; Joshua 8:32)—which says a lot about its essence as a recapitulation of the earlier books of the Torah.

In his commentary on the Torah, Richard Elliott Friedman observes that during his first prophetic revelation at the burning bush, Moses said, "Please, O Lord, I have never been a man of words (*lo ish devarim anokhi*), either in times past or now that You have spoken to Your servant; I am slow of speech and slow of tongue" (Exodus 4:10). Though he initially said that he was not a man of *devarim*, his closing speech to the people is called *Devarim*. Moses had progressed immensely over his 40 years of leadership.

In Deuteronomy 17:18, the term *mishneh Torah* is used: "When [the king] is seated on his royal throne, he shall have a copy of this Teaching (*mishneh Torah*) written for him on a scroll by the levitical priests." In this verse, *mishneh Torah* refers to a copy of the Torah, or at least a part of it. The term expanded for naming the Book of Deuteronomy. It is not a repetition as much as a selective interpretation of Israelite history and laws.

Although tradition speaks of God's revelation of all five books of the Torah, Deuteronomy stands apart from the other four books in that Moses speaks for much of it. The Talmud makes a halakhic distinction between reading the blessings and curses in Leviticus, chapter 26, where no break in the reading is permitted; and those in Deuteronomy, chapter 28, where the reader may insert a break between those called to the Torah:

Said Abaye . . . . What is the reason? In the former, [the people of] Israel are addressed in the plural number and Moses uttered them [the blessings and

curses] on behalf of the Almighty ('if you shall not hearken unto me, etc.');
in the latter, [the people of] Israel are addressed in the singular, and Moses
uttered them in his own name ('if you shall not hearken unto the voice of
the Lord thy God, etc.'). (*Megillah* 31b)

Abarbanel explains that throughout his leadership in the wilderness,
Moses composed speeches and spoke in his own name. God then commanded Moses to edit and organize some of these speeches into the Book
of Deuteronomy. It was that divine command that elevated Moses' speeches to the level of revelation. The same principle applies to passages in the
Torah such as the Song at the Sea (Exodus, chapter 15). Moses and Israel
composed this song on their own, and afterward, God commanded Moses
to include it in the Torah. The revelation of the Torah itself thus reflects a
partnership between God and Israel.

RASHI AND RAMBAN ON THE CONFLICTING SPIES NARRATIVES

*T*here is a discrepancy between the accounts of the Spies in
Numbers and Deuteronomy. First, God appears to have initiated this mission (Numbers 13:1). However, Moses retells this
episode in Deuteronomy and relates that the people, and not God, initiated the mission (Deuteronomy 1:22). Moreover, Moses appears to cast the
people as faithless for requesting spies immediately following God's promise of the Land (1:20–22).

Attempting to harmonize the two narratives, Rashi asserts that the
people initiated the mission, thereby demonstrating a lack of faith in God's
promises, as related in Deuteronomy. Moses expressed support not
because he agreed with the people, but rather because he was using
reverse psychology. He surmised that the people would be impressed by
his assuredness and conclude that there was no reason to send spies
(Deuteronomy 1:23). When Moses' efforts failed, God responded *shelah
lekha* (Numbers 13:1)—send for *your* benefit, but not with My blessing.

God acquiesced so that He could expose what He knew from the outset, namely, that this generation lacked faith. Thus Israel's downfall occurred before the Numbers narrative even begins.

However, the Numbers account offers no indication that God was upset at the outset of the narrative. The plain reading suggests that the nation sinned only with their hasty acceptance of the spies' negative report. Similarly, Moses hardly appears to be feigning agreement only to encourage the abortion of the mission.

Consequently, Ramban rejects Rashi's approach, and proposes an alternate methodology. Numbers presents the "objective" story as it unfolded. There was nothing wrongful in sending spies on a military mission, and Tanakh presents other occasions where spying was legitimate (see, for example, Numbers, chapter 21; Joshua, chapter 2). God approved, but the people sinned by accepting the negative account of the majority of spies. When Moses recounted this event at the end of his life in Deuteronomy, however, he already knew the conclusion of the episode. Therefore, he projected the people's faithlessness back onto their initial request, saying that they did not trust God's assurances from the outset.

Ramban accepts Rashi's view that the people first requested sending spies (Deuteronomy), and then God approved of their request (Numbers). Moses likewise approved because the initial request was valid. Ramban demonstrates how both texts may be read smoothly based on the respective contexts of each narrative. It is undesirable to impose the meaning of one account onto the other at the expense of either text's plain sense.

Vaethannan

WHY DID MOSES NOT APOLOGIZE AFTER HIS SIN AT MERIBAH?

*B*eing one of the most cryptic narratives in the Torah, Numbers 20 has received much exegetical attention. What was Moses' actual sin that led to his forfeiture of entering the Land? Why did Aaron deserve punishment? These enigmas never have received compelling explanations despite a millennium of efforts by the greatest commentators.

Rather than attempt yet another solution to this age-old conundrum, I will approach this passage from a different angle. The Torah blames Moses for "lacking faith." What constituted that lack of faith, and why did he lack faith? This line of questioning may shed light on the passage without having to resolve precisely what he did wrong.

At the very beginning of his prophetic calling, Moses stalled at the burning bush. After he claimed that he was slow of speech, God responded that He always would be there to help him speak (Exodus 4:11–12). Within Rashi's reading of Numbers 20, one might suggest that Moses did not have faith that God would instruct him what to say. Instead, Moses struck the rock. This reading connects Moses' rebellion in the 40th year of his leadership to his insecurities from the beginning of his career. However, the question remains: Why would Moses lack faith in God after 40 years of steady guidance?

Moses' reaction at Meribah appears to parallel an earlier crisis in Numbers 11, when the people complained regarding meat: "Moses heard the people weeping, every clan apart, each person at the entrance of his tent. The Lord was very angry, and Moses was distressed" (Numbers 11:10). When "Moses was distressed," at whom was he distressed? From the parallel with the first half of the verse, "the Lord was very angry," it would appear that Moses also was angered with the people for their unwarranted complaint.

However, his ensuing outburst indicates that Moses was distressed with God as well:

And Moses said to the Lord, "Why have You dealt ill with Your servant, and why have I not enjoyed Your favor, that You have laid the burden of all this people upon me? Did I conceive all this people, did I bear them, that You should say to me, 'Carry them in your bosom as a nurse carries an infant,' to the land that You have promised on oath to their fathers? Where am I to get meat to give to all this people, when they whine before me and say, 'Give us meat to eat!' I cannot carry all this people by myself, for it is too much for me. If You would deal thus with me, kill me rather, I beg You, and let me see no more of my wretchedness!" (Numbers 11:11–15)

Moses complained that God had set him up for failure. How could he care for this nation and supply all their needs? Returning to his primal fears from the burning bush, Moses was prepared to resign and even die rather than remain in a situation where God appeared to be failing him.

This reading is strengthened by a literary parallel to Exodus 5:22, immediately following Moses' first disappointment. Pharaoh denied Moses' request for three days of worship and also deprived the Israelites of straw for their brickmaking. Moses protested, *lamah hare'ota la-am ha-zeh* (O Lord, why did You bring harm upon this people?). In Numbers 11:11 he complained *lamah hare'ota le-avdekha* (Why have You brought harm upon Your servant?).

God solved the crisis in Exodus 5 by beginning the plagues and exodus; He did so in Numbers 11 by supplying meat and appointing leaders to help Moses. Yet Moses appears to have been wounded by God's allowing him to fail—if only temporarily. In the 40th year, when the people again complained about water, Moses again felt abandoned by God. Though God had promised that He would always instruct Moses what to say (Exodus 4:12), Moses had a brief lapse of faith in God's support. Therefore, Moses struck the rock instead of speaking.

We may offer a symbolic interpretation to Moses' striking the rock *twice* (Numbers 20:11). Parallel to his negative experience in chapter 11, Moses now was frustrated with the people and with God. Moses consequently struck the rock twice as a sign of his double distress.

This discussion elucidates a question seldom raised by our commentators: Whatever Moses' sin may have been at Meribah, why did he never apologize to God? He did not repent immediately following God's stark decree, and God offered him no fewer than three further opportunities to repent by reiterating the sin (Numbers 20:24; 27:12–14; Deuteronomy 32:49–52). In all three cases, Moses listened obediently but never expressed remorse.

Even more remarkably, although God always blamed Moses for his lack of faith at Meribah, Moses repeatedly transferred blame to the people when reviewing the nation's history in Deuteronomy: "*Because of you* the Lord was incensed with me too, and He said: You shall not enter it either" (Deuteronomy 1:37; cf. 4:21). It appears that there was a debate between God and Moses over whose fault the sin at Meribah was!

The divergence between the views of God and Moses may relate to our previous discussion. Moses believed that God had failed him during his initial encounter with Pharaoh (Exodus 5), with the meat (Numbers 11), and again at Meribah. In contrast, God maintained at Meribah that Moses let Him down. This was a battle over principle. Of course, God wins all battles over principle. Moses was punished, and God did not reprimand the people for their complaints.

However, the Torah affords Moses a sympathetic view as well:

> I pleaded with the Lord at that time, saying…Let me, I pray, cross over and see the good land on the other side of the Jordan, that good hill country, and the Lebanon. But the Lord was wrathful with me on your account and would not listen to me. The Lord said to me, "Enough! Never speak to Me of this matter again!" (Deuteronomy 3:23–26)

In this heart-wrenching plea, Moses again blamed the people and again did not apologize. Instead, he asked God to allow him into the Land as a personal favor. He did not express remorse, because he did not feel himself guilty. Moses went to his grave after looking at the Promised Land, not convinced that he should be left out, but obediently following God's command to the end.

This story often is used to illustrate the principle that even the greatest human being is not perfect. It also teaches that God does not necessarily respond affirmatively to prayer—not even to Moses. We have explored the possibility that also included in this series of messages is the fact that even the greatest person has a blind spot in seeing his own mistakes. There is much that one can learn from these central lessons.

Hayyim Angel, "Why Did Moses Not Apologize After His Sin at Meribah?" in Angel, *Creating Space Between Peshat and Derash: A Collection of Studies on Tanakh* (Jersey City, NJ: Ktav-Sephardic Publication Foundation, 2011), pp. 45–51.

—

Ekev

THE DESIRE TO RETURN TO EGYPT

*R*abbi Francis Nataf explores the religious ramifications of living in Israel versus living in Egypt. The Torah teaches that Israel's dependence on rainfall is a sign of divine providence (Deuteronomy 11:10–12). We hear the opposite perspective in the writings of the ancient Greek historian Herodotus. He writes that the Egyptians viewed the consistent rising of the Nile as proof that they were chosen by the gods. In contrast, they viewed Greek dependence on rainfall as a sign of their being out of favor of the gods.

Because of its consistent agricultural cycle, Egypt became a place of refuge during famines. The Torah likens Egypt to the Garden of Eden (Genesis 13:10). Abraham's nephew Lot moved to Sodom because it resembled Egypt in that the Jordan River watered the area and therefore guaranteed fertility.

The Torah also casts Egypt as an immoral, sexually depraved society (Leviticus 18:3). The progenitor of the Egyptian nation, Noah's son Ham, behaved in a disgraceful manner with his father (Genesis 9:20–27). Ham was the father of Mitzrayim, the ancestor of Egypt (Genesis 10:6). Sodom also is associated with moral depravity.

Climates contribute to religious outlooks. The Nile led to a concept of God wherein people felt a sense of security and entitlement. There are no consequences to behavior since the Nile always rises. In contrast, In contrast, Israel's dependence on its climate led to a culture of introspection and relationship-building with a personal God. At the same time, Israel always found the security of Egypt alluring. The generation leaving Egypt reminisced about the good old days in Egypt despite their having been oppressed slaves there. Dathan and Abiram bitingly refer to Egypt as a land flowing with milk and honey during the Korah rebellion (Numbers 16:13).

Being a good Israelite means to accept some instability and the need for constant work in exchange for a heightened religious consciousness. By appreciating our dependence on God, we never become complacent.

Rabbi Francis Nataf, *Redeeming Relevance in the Book of Exodus: Explorations in Text and Meaning* (Jerusalem: Urim, 2009), pp. 21–36.

MOSES' HIGH SPIRITUAL LEVEL AS AN IMPEDIMENT TO RELATING TO THE PEOPLE

*J*oshua was one of Israel's most effective leaders. The only recorded sin of his period was that of Achan (Joshua 7:1). More impressively, a nation that persistently complained throughout Moses' leadership grumbled only once in the Book of Joshua—to the *elders* after they mistakenly struck a treaty with the Gibeonites (Joshua 9:18). Most remarkably, even after their hearts "sank in total dismay" following their defeat at Ai (Joshua 7:5), they did not complain to Joshua.

Paradoxically, it may be that the people had more confidence in Joshua than in Moses, precisely because Joshua himself was terrified after the loss at Ai:

"Ah, Lord God!"cried Joshua. "Why did You lead this people across the Jordan only to deliver us into the hands of the Amorites, to be destroyed by them? If only we had been content to remain on the other side of the Jordan! O Lord, what can I say after Israel has turned tail before its enemies? When the Canaanites and all the inhabitants of the land hear of this, they will turn upon us and wipe out our very name from the earth. And what will You do about Your great name?" (Joshua 7:7–9)

Joshua sounded like the majority of the spies and their followers in the wilderness (Numbers 14:1–3; Deuteronomy 1:27). At the same time, Joshua made an appeal similar to that of Moses, that God should be concerned with His reputation among the nations of the world (Numbers 14:13–16).

In contrast, it may have been difficult for the people to trust the ever-resolute Moses. They could not even look at his face without a veil (Exodus 34:29–35). Moses was privileged to speak with God face to face (Numbers 12:8), but the people were unable to speak to Moses face to face!

This tension is captured by another talmudic passage:

> Rabbi Hanina further said: Everything is in the hand of heaven except the fear of heaven, as it says, "And now, O Israel, what does the Lord your God demand of you? Only this: to revere" (Deuteronomy 12:10). Is the fear of heaven such a little thing. . . . Yes; for Moses it was a small thing; as Rabbi Hanina said: To illustrate by a parable, if a man is asked for a big article and he has it, it seems like a small article to him; if he is asked for a small article and he does not possess it, it seems like a big article to him. (*Berakhot* 33b)

Moses' awe of God was so great that he could not fathom why his people did not trust God also. Ironically, Moses' incomparable faith may have been at the root of his struggles in leading the Israelites. In contrast, the people never rebelled against Joshua, because they detected his fears and therefore viewed him as one of them. Joshua was able to bridge the world of Moses with the world of the people.

Hayyim Angel, "Moonlit Leadership: A Midrashic Reading of Joshua's Success," *Jewish Bible Quarterly* 37:3 (2009), pp. 144–152; reprinted in Angel, *Creating Space Between Peshat and Derash: A Collection of Studies on Tanakh* (Jersey City, NJ: Ktav-Sephardic Publication Foundation, 2011), pp. 64–73.

Re'eh

GOD'S CHOICE OF JERUSALEM AS ISRAEL'S ETERNAL CAPITAL

*I*n Deuteronomy, chapter 12, God commands the Israelites not to serve Him as pagans serve their deities, wherever they want. Rather, they may bring offerings only on "the site that the Lord your God will choose amidst all your tribes as His habitation, to establish His name there" (Deuteronomy 12:5).

God ultimately selected Jerusalem as this singular location. The history of how Jerusalem became the place for God's Presence is fascinating. The Torah never mentions Jerusalem by name. Some think that King Melchizedek of Salem in Genesis, chapter 14 lived in Jerusalem. However, Genesis 33:18 relates that "Jacob arrived safe in the city of Shechem (*va-yavo Yaakov shalem ir Shechem*) which is in the land of Canaan—having come thus from Paddan-aram—and he encamped before the city." "*Shalem*" could mean that he arrived safely, but it also could be another name for Shechem (Rashbam). At any rate, the Melchizedek narrative does not mention Jerusalem by that name.

Similarly, the Binding of Isaac (Genesis, chapter 22) took place at Mount Moriah, which is linked to the Temple Mount in II Chronicles 3:1: "Then Solomon began to build the House of the Lord in Jerusalem on Mount Moriah, where [the Lord] had appeared to his father David." Once again, Jerusalem is not named. Jerusalem is mentioned by name for the first time in Joshua 10:1, where its king participated in a Canaanite coalition against Joshua.

The most important cities from the time of the Patriarchs were Hebron and Shechem. Abraham and Sarah lived near Hebron, and Abraham purchased the cave and field of Machpelah as a family burial ground. Jacob later purchased land for his family in Shechem.

When David became king over Judah, he inquired of God as to where the capital of Judah should be located. God responded with the obvious choice—Hebron (II Samuel 2:1). After achieving national unity and bridging the gap between the Tribes of Judah and Benjamin, David moved the nation's capital from Hebron to Jerusalem on his own.

Malbim explains that David chose Jerusalem on the border between the lands of Judah and Benjamin in order to make peace with rival-tribe Benjamin, which had just lost King Saul and with it the kingship. In essence, Jerusalem was the world's first Washington, D.C. This gesture of peace and goodwill bore fruit. Two generations later when the northern tribes seceded and formed the Kingdom of Israel, the Tribe of Benjamin remained loyal to the Kingdom of Judah.

Aside from its political ramifications, God approved of David's choice of Jerusalem, and an angel selected the location of the Temple Mount in Jerusalem (II Samuel, chapter 24). Jerusalem thus became the place that God would choose as His habitation, and Israel's eternal capital.

JEREMIAH'S USE OF DEUTERONOMY TO COMBAT FALSE PROPHETS

*H*ow were people—even the most sincerely religious ones— to distinguish between true and false prophets? Jeremiah's forecast of 70 years of Babylonian rule (Jeremiah 25:10–11; 29:10) came with political ramifications: Remain loyal to Babylonia or else they will destroy the country. By predicting the miraculous demise of Babylonia, the false prophets supported revolt against Babylonia.

Some false prophets were easier to detect than others. Some were adulterers (Jeremiah 29:21–23). Their flagrant disregard for the Torah discredited them as true prophets. However, Hananiah (Jeremiah 28:1–17) and Shemaiah (Jeremiah 29:24–32) both sounded righteous. Both spoke in the name of God. The nation would have to wait to see whose prediction would be fulfilled. Waiting, however, was not a realistic option. The false prophets were calling for an immediate revolt, at the same time that Jeremiah was calling for loyalty to Babylonia. Thus Jeremiah could not appeal to one of the Torah's primary tests for distinguishing true prophets from false prophets, namely, that one's predictions can determine the truthfulness or falsity of the prophet (Deuteronomy 18:21–22).

To address these difficulties, Jeremiah presented alternative criteria by which to ascertain false prophets. He staked his argument in the Torah's assertion that a wonder worker who preaches idolatry is a false prophet regardless of successful predictions or signs:

> As for that prophet or dream-diviner, he shall be put to death; for he urged disloyalty to the Lord your God (*ki dibber sarah al A-donai Elokekhem*)—who freed you from the land of Egypt and who redeemed you from the house of bondage—to make you stray from the path that the Lord your God commanded you to follow. Thus you will sweep out evil from your midst. (Deuteronomy 13:6)

Jeremiah extended the Torah's example of idolatry to include anyone who does not actively promote repentance. Since the false prophets predicted the unconditional downfall of Babylonia regardless of any repentance on Israel's part, they must be fraudulent (Jeremiah 23:13–14).

More subtly, the Torah uses the expression, "for he urged disloyalty to the Lord your God" (*ki dibber sarah al A-donai Elokekhem*). This phraseology is used to refer to prophets only twice in Tanakh—specifically when Jeremiah censured Hananiah and Shemaiah, the two false prophets who appeared the most righteous (Jeremiah 28:16; 29:32).

In contrast, Jeremiah was committed to God's word no matter how unpopular that made him. Though Jeremiah was unhappy for a majority of his career, his prophecies gave him strength knowing that there would be an eternal future for Israel and her relationship with God: "At this I awoke and looked about, and my sleep had been pleasant to me" (Jeremiah 31:25).

Hayyim Angel, "Jeremiah's Confrontation with the Religious Establishment: A Man of Truth in a World of Falsehood," in Angel, *Revealed Texts, Hidden Meanings: Finding the Religious Significance in Tanakh* (Jersey City, NJ: Ktav-Sephardic Publication Foundation, 2009), pp. 127–138.

Shofetim

MONARCHY

If, after you have entered the land that the Lord your God has assigned to you, and taken possession of it and settled in it, you decide, "I will set a king over me, as do all the nations about me," you shall be free to set a king over yourself, one chosen by the Lord your God. Be sure to set as king over yourself one of your own people; you must not set a foreigner over you, one who is not your kinsman. (Deuteronomy 17:14–15)

This passage may be read as a positive commandment for establishing a monarchy, or it could permit monarchy only were the people to request it.

In the prophet Samuel's time, at a time of political unrest, the people finally did request a king. God and Samuel were furious:

Samuel was displeased that they said "Give us a king to govern us." Samuel prayed to the Lord, and the Lord replied to Samuel, "Heed the demand of the people in everything they say to you. For it is not you that they have rejected; it is Me they have rejected as their king. Like everything else they have done ever since I brought them out of Egypt to this day—forsaking Me and worshiping other gods—so they are doing to you." (I Samuel 8:6–8)

As a result of the ambiguity in the Torah law, and the negative response of God and Samuel, the *tannaim* debate whether the Torah commands monarchy or whether it only permits it if the people request a king. Rabbi Yehudah (*Sanhedrin* 20b) considers monarchy a positive commandment. Rabbi Nehorai maintains that it is permitted yet frowned upon. Rambam rules like Rabbi Yehudah, that monarchy is a positive commandment (*Hil. Melakhim* 1:1–2). The people in Samuel's time therefore must have asked inappropriately. Many commentators and codifiers adopted this position.

Abarbanel, however, dissents and critiques Rambam's view. God and Samuel were incensed at the people's very asking for a king, rather than at the formulation or timing of their request (cf. I Samuel 10:19; 12:17). If the Torah commands monarchy, why did Joshua and his successors fail to appoint a king? When Samuel rebuked the people, why did they not respond that they wanted to fulfill a Torah commandment?

Abarbanel therefore adopts Rabbi Nehorai's view that although monarchy is permitted if requested, it is a negative political institution. Abarbanel invokes the talmudic principle, "the Torah states this in consideration of the evil inclination" (*Kiddushin* 21b). In Abarbanel's view, the Torah permitted monarchy only as a concession to the people's wrongful desires.

The relevance of this debate goes beyond the textual analysis. Those who maintain that monarchy is a positive commandment assert that the Torah's ideal form of government is a monarchy. Alternatively, those who view monarchy as optional maintain that the Torah leaves open the form of government desired by the people in a given time. This debate has taken on new meaning with the founding of the modern State of Israel as a democracy. For some contemporary ramifications in halakhah and religious philosophy, see the articles by Rabbi Aharon Lichtenstein and Professor Gerald Blidstein cited below.

Hayyim Angel, "Abarbanel: Commentator and Teacher: Celebrating 500 Years of his Influence on Tanakh Study," *Tradition* 42:3 (Fall 2009), pp. 9–26; reprinted in Angel, *Creating Space Between Peshat and Derash: A Collection of Studies on Tanakh* (Jersey City, NJ: Ktav-Sephardic Publication Foundation, 2011), pp. 1–24.

Rabbi Aharon Lichtenstein, "Communal Governance, Lay and Rabbinic: An Overview," pp. 19–52, esp. pp. 21–26; Prof. Gerald Blidstein, "On Lay Legislation in Halakhah: The King as Instance," pp. 1–17, in *Rabbinic and Lay Communal Authority*, ed. Suzanne Last Stone (New York: Yeshiva University Press, 2006).

BREAKING THE CALF'S NECK

*D*euteronomy 21:1–9 contains the law of what to do when a murdered individual is found on the roadside between two towns, and it is not known which town is responsible for the murder. Communal leaders conducted a ceremony involving breaking the neck of a calf as a form of atonement. One midrash (*Tanhuma Mishpatim* 7) remarks that the ceremony sounds pagan and cruel. Perhaps there is some consolation in knowing that there is no record of this ceremony's ever having taken place. Regardless, it is important to examine the text and rabbinic tradition to uncover the underlying values of this unusual law.

The Torah refers to town elders and priests who needed to be present at this ceremony. In the Talmud, Rabbi Eliezer rules that in addition to the local leadership, the king and High Priest had to be present (*Sotah* 45a). The prevailing talmudic view is that members of the Sanhedrin from Jerusalem joined the local leadership. Both views express the idea that a roadside murder anywhere in the country is a national disaster and therefore the nation's leaders must participate.

This ceremony also calls on leaders to build an ethical society before crises arise. The town elders should be able to state with confidence: "Our society *could not have* produced a murderer." The horror of one murder became a public spectacle so all would internalize the gravity of this crime.

The prayer was central to this ceremony: "Absolve, O Lord, Your people Israel whom You redeemed, and do not let guilt for the blood of the innocent remain among Your people Israel" (21:8). Bloodguilt defiles the land, and the community prays to God that they should live holy lives so that they can build an ethically perfected society.

The Talmud states that when murder became more common in Israel, this ceremony was abolished (*Sotah* 47a). The absolute shock of this ceremony was effective only when people recoiled in horror at a single murder. As society's morality declined, this dramatic measure became superfluous and was discontinued.

One also may contrast the Torah's laws with the ancient Hittite and Hammurabi Codes. In the Hittite Code, if one finds a corpse in a field, the members of the city living closest to where it was found had to pay compensation to the family of the deceased. Similarly, the Code of Hammurabi states if there was a kidnapping, the community closest to where it happened had to pay compensation to the family. In both codes, family members are treated as commodities; they can be "replaced" by financial compensation. In contrast, the Torah presents a comprehensive religious-ethical system wherein the entire society is answerable to God.

Ki Tetzei

REASONS FOR THE COMMANDMENTS

If, along the road, you chance upon a bird's nest, in any tree or on the ground, with fledglings or eggs and the mother sitting over the fledglings or on the eggs, do not take the mother together with her young. Let the mother go, and take only the young, in order that you may fare well and have a long life. (Deuteronomy 22:6–7)

At first glance, this commandment appears to teach compassion. Rambam (*Guide for the Perplexed* III:48) argues that this law teaches that we must have mercy on animals, which also have feelings. Alternatively, Ramban maintains that this law teaches *people* the trait of compassion by being kind to animals. Despite their differences, both authorities agree that this law teaches some form of compassion.

One passage in the Talmud, however, objects to this line of thinking (*Berakhot* 33b). The Mishnah rules that one leading prayer services is prohibited from imploring God to be merciful as God is to birds in this commandment. The Gemara offers two explanations of this law: (1) invoking God's mercy in this context could raise the question of why God had mercy only on birds; and (2) the prayer offers a rationale—that God is merciful—for the commandment, when all of the Torah's commandments are simply divine decrees.

Adopting this second perspective, Rabbi Yehudah Halevi maintains that ideally, one should not seek reasons behind the commandments. We observe them because God gave them to help us build a relationship with God. Only one who unfortunately asks the philosophical question should then speculate on reasons for the commandments rather than remaining in doubt (*Kuzari* II:26). Several other rabbinic thinkers similarly maintained this position.

Rambam vehemently disagrees with this approach, which he maintains reflects negatively on God. Even people generally act purposefully; how could one think that God creates purposeless laws merely to create subservience? (*Guide for the Perplexed* III:31). Many other great thinkers likewise assume that God had a purpose for every commandment.

Rabbi David Hartman adds a religious-social component to Rambam's theological position (*A Heart of Many Rooms*, 2002, pp. 101–103). People who have faith in God and observe the commandments blindly can have no shared language with those who do not believe and observe. In contrast, Rambam's approach fosters intelligent discourse between observant Jews and the rest of world, including less-observant Jews. Rambam stresses that every commandment teaches justice and noble qualities, or wards off injustice or negative qualities. The Torah wants others to appreciate its wisdom, and Rambam cites these verses in support of his view:

> Observe them faithfully, for that will be proof of your wisdom and discernment to other peoples, who on hearing of all these laws will say, "Surely, that great nation is a wise and discerning people." For what great nation is there that has a god so close at hand as is the Lord our God whenever we call upon Him? Or what great nation has laws and rules as perfect as all this Teaching that I set before you this day? (Deuteronomy 4:6–8)

—

LEVIRATE MARRIAGE

*T*he Torah legislates levirate marriage (Deuteronomy 25:5–10) for the circumstance when a married man dies childless. His brother was supposed to marry the widow and have a child who would bear the title of the deceased and inherit his land. If the brother refused to marry his sister-in-law, there would be a *halitzah*, a ceremony of public humiliation of the brother who refuses to do his duty, after which the widow was free to marry anyone.

Although levirate marriage is foreign to our modern world, and we almost invariably practice *halitzah* when this tragic situation arises, it teaches absolute responsibility for one's family. The narrative of Judah and Tamar in Genesis, chapter 38, teaches that a form of levirate marriage was practiced prior to the revelation of the Torah to Israel (Rambam, Abarbanel). Some suggest further that in addition to Tamar's desperation, she actually was following ancient convention. In the Hittite code (#193), there was an order of precedence for levirate marriages. If there were no brothers, the father-in-law (in this case Judah) was next in line. After Onan refused his responsibility and Judah withheld Shelah from Tamar, Tamar seduced Judah and had children through him, thereby continuing Er's family line.

In Leviticus 25:25–28, the Torah legislates the redemption of fields for relatives. One never wanted to part with his ancestral land and did so only under deep financial distress. Family members had a responsibility to buy the field back for their destitute relative. Although the Torah does not link levirate marriage with field redemption, the underlying family values are the same.

Levirate marriage and field redemption were weighty burdens. Marrying one's sister-in-law came with financial obligations and also could create difficulties in a family dynamic if the brother-in-law already had a family of his own. Moreover, the Torah generally views marriage between a brother and sister-in-law as incestuous (Leviticus 18:16). The exception made for levirate marriage is all the more remarkable in this context. Field redemption likewise placed great financial pressure on the redeemer. They were heroic acts of family loyalty that preserved the title of one's relative.

In the Book of Ruth, Boaz linked these two laws by redeeming Elimelech's field and marrying Ruth. Ramban (on Genesis 38:9) explains that Judean society was so impressed by the Torah's teaching of family loyalty that they extended the practice of levirate marriage to other male relatives if there were no brothers-in-law.

King David was descended from the levirate marriages of Judah-Tamar, and Ruth-Boaz. Ruth 4:12 links the two stories when the townsfolk bless Boaz and Ruth to be like the house of Judah's son Perez. Thus, David's pedigree attests to the importance of the levirate laws. He owed his very existence to Tamar and to Boaz for their deep loyalty and sacrifice to preserve their family lines.

—

AMALEK

*O*ne branch of Esau's family descends from his grandson Amalek (Genesis 36:10–12). Amalek plays a singularly negative role in Tanakh. Soon after the exodus, Amalek attacked Israel from the rear—the first instance of terrorism in Tanakh (Exodus 17:8–16; Deuteronomy 25:17–19). God Himself declares war against Amalek. A midrash states that God's kingdom is incomplete as long as Amalek exists (*Tanhuma Ki Tetzei* 11).

Throughout biblical history, the Amalekites distinguished themselves by joining wars that were not theirs (see, for example, Judges 3:13; 6:3, 33; 7:12). In I Samuel, chapter 15, King Saul defeats the Amalekite power base but spares their King Agag. Consequently, God rejects Saul's kingship since he violated God's commandment to destroy all of the Amalekites, including their king. After the nation of Amalek finally was destroyed, their evil influence remained. In the Purim story, Haman is called an "Agagite," a representative of the abject evil for which Amalek stands.

Amalek's mother was Timna (see Genesis 36:12). Timna was a concubine to Esau's son Eliphaz, and we know nothing further about her. The Talmud offers a surprising analysis of how Amalek came to be:

> Desiring to become a proselyte, [Timna] went to Abraham, Isaac, and Jacob, but they did not accept her. So she went and became a concubine to Eliphaz the son of Esau, saying, I would rather be a servant to this people than a

mistress of another nation. From her Amalek was descended who afflicted Israel. Why so? Because they should not have repulsed her. (*Sanhedrin* 99b)

Incredibly, this Sage appears to blame our Patriarchs for adopting a hard-line posture against Timna's conversion, thereby contributing to the creation of Amalek! Although the Torah makes it amply clear that Israel should not bear blame for the existence of Amalek, one may derive lessons from this talmudic passage: (1) We should be as open and welcoming as possible. Although no doubt the Patriarchs had good reason to prevent Timna from entering their family, it is better to err on the side of being overly welcoming than being overly exclusive. (2) While in no way excusing the evil behavior of Amalek, this talmudic passage teaches the constant need for sensitivity and introspection rather than creating a culture of victimhood or a position where we feel no moral responsibilities when confronting evil.

Ki Tavo

THE COVENANT AT MOUNT GERIZIM AND EBAL

*D*euteronomy, chapters 11 and 27 command the Israelites to make a covenant in the area of Shechem when they enter the Land. Tribal delegates would ascend Mount Gerizim and Mount Ebal, and proclaim blessings for fulfilling God's covenant in the Torah and curses for violating the covenant.

In the following generation, Joshua fulfilled this commandment:

At that time Joshua built an altar to the Lord, the God of Israel, on Mount Ebal.... And there, on the stones, he inscribed a copy of the Teaching that Moses had written for the Israelites. All Israel—stranger and citizen alike

. . . stood on either side of the Ark. . . . Half of them faced Mount Gerizim and half of them faced Mount Ebal. . . . There was not a word of all that Moses had commanded that Joshua failed to read in the presence of the entire assembly of Israel, including the women and children and the strangers who accompanied them. (Joshua 8:30–35)

While emulating the Sinaitic Revelation, it was the people who engraved the laws onto stones and who proclaimed the Torah's covenant from mountaintops, rather than God. The people accepted a preexisting Torah but were far more actively involved than the previous generation, who had received the Torah directly from God.

It is difficult to ascertain when this covenant occurred. Some commentators (e.g., Abarbanel, Malbim, Yehudah Kiel) maintain that that the narratives are in chronological sequence. Joshua conducted this ceremony after the conquest of Jericho and Ai in Joshua, chapters 6–8.

Some commentators, however, observe that Deuteronomy 27:2 commands that the ceremony be performed *ba-yom asher ta'avru et ha-Yarden,* literally, "on the *day* you cross the Jordan." These commentators assert that this ceremony was performed on the actual day that the people crossed the Jordan, following Joshua, in chapters 3–4 (*Tosefta Sotah* 8; *Sotah* 36a, Rashi, Kara, and Radak).

Alternatively, Rabbi Yishmael (J.T. *Sotah* 7:3, 21c) suggests that Joshua brought the nation to Gerizim and Ebal after the conquest and distribution of the land were completed.

Those who do not believe that the ceremony is in its proper chronological location may ask: Why did the narrator place the event here? First, observance of the Torah must be at the forefront of the conquest. This dramatic affirmation of Israel's faithfulness to the Torah fittingly was placed after the first loss and reprieve as a result of Achan's sin, driving home the point that Israel's success was dependent on its following God's commandments.

In his *Berit Olam* commentary (2000, pp. 32–33), L. Daniel Hawk derives further meaning from the flow of chapters 6–8. Rahab's joining the Israelites in chapter 6, followed by Achan's being treated as a Canaanite in chapter 7, accentuates that the battle was not an ethnic cleansing. Religious and ethical choices were the determining factors for inclusion in or exclusion from the nation. Significantly, both Israelites and non-Israelites who accepted the covenant were present at this ceremony at Gerizim and Ebal, and the brief narrative twice notes the outsiders' inclusion (8:33, 35).

Thus, by (possibly) deviating from the chronological sequence, the prophetic author of the Book of Joshua uses the covenant at Gerizim and Ebal to teach lessons central to its religious and educational purposes.

Hayyim Angel, "'There Is No Chronological Order in the Torah': An Axiom for Understanding the Book of Joshua," *Jewish Bible Quarterly* 36:1 (2008), pp. 3–11; reprinted in Angel, *Revealed Texts, Hidden Meanings: Finding the Religious Significance in Tanakh* (Jersey City, NJ: Ktav-Sephardic Publication Foundation, 2009), pp. 85–95.

FREE WILL AND DIVINE PLANS

The covenants and exhortations in Deuteronomy, chapters 27–30 base their central message on free will. Israel may do good or evil, and should choose the good. If they remain faithful to God's covenant, they will be blessed in their land. If they sin and suffer the consequences of that sin, they should choose to repent—and then God will restore the relationship.

In contrast, Deuteronomy, chapters 31–32 are fatalistic. God informs Israel that they *will* sin. God gives Moses the *Ha'azinu* poem as testimony that they will fail and suffer. When Israel suffers the consequences of unfaithfulness in the future, the poem will testify "I told you so" so that Israel cannot blame God for abandoning them.

In these chapters, God redeems Israel to protect His own reputation, rather than because Israel chooses to repent: "I might have reduced them to naught, made their memory cease among men, but for fear of the taunts of the foe, their enemies who might misjudge and say, 'Our own hand has prevailed; none of this was wrought by the Lord!'" (32:26–27).

Different prophets focus on aspects of this dichotomy. Most prophets tend toward a free choice-repentance model for redemption. Others—notably Ezekiel—envision God's restoration of Israel as largely unconditional on Israel's repentance. Rather, God wants to avoid the desecration of His name and therefore redeems Israel.

As a result of the diversity of perspectives within prophetic sources, the Sages of the Talmud debate whether the final redemption is contingent on repentance or not (*Sanhedrin* 97b). They adduce verses from prophetic literature without reaching a resolution since the prophets adopt different approaches to this complex issue.

Although we cannot resolve the messianic debate with prooftexts, the prophets certainly pushed toward an active approach to repentance and improving the world. Rabbi Haim David Halevy wrote that unfortunately, many Jews gradually adopted the idea of a supernatural redemption since they had suffered so much during their exile and felt powerless.

As Jews began to build the State of Israel, most religious Jews rejected the very possibility of a natural redemption through human efforts. Yes, some religious Jews were involved, but the majority of modern Zionists were not religiously observant. In retrospect, it had become evident that the process of establishing and defending the State had been miraculous. God's plan of redemption was achieved, but most of the religious community failed to respond. Unwittingly, the secularists became God's primary agents of redemption (*Asei Lekha Rav* 1:3).

Rabbi Halevy expressed disappointment that many contemporary Jews still had not recognized the religious potential of today, mistakenly waiting passively for supernatural miracles (*Asei Lekha Rav* 1:4–5). It is up to us to take an active role in builidng a better society and nation.

Hayyim Angel, "*At'halta deGe'ulah*: The State of Israel as Prelude to the Messianic Era," in Marc D. Angel and Hayyim Angel, *Rabbi Haim David Halevi: Gentle Scholar, Courageous Thinker* (Jerusalem: Urim, 2006), pp. 218–236; abridged in *Conversations* 10 (Spring 2011), pp. 9–20.

Nitzavim

WESTERN REJECTION OF
THE CONCEPT OF SIN

*D*euteronomy, chapter 30 contains one of the greatest exposi-tions on repentance in the Torah. Dr. Meir Seidler of Bar-Ilan University addresses a modern phenomenon that threatens the Torah's framework. Contemporary Western society does not acknowl-edge "sins," only "crimes."

According to this outlook, human beings have rights, including the right to life, body, and property. In addition, obligations do not have an independent existence; they stem from human rights. The right to one's life and body implies the obligation not to injure others. The right to prop-erty implies the obligation not to steal. When we speak of crime, we mean the infringement of a person's rights.

In contrast, sin can be defined in light of an additional normative dimension. Judaism does not perceive every obligation as stemming from the rights of one's fellow human being. Transgressions concerning rela-tions with others not only violate the rights of another person but also vio-late the divine command.

"Whoever sheds the blood of man, by man shall his blood be shed, for in His image did God make man" (Genesis 9:6). God's prohibition of mur-der captures the difference between the Western concept of human rights and the Jewish concept. Both approaches give supreme value to human life, but the reasons are different. According to the Torah, the prohibition against shedding blood does not stem simply from a person's right to life, but because that person was created in God's image.

Duties that do not stem from the rights of one's fellow but from an obli-gation to the image of God in us give human beings an additional moral quality. For people who seek only to realize rights, morality is likely to degenerate to the purely functional, intended solely to mediate and maneu-ver between the rights of individuals, without reflecting any loftier ideal.

In *The Death of Satan* (1995), Professor Andrew Delbanco of Columbia University traces the gradual elimination of the concept of sin from American literature, and discusses some of its moral implications. The Western world has no vocabulary for dealing with evil, and often refuses even to call it evil. One historian refers to Hitler and Stalin as having mental disorders. Many call terrorists madmen, rather than evil people. The idea that there is no sin also makes it easy to shift responsibility away from even the greatest of criminals.

We need a way of keeping the concept of sin alive while also not slipping into a black-and-white morality. Our challenge is to translate our ancient terminology of sin into something that can meaningfully transform our lives and society.

Meir Seidler, "Forgive Us: The Difference Between Sins and Crimes," Bar-Ilan University, Yom Kippur 2001, athttp://www.biu.ac.il/JH/Parasha/eng/yomk/suc.html.

HEART CIRCUMCISIONS AND TRANSPLANTS

*D*euteronomy 30:1–5 envisions that after the curses enumerated in chapters 28–29 befall the people, the people will return to God. God will assist Israel: "Then the Lord your God will open up your heart and the hearts of your offspring to love the Lord your God with all your heart and soul, in order that you may live" (Deuteronomy 30:6). Literally, the verse says that God will "circumcise" Israel's heart. Israel's sin is a layer of spiritual blockage around an otherwise pure heart. By removing that blockage, Israel's heart will be restored to its pristine state.

Following this lead, Jeremiah employs the same imagery: "Open your hearts to the Lord (literally, circumcise your hearts), remove the thickening about your hearts—O men of Judah and inhabitants of Jerusalem…" (Jeremiah 4:4).

In a related prophecy, Jeremiah envisions God's looking back to the good old days at the time of the exodus: "Thus said the Lord: I accounted to your favor the devotion of your youth, your love as a bride—how you followed Me in the wilderness, in a land not sown. Israel was holy to the Lord, the first fruits of His harvest" (Jeremiah 2:2–3). Israel's history began perfectly, but then Israel betrayed her covenant with God. Jeremiah invokes the heart circumcision terminology of the Torah in order to encourage Israel to repent in order to restore the original relationship.

In contrast, Jeremiah's contemporary, Ezekiel, depicts Israel as being rotten to the core throughout its history, and therefore changes the imagery: "I will give them one heart and put a new spirit in them; I will remove the heart of stone from their bodies and give them a heart of flesh" (Ezekiel 11:19). Instead of heart circumcision, Ezekiel envisions a heart transplant.

These imageries present alternative models of repentance. Sometimes, we have a great relationship with God and then fail through sin. The road to repentance involves eliminating the barriers that were created. On other occasions, the road to God was opaque from the outset. In such circumstances, one must take the more radical approach of a transplant and then build going forward.

After King David's catastrophic sin with Uriah and Bathsheba, he felt so alienated from God that it was inadequate to "circumcise" his heart. He needed to rebuild his spiritual connection to God at the most fundamental level: "Fashion a pure heart for me, O God; create in me a steadfast spirit. Do not cast me out of Your presence, or take Your holy spirit away from me" (Psalm 51:12–13).

These imageries of repentance are relevant for every individual, regardless of one's personal spiritual history. God is open to a rewarding and enduring relationship to anyone who pursues it either by removing barriers to religious growth—or by undergoing a religious transformation.

Vayelekh

THE MOSES-JOSHUA SUCCESSION

ollowing the death of Moses, his disciple Joshua led the nation into the Promised Land, attaining religious heights for the nation virtually unparalleled through the rest of biblical history. What were the roots of this success story?

The Torah and Book of Joshua highlight several elements: (1) Joshua had God's help and support, and the religious mission of Joshua's leadership energized him. (2) Joshua had the unqualified support of his nation. (3) The people were actively involved, helping to develop the community together with Joshua. (4) Joshua's foremost charge was to study Torah and teach it. Without this constant self-growth and sharing with others, Jewish communal leadership will fail.

One other aspect played a prominent role: Moses' unwavering love and support for Joshua:

> And the Lord answered Moses, "Single out Joshua son of Nun, an inspired man, and lay your hand upon him". . . Moses did as the Lord commanded him . . . He laid his hands upon him and commissioned him—as the Lord had spoken through Moses. (Numbers 27:18–23)

The Sages of the Talmud (*Sanhedrin* 105b) observe that God commanded Moses to lay his "hand" on Joshua, but Moses in fact laid both of his "hands" on his disciple, indicating full generosity and a complete heart. Generosity in teaching means transmitting everything one knows, while simultaneously fostering critical and independent thinking rather than creating watered-down clones one oneself.

Rabbi Shlomo Riskin recalls Rabbi Joseph Soloveitchik's address at his *semikhah* convocation at Yeshiva University. The concept of *semikhah* (literally, the teacher's leaning of his hands on a student to invest him with authority, as Moses did to Joshua) is that the older rabbi places his hands on the younger one as a means of demonstrating how the student depends on his teacher. However, Rabbi Soloveitchik understood this differently as well. When an older man leans on a younger one, it is for support. "We, the older generation must lean upon you, the younger generation, for our future, for our eternity. If you don't carry on our teachings, we are consigned to oblivion. If you convey our teachings, we live through you, into succeeding generations, as 'part of eternal Torah. . . .'" (*Memories of a Giant*, 2003, p. 270).

Thus, the older generation teaches and supports the younger generation. Simultaneously, the younger generation bears the weight of tradition, and is responsible to carry on the legacy of its forebears. In this manner, it can achieve great success.

—

Ha'azinu

WHAT WERE MOSES' LAST WORDS TO THE PEOPLE?

*T*he final four chapters of Deuteronomy contain Moses' final words to his people. Chapters 31–32 present *Ha'azinu*, the bleak prediction of Israel's upcoming failures followed by a restoration. When Israel sins and suffers in the future, God will have testimony that they were properly warned beforehand. Once Israel recognizes her responsibility for sin and exile, they can return to God rather than wrongly concluding that God had abandoned them.

Chapter 33 contains Moses' loving blessing of his people. He blesses each tribe, and then concludes with a sweeping blessing for all Israel: "Who is like you, a people delivered by the Lord, your protecting Shield, your Sword triumphant! Your enemies shall come cringing before you, and you shall tread on their backs" (Deuteronomy 33:29). Chapter 34 then recounts that Moses ascends Mount Nebo, sees the Land of Israel, and then dies.

Let us return to the first verse in this section, "Moses went and spoke these things to all Israel" (Deuteronomy 31:1). Where did he go? Following midrashic precedents, Rashi explains that Moses walked to each tribe to wish farewell to his people. Ibn Ezra adds a significant dimension to this idea: As he walked from tribe to tribe, Moses blessed each one. This is the blessing recorded in chapter 33.

If Moses blessed Israel in chapter 31, then his final words to the people actually were the bleak predictions in the *Ha'azinu* poem. From a narrative perspective, Ibn Ezra's suggestion appears likely. After the *Ha'azinu* poem, God commands Moses to ascend the mountain, see the land, and die (32:48–52). This narrative is followed by Moses' doing so in chapter 34. The blessings in chapter 33 appear to have been inserted in the middle of the narrative flow about Moses' death.

If Ibn Ezra is correct, then the Torah deliberately placed Moses' blessing after *Ha'azinu* to teach a lesson. The Torah wanted the last words of Moses—his climactic message—to end on a note of love and blessing, rather than on the bleak prediction of *Ha'azinu*.

Although Moses rebuked his people throughout his life and knew that they would lapse into sin after he died, his rebukes emanated from the deepest love of his people. Moses' life work was to bring God and Israel closer together. Rather than using his position of leadership to lord over the people, there is nothing he wanted more than for everyone to have access to God and to experience the blessing of that relationship. As Moses had exhorted his student Joshua many years earlier, "Would that all the Lord's people were prophets, that the Lord put His spirit upon them!" (Numbers 11:29).

Ve-Zot Ha-Berakhah

REUBEN

*D*uring Moses' final blessing to the tribes, he opens with a surprising wish for the tribe of Reuben: "May Reuben live and not die, though few be his numbers" (Deuteronomy 33:6). Was there nothing better to which they might aspire? Was there any indication that they were an endangered tribe facing imminent extinction?

From the desert census statistics, there is no obvious answer these questions. In the 40th year, the tribe of Reuben numbered 43,730, ranked ninth out of the 12 tribes (Numbers 26:7). They were not the smallest tribe, nor had they declined significantly in the desert. In the first year, they numbered 46,500 (Numbers 1:21). Compare this relatively minor drop with that of the tribe of Simeon, who drastically plummeted from 59,300 to 22,200 during the 40-year trek through the wilderness (Numbers 1:23, 26:14).

It appears that we may approach this problem of Moses' blessing by tracing the history of Reuben and his tribe in Tanakh. Reuben was the firstborn of a less-beloved mother, Leah. His very name reflected his mother's humiliation and yearning for Jacob's love: "Leah conceived and bore a son, and named him Reuben; for she declared, 'It means: "The Lord has seen my affliction"; it also means: 'Now my husband will love me'" (Genesis 29:32).

One day, the young Reuben brought his mother mandrakes. Rachel immediately coveted the flowers, which may be interpreted as a sign of Reuben's love of his mother. Leah exchanged them with Rachel for a night with Jacob, so that each sister could temporarily enjoy what she lacked. Leah spent the night with Jacob, and Rachel vicariously experienced the affection of a child by holding her sister's gift from Reuben (Genesis 30:14–16). At that stage, Reuben's gesture of love for his mother triggered the deep anguish Leah and Rachel felt constantly.

As he grew older, Reuben's sensitivity regarding his mother's rejection continued to fester. Things came to a head when Reuben performed a rashly inappropriate act with Bilhah (Genesis 35:22). One view in the Talmud (*Shabbat* 55b) explains that after Rachel's death, Jacob set up his primary tent with Rachel's maid, Bilhah, and Reuben was outraged. It was enough that his mother had to play second fiddle to Rachel; but now Leah would lose precedence to Rachel's *maid*! Jacob did not confront Reuben immediately, waiting instead until his deathbed to vent his displeasure with his son's behavior.

Leah's firstborn Reuben was the direct loser in Jacob's conspicuous favoritism toward Joseph, Rachel's firstborn. However, despite the slight to Reuben (and to his mother), it was Reuben who heroically stepped forward to oppose his brothers' attempt to murder Joseph: "And Reuben went on, 'Shed no blood! Cast him into that pit out in the wilderness, but do not touch him yourselves'—intending to save him from them and restore him to his father" (Genesis 37:22).

Several midrashim portray Reuben engrossed in deep repentance after his act with Bilhah (see, for example, *Genesis Rabbah* 85:1). Reuben overcame his own self-interests as firstborn, and courageously stood up against his brothers on behalf of one who was his direct competitor.

With Joseph gone, Reuben believed that he would reassume the mantle of the family leadership. When Joseph, the Egyptian prime minister, held Simeon hostage while waiting for the brothers to return with Benjamin, the brothers met with the expected resistance from their father. Reuben immediately offered Jacob his own two sons as guarantee that Benjamin would return safely (Genesis 42:37). Jacob rejected this offer, because, as Rashi explains, Reuben's sons were also Jacob's grandsons. Reuben's guarantee sounded heroic, but was actually meaningless. In contrast, Judah offered himself as guarantor of Benjamin's safety (Genesis 43:8–9). At this decisive moment, Judah became the leader of his brothers, courageously willing to challenge even the prime minister of Egypt when Benjamin was threatened.

On his deathbed, Jacob officially pronounced Reuben's banishment from family leadership: "Reuben, you are my first-born, my might and first fruit of my vigor, exceeding in rank and exceeding in honor. Unstable as water, you shall excel no longer; for when you mounted your father's bed, you brought disgrace—my couch he mounted!" (Genesis 49:3–4). Jacob told his eldest son that he had lost his prominence because of the Bilhah episode. In the remainder of his blessings to his sons, Jacob prophetically recognized Judah as the kingly tribe, and Joseph received the balance of the family leadership.

The tribe of Reuben did not quickly forget this painful rejection. During Korah's rebellion against Moses, much of the rebel leadership came from the tribe of Reuben. Ibn Ezra explains that at the root of their rebellion lay the desire to regain their firstborn leadership status. Of course, that rebellion failed, and Reuben remained a peripheral tribe.

This outsider self-perception came to a head a generation later as the nation prepared to enter the Promised Land. The tribal leaders of Reuben and Gad requested permission to live outside of Israel, on the east bank of the Jordan River. Moses was furious, viewing this appeal as a rebellion tantamount to that of the spies: "Moses replied to the Gadites and the Reubenites, 'Are your brothers to go to war while you stay here? Why will you turn the minds of the Israelites from crossing into the land that the Lord has given them?'" (Numbers 32:6–7). Although commentators debate whether or not Moses properly understood the request, one can see the deep suspicion Moses and the nation harbored toward Reuben (and its affiliate tribe Gad—Gad was the firstborn of Zilpah, Leah's maidservant).

This suspicion carried over into Joshua's time. After Reuben and Gad had sent fighters as promised to help in the conquest of Canaan, they built an altar near the Jordan River. The other tribes viewed this gesture as a means of breaking away from the central religious authority of the Tabernacle. Only by the righteous declaration of Reuben and Gad was civil war avoided. They claimed that their purpose in building the altar was to preserve national unity, not to cause division (Joshua, chapter 22).

Despite these assurances, however, the tribes of Reuben and Gad in fact used the natural boundary of the Jordan River to separate themselves from the nation. After Deborah's victory against the Canaanites a few generations later, she composed a song praising those tribes who assisted in the national effort, and criticized those who failed to support it. Her scathing words against Reuben are immortalized: "Among the clans of Reuben were great decisions of heart. Why then did you stay among the sheepfolds and listen as they pipe for the flocks? Among the clans of Reuben were great searchings of heart!" (Judges 5:15–16).

One can surmise that the tribal leaders of Reuben sent letters of solidarity to Deborah, expressing "heartfelt support" of her efforts. They did not send troops, remaining safely across the Jordan. Deborah saw the realization of the fears of Moses and Joshua. The Tribe of Reuben's choice of land apart from the other tribes led them to prefer a quiet life with their sheep, rather than casting their lot with their compatriots west of the Jordan River.

Remarkably, this is the last that we hear specifically about the Tribe of Reuben until the Assyrians exiled the tribe, together with the rest of the Northern Kingdom centuries after Deborah's rule. Tanakh does not mention any judges or other national leaders arising from the tribe, and very little of biblical consequence happened in its territory.

Deborah lived only four or five generations after Moses' blessing, and already then, Reuben was fading off of the Jewish map. We now may begin to understand Moses' unusual blessing to the tribe of Reuben at the end of his own life. He realized that although they had expressed a reasonable excuse for their choice to live across the Jordan (good pastureland), Reuben's long history of rejection might lead them to break away from the nation.

Reuben's life was characterized by feeling second-best, always the "could have been" tribe of Israel. Frustrated and impetuous, Reuben tried to reclaim the post he believed was his both in Joseph's absence and later on a tribal level during the Korah rebellion. When these efforts failed, the tribe distanced itself from its people, even living outside the intended Promised Land. Only a few short generations later, it all but faded from the national history. Moses, in his prophetic greatness, recognized this concern, and prayed that Reuben live on, rather than dying out from the nation's destiny.

In Ezekiel's vision of the new land distribution during messianic times (Ezekiel 48), Reuben will be included within the boundaries of the Promised Land, no longer separated and alienated from the rest of the people.

Hayyim Angel, "May Reuben Live!" *AMIT Magazine*, Fall 2003, pp. 32–34.

SIMEON AND LEVI

*W*hen Shechem raped Leah's daughter Dinah, Leah's sons Simeon and Levi led a massacre against the people of Shechem (Genesis, chapter 34). Although Jacob rebuked them lightly at the time, this event permanently altered their relationship. When the brothers came to Egypt during the famine, Joseph imprisoned Simeon as collateral for the brothers to return to fetch Benjamin (Genesis 42:18–24). Jacob refused to send Rachel's remaining son until the family became desperate for food.

Jacob probably felt more intense love for Benjamin since he was Rachel's only remaining son (as far as he knew). Ramban suggests further that after Shechem, Jacob lost his love of Simeon and therefore was unwilling to sacrifice to rescue him. Another possible sign of this alienation is manifest in Jacob's referring to Simeon as "your other brother" (43:14), rather than using his name (Yehudah Kiel).

At the end of his life, Jacob condemned Simeon and Levi for their massacre at Shechem: "Simeon and Levi are a pair; their weapons are tools of lawlessness. Let not my person be included in their council, let not my being be counted in their assembly. For when angry they slay men, and when pleased they maim oxen. Cursed be their anger so fierce, and their wrath so relentless. I will divide them in Jacob, scatter them in Israel" (49:5–7). In fact, neither tribe received a block of land as inheritance.

Although Jacob's blessings appear prophetic and therefore ostensibly irreversible, these tribes channeled their traits differently in Moses' time. During the Golden Calf episode, the Tribe of Levi remained faithful to God and eliminated the main perpetrators (Exodus 32:26). Their religious commitment during that national crisis led to their elevation as the spiritual caste for Temple service (Deuteronomy 10:8–9).

At the parallel sin of Baal Peor (Numbers, chapter 25), the tribal leader of Simeon, Zimri, took a Midianite princess and publicly displayed disdain for God and Moses. Phinehas, from the Tribe of Levi, ended the plague by killing Zimri.

Both tribes were still characterized by the violence we saw in their ancestors in Genesis. However, Simeon channeled these energies in a negative direction, whereas Levi channeled them for holy purposes. Levi still would be scattered throughout Israel, but so that they could serve as teachers.

Moses' blessing to Levi (Deuteronomy 33:8–11) is the second longest blessing of the tribes. In contrast, Moses blessed all the tribes at the end of his life except for Simeon! They had failed to improve, and would fade away as a tribe without any distinctive character. In Judges, chapter 1, they merged into Judah and essentially vanished as an independent tribe.

Thus Jacob's "blessing" came true, that these two tribes would not receive independent inheritance. However, Levi became the spiritual caste in Israel, whereas Simeon sunk into oblivion. The saga of these two tribes demonstrates channeling one's traits to serve God could help avert Jacob's negative prophetic "decree."

MOSES' "MIGHTY DEEDS"

The last verses in the Torah refer to Moses' unparalleled prophecy and mighty deeds he performed in the sight of all the people (Deuteronomy 34:10–12). Which "mighty deeds"? Strikingly, Rashi closes his commentary on the Torah by quoting a midrash: "All the mighty deeds . . . that he smashed the tablets before their eyes . . . and God agreed with him. . . ."

What does Rashi want to teach by focusing on Moses' shattering the tablets? According to Professor Yeshayahu Leibowitz, Moses' greatest act was not the exodus or even teaching Torah. His ultimate "mighty deed" was to protect the tablets from desecration when the people worshipped an idol.

When human interests are considered holy, they must be smashed. Professor Leibowitz views Rashi's comment as corroborating everything that Professor Leibowitz himself stood for. Leibowitz was famed for his forceful attacks on those elements in society that he deemed idolatrous, and considered these attacks the most important thing a leader can do.

A different approach is offered by Rabbi Yosef Blau of Yeshiva University. In that same chapter (Deuteronomy 34:5), Moses is called God's servant. This term suggests a loyal follower who obeys his master.

When Moses shattered the tablets, he acted independently because of the urgency of the situation. Additionally, Moses' hallmark characteristic was humility. When the spiritual state of his people was threatened, however, Moses acted decisively. This act was Moses' greatest achievement, according to Rashi.

That being said, Rashi is saying something different from either view. Following in classical midrashic analysis, Rashi is explaining poetically redundant clauses as each referring to something specific. He plays off of related phraseology found elsewhere in the Torah. The verse reads, "And for all the great might and awesome power that Moses displayed before all Israel."

Rashi interprets the elements in this verse as referring to three aspects of Moses' leadership. "And for all the great might": he received the Torah and tablets in his hands (referring to Moses' mighty arms, *yad ha-hazakah*). "And awesome power": the miracles and wonders in the great and fearful desert (*mora ha-gadol*, playing off of *ba-midbar ha-gadol ve-ha-nora* in Deuteronomy 8:15). "Before all Israel" (*le-enei kol Yisrael*): that he shattered the tablets in their presence (Deuteronomy 9:17, *le-enehem*).

Rashi is not teaching that the most impressive act of Moses was in shattering the tablets. Rashi is presenting a multifaceted picture of Moses' leadership. He exhibited incredible physical energy in leading the people and taught them Torah. He was God's servant and agent guiding the community from Egyptian slavery to the doorstep of the Promised Land. He was a strong leader who took initiative.

Rabbi Yosef Blau, "The Greatness of Moses," in *Mitokh Ha-Ohel: Essays on the Weekly Parashah from the Rabbis and Professors of Yeshiva University*, ed. Daniel Z. Feldman & Stuart W. Halpern (New York: Yeshiva University Press, 2010), pp. 483–485.

Yeshayahu Leibowitz, *Accepting the Yoke of Heaven: Commentary on the Weekly Torah Portion*, trans. Shmuel Himelstein (Jerusalem: Urim, 2006), pp. 202–203.

WHAT HAPPENED TO THE ARK OF THE COVENANT?

*A*t the heart of the Tabernacle and later the Temple lay the Ark. It contained the Ten Commandments, symbolizing the mutual covenant between God and Israel. After the destruction of the First Temple (586 BCE), we do not hear of it again. The Talmud (*Yoma* 21b) explains that the Ark was missing from the Second Temple. Where did it go?

One frightening possibility is that it was destroyed along with the First Temple. However, ancient rabbinic traditions assume that it still exists somewhere. One talmudic Sage (*Yoma* 52b) suggests that the righteous King Josiah (640–609 BCE) anticipated the destruction. Therefore he removed the Ark from the Temple and buried it somewhere in the Temple Mount. Rambam (*Hil. Bet ha-Behirah* 4:1) adopts this viewpoint as well.

Other Sages propose alternatives (*Yoma* 53b–54a). Perhaps it was captured by the Babylonians and brought to Babylonia. Perhaps it still is located there, or perhaps it was subsequently captured and could have been taken anywhere. Alternatively, perhaps it was buried in other areas in Jerusalem.

One of the most fascinating of the ancient traditions is found in the apocryphal Book of Maccabees:

> In our documents we find that it was Jeremiah the prophet...on receiving a divine revelation, ordered that the tabernacle and the ark should go with him. [One of these documents said] . . . that Jeremiah went out to the mountain which Moses ascended to see the heritage promised by God. There, Jeremiah found a save chamber and brought into it the tabernacle and the ark and the incense altar and blocked up the entrance. Some of those who had come along went back to mark the path, but they could not find it. When Jeremiah found out, he rebuked them, saying, "The place will remain unknown until God gathers His people together in the Age of Mercy. At that time the Lord will bring these things to light again, and the glory of the Lord and the cloud will be seen, as they were over Moses and as Solomon, too, requested, in order that the Place should be greatly sanctified." (II Macc. 2:1–8)

According to this tradition, God revealed the burial place of Moses to Jeremiah, the prophet at the time of the destruction of the First Temple. Jeremiah had the Ark moved to Moses' grave, a fitting resting place for the most sacred object in world history. When the Third Temple is built, we hopefully will regain the Ark and restore it to its rightful location in the Holy of Holies.

SELECTED BIBLIOGRAPHY:
TORAH

I have listed the main traditional commentaries consulted, followed by a selection of contemporary books and articles that I found particularly helpful.

CLASSICAL COMMENTARIES

Rabbi Saadiah Gaon	Babylonia	882–942
Rashi	Northern France	1040–1105
Rabbi Shemuel ben Meir (Rashbam)	Northern France	1080s–1174
Rabbi Abraham ibn Ezra	Spain, Italy	1089–1164
Rabbi Joseph Bekhor Shor	Northern France	1130–1200
Rabbi Moshe ben Maimon (Rambam)	Spain, Egypt	1138–1204
Rabbi David Kimhi (Radak)	Provence	1160–c.1235
Rabbi Moshe ben Nahman (Ramban)	Spain	1194–1270
Rabbi Hizkiyah ben Manoah (Hizkuni)	Northern France	13th century
Rabbenu Bahya ben Asher	Spain	d. 1340
Rabbi Joseph ibn Caspi	Provence, Spain	1279–1340
Rabbi Levi ben Gershon (Ralbag)	Provence	1288–1344
Rabbi Yitzhak Arama	Spain	1420–1494
Rabbi Isaac Abarbanel	Spain, Italy	1437–1508
Rabbi Ovadiah Sforno	Italy	1470–1550
Rabbi Hayyim Ben-Attar (Or HaHayyim)	Morocco	1696–1743
Rabbi Samuel David Luzzatto (Shadal)	Italy	1800–1865
Rabbi Samson Raphael Hirsch	Germany	1808–1888
Rabbi Meir Leibush b.Yehiel Michel (Malbim)	Romania, Germany	1809–1879
Rabbi Naftali Tzvi Yehudah Berlin (Netziv)	Lithuania	1817–1893
Rabbi David Zvi Hoffmann	Germany	1843–1921

BOOKS

Rabbi Marc D. Angel, *Angel for Shabbat: Thoughts on the Weekly Torah Portion* vol. 1 (New York: Institute for Jewish Ideas and Ideals, 2010).

Rabbi Marc D. Angel, *Angel for Shabbat: Thoughts on the Weekly Torah Portion* vol. 2 (New York: Institute for Jewish Ideas and Ideals, 2013).

Rabbi David Bigman, *The Fire and the Cloud* (Jerusalem: Gefen, 2011).

Rabbi Yoel Bin-Nun, *Pirkei ha-Avot: Iyyunim be-Parshiyot ha-Avot be-Sefer Bereshit* (Hebrew) (Alon Shevut: Tevunot, 2003).

Rabbi Mordechai Breuer, *Pirkei Bereshit* (Hebrew) (Alon Shevut: Tevunot, 1999).

Rabbi Mordechai Breuer, *Pirkei Mikraot* (Alon Shevut: Tevunot, 2009).

Umberto Cassuto, *Commentary on the Book of Genesis* (Hebrew) (Jerusalem: Magnes Press, 1987).

Umberto Cassuto, *Commentary on the Book of Exodus* (Hebrew) (Jerusalem: Magnes Press, 1988).

Richard Elliott Friedman, *Commentary on the Torah* (San Francisco: Harper, 2003).

Rabbi Shmuel Goldin, *Unlocking the Torah Text: An In-Depth Journey into the Weekly Parsha: Genesis, Exodus, Leviticus, and Numbers* (Jerusalem: Gefen Publishing House, 2007).

Leon Kass, *The Beginning of Wisdom: Reading Genesis* (New York: Free Press, 2003).

Nehama Leibowitz, *Studies in the Torah* (seven volumes), translated and adapted by Aryeh Newman (Jerusalem: Eliner Library).

Jacob Milgrom, *Anchor Bible: Leviticus* (New York: Doubleday, 1991).

Rabbi Yehudah Nachshoni, *Studies in the Weekly Parashah* (five volumes), trans. Shmuel Himelstein (Brooklyn: Mesorah Publications, 1988).

Rabbi Chaim Navon, *Genesis and Jewish Thought*, translated by David Strauss (Jersey City, NJ: Ktav in association with Yeshivat Har Etzion, 2008).

William Propp, *Anchor Bible: Exodus* (New York, Doubleday, 1999).

Rabbi Shlomo Riskin, *Torah Lights: Genesis, Exodus, Leviticus, and Numbers* (Jerusalem: Urim, 2005).

Rabbi Jonathan Sacks, *Covenant & Conversation: A Weekly Reading of the Jewish Bible: Genesis and Exodus* (New Milford, CT: Maggid Books, 2009).

Rabbi Elhanan Samet, *Iyyunim be-Parashot ha-Shavua* (first series) (Hebrew) ed. Ayal Fishler (Ma'aleh Adumim: Ma'aliyot Press, 2002).

Rabbi Elhanan Samet, *Iyyunim be-Parashot ha-Shavua* (second series) (Hebrew) ed. Ayal Fishler (Ma'aleh Adumim: Ma'aliyot Press, 2004).

Rabbi Elhanan Samet, *Iyyunim be-Parashot ha-Shavua* (third series) (Hebrew) ed. Ayal Fishler (Tel Aviv: Yediot Aharonot, 2012).

Nahum Sarna, *Understanding Genesis: The Heritage of Biblical Israel* (New York: Schocken Books, 1966).

Nahum Sarna, *Exploring Exodus* (New York: Schocken Books, 1986–1996).

Rabbi Moshe Shamah, *Recalling the Covenant: A Contemporary Commentary on the Five Books of the Torah* (Jersey City, NJ: Ktav, 2011).

Da'at Mikra on the Torah (Jerusalem: Mossad HaRav Kook).

The JPS Torah Commentary on the Torah (Philadelphia: Jewish Publication Society).

Olam HaTanakh on the Torah (Tel Aviv: Dodson-Iti).

ARTICLES

Hayyim Angel, "*Elleh Toledot*: A Study of the Genealogies in the Book of Genesis," in *Haham Gaon Memorial Volume*, ed. Marc D. Angel (Brooklyn: Sefer Hermon Press, 1997), pp. 163–182; reprinted in Angel, *Through an Opaque Lens* (New York: Sephardic Publication Foundation, 2006), pp. 111–126.

Hayyim Angel, "The Tower of Babel: A Case Study in Combining Traditional and Academic Bible Methodologies," in *Where the Yeshiva Meets the University: Traditional and Academic Approaches to Tanakh Study*, ed. Hayyim Angel, *Conversations* 15 (Winter 2013), pp. 135–143.

Hayyim Angel, "'The Chosen People': An Ethical Challenge," *Conversations* 8 (Fall 2010), pp. 52–60; reprinted in Angel, *Creating Space Between Peshat and Derash: A Collection of Studies on Tanakh* (Jersey City, NJ: Ktav-Sephardic Publication Foundation, 2011), pp. 25–34.

Hayyim Angel, "Learning Faith from the Text, or Text from Faith: The Challenges of Teaching (and Learning) the Avraham Narratives and Commentary," in *Wisdom from All My Teachers: Challenges and Initiatives in Contemporary Torah Education*, ed. Jeffrey Saks & Susan Handelman (Jerusalem: Urim Publications, 2003, ATID), pp. 192–212; reprinted in Angel, *Through an Opaque Lens* (New York: Sephardic Publication Foundation, 2006), pp. 127–154.

Hayyim Angel, "Sarah's Treatment of Hagar (Genesis 16): Morals, Messages, and Mesopotamia," *Jewish Bible Quarterly* 41:4 (2013), pp. 211–218.

Hayyim Angel, "When Other Languages May Help Us Understand," *Enayim LeTorah*, Lekh Lekha 5767, 2006.

Hayyim Angel, "Joseph's Bones: *Peshat, Derash*, and in Between," *Intersession Reader 2013* (New York: Tebah, 2013), pp. 83–94.

Hayyim Angel, "Chur and Pharaoh's Daughter: Midrashic Readings of Silent Heroes," in *Mitokh Ha-Ohel: Essays on the Weekly Parashah from the Rabbis and Professors of Yeshiva University*, ed. Daniel Z. Feldman & Stuart W. Halpern (New York: Yeshiva University Press, 2010), pp. 205–213; reprinted in Angel, *Creating Space Between Peshat and Derash: A Collection of Studies on Tanakh* (Jersey City, NJ: Ktav-Sephardic Publication Foundation, 2011), pp. 35–43.

Hayyim Angel, Review Essay: "A Modern *Midrash Moshe*: Methodological Considerations." Review of *Tsir va-Tson*, by Rabbi Mosheh Lichtenstein, *Tradition* 41:4 (Winter 2008), pp. 73–86; reprinted in Angel, *Revealed Texts, Hidden Meanings: Finding the Religious Significance in Tanakh* (Jersey City, NJ: Ktav-Sephardic Publication Foundation, 2009), pp. 48–64.

Hayyim Angel, "An Amazing Comment of Rabbi Yosef Bekhor Shor," *Enayim LeTorah*, Beshallah 5767, 2007.

Hayyim Angel, "The Genesis-Exodus Continuum: What Happens When They Are Viewed as a Larger Unit," *Intersession Reader* (New York: Tebah, 2009), pp. 43–52; reprinted in Angel, *Revealed Texts, Hidden Meanings: Finding the Religious Significance in Tanakh* (Jersey City, NJ: Ktav-Sephardic Publication Foundation, 2009), pp. 65–74.

Hayyim Angel, "Rambam's Continued Impact on Underlying Issues in Tanakh Study," in *The Legacy of Maimonides: Religion, Reason and Community*, ed. Yamin Levy & Shalom Carmy (Brooklyn: Yashar Books, 2006), pp. 148–164; reprinted in Angel, *Through an Opaque Lens* (New York: Sephardic Publication Foundation, 2006), pp. 35–55.

Hayyim Angel, "Zephaniah's Usage of the Genesis Narratives," in Angel, *Revealed Texts, Hidden Meanings: Finding the Religious Significance in Tanakh* (Jersey City, NJ: Ktav-Sephardic Publication Foundation, 2009), pp. 162–170.

Hayyim Angel, "Abarbanel: Commentator and Teacher: Celebrating 500 Years of his Influence on Tanakh Study," *Tradition* 42:3 (Fall 2009), pp. 9–26; reprinted in Angel, *Creating Space Between Peshat and Derash: A Collection of Studies on Tanakh* (Jersey City, NJ: Ktav-Sephardic Publication Foundation, 2011), pp. 1–24.

Hayyim Angel, "When God's Will Can and Cannot Be Altered: The Relationship between the Balaam Narrative and 1 Kings 13," *Jewish Bible Quarterly* 33:1 (2005), pp. 31–39; reprinted in Angel, *Through an Opaque Lens* (New York: Sephardic Publication Foundation, 2006), pp. 215–225.

Hayyim Angel, "Why Did Moses Not Apologize After His Sin at Meribah?" in Angel, *Creating Space Between Peshat and Derash: A Collection of Studies on Tanakh* (Jersey City, NJ: Ktav-Sephardic Publication Foundation, 2011), pp. 45–51.

Hayyim Angel, "Moonlit Leadership: A Midrashic Reading of Joshua's Success," *Jewish Bible Quarterly* 37:3 (2009), pp. 144–152; reprinted in Angel,

Creating Space Between Peshat and Derash: A Collection of Studies on Tanakh (Jersey City, NJ: Ktav-Sephardic Publication Foundation, 2011), pp. 64–73.

Hayyim Angel, "Jeremiah's Confrontation with the Religious Establishment: A Man of Truth in a World of Falsehood," in Angel, *Revealed Texts, Hidden Meanings: Finding the Religious Significance in Tanakh* (Jersey City, NJ: Ktav-Sephardic Publication Foundation, 2009), pp. 127–138.

Hayyim Angel, "'There Is No Chronological Order in the Torah': An Axiom for Understanding the Book of Joshua," *Jewish Bible Quarterly* 36:1 (2008), pp. 3–11; reprinted in Angel, *Revealed Texts, Hidden Meanings: Finding the Religious Significance in Tanakh* (Jersey City, NJ: Ktav-Sephardic Publication Foundation, 2009), pp. 85–95.

Hayyim Angel, "*At'halta deGe'ulah*: The State of Israel as Prelude to the Messianic Era," in Marc D. Angel and Hayyim Angel, *Rabbi Haim David Halevi: Gentle Scholar, Courageous Thinker* (Jerusalem: Urim, 2006), pp. 218–236; abridged in *Conversations* 10 (Spring 2011), pp. 9–20.

Hayyim Angel, "May Reuben Live!" *AMIT Magazine*, Fall 2003, pp. 32–34.

Nathan Aviezer, "The Extreme Longevity of the Early Generations in Genesis," Bar-Ilan University, Noah 5759/1999, at http://www.biu.ac.il/JH/Parasha/eng/noah/avi.html.

Yair Barkai, "The Copper Serpent," Bar-Ilan University, Hukkat 5764/2004, at http://www.biu.ac.il/JH/Parasha/eng/chukath/bar1.html.

David Berger, "Miracles and the Natural Order in Nahmanides," in *Rabbi Moses Nahmanides (Ramban): Explorations in His Religious and Literary Virtuosity*, ed. Isadore Twersky (Cambridge, MA: Harvard University, Center for Jewish Studies, 1983), pp. 107–128.

David Berger, "On the Morality of the Patriarchs in Jewish Polemic and Exegesis," in *Modern Scholarship in the Study of Torah: Contributions and Limitations*, ed. Shalom Carmy (New Jersey: Jason Aronson Inc., 1996), pp. 131–146.

Rabbi Yoel Bin-Nun, "*Ha-Pilug ve-ha-Ahdut: Kefel ha-Ta'ut ve-Halom ha-Gilui—Mippenei Ma Lo Shalah Yosef (Shali'ah) el Aviv?*" (Hebrew), *Megadim* 1 (1986), pp. 20–31.

Rabbi Yoel Bin-Nun. "The Eighth Day and Yom Kippur" (Hebrew), *Megadim* 8 (1989), pp. 9–34.

Rabbi Yosef Blau, "The Greatness of Moses," in *Mitokh Ha-Ohel: Essays on the Weekly Parashah from the Rabbis and Professors of Yeshiva University*, ed. Daniel Z. Feldman & Stuart W. Halpern (New York: Yeshiva University Press, 2010), pp. 483–485.

Rabbi J. David Bleich, *Contemporary Halakhic Problems*, vol. 3 (New York: Ktav, 1977), pp. 237–250.

Barry Eichler, "On Reading Genesis 12:10–20," in *Tehillah Le-Moshe: Biblical and Judaic Studies in Honor of Moshe Greenberg*, ed. Mordechai Cogan, Barry Eichler & Jeffrey Tigay (Eisenbrauns, Indiana: 1997), pp. 23–38.

Barry Eichler, "Study of Bible in Light of Our Knowledge of the Ancient Near East," in *Modern Scholarship in the Study of Torah*, ed. Shalom Carmy (New Jersey: Jason Aronson Inc., 1996), pp. 81–100.

Rabbi Yehoshua Engelman, "Hasidic-Psychological Readings: Revelation and Korah," in *Where the Yeshiva Meets the University: Traditional and Academic Approaches to Tanakh Study*, ed. Hayyim Angel, *Conversations* 15 (Winter 2013), pp. 200–208.

Moshe Greenberg, "Some Postulates of Biblical Criminal Law," and "The Biblical Concept of Asylum," in Greenberg, *Studies in the Bible and Jewish Thought* (Philadelphia: JPS, 1995), pp. 25–50.

Rabbi Yonatan Grossman, "The Priests of Egypt and the Kohanim of Israel," Yeshivat Har Etzion Vayigash 1998, at http://www.vbm-torah.org/parsha.58/11vayig.htm.

Rabbi Yonatan Grossman, "The Two Consecrations of Moshe," Yeshivat Har Etzion Virtual Beit Midrash, Vaera 5759, at www.vbm-torah.org/parsha.59/14vaera.htm.

Moshe Halbertal, *On Sacrifice* (Princeton, NJ: Princeton University Press, 2012).

Rabbi Raymond Harari, "Abraham's Nephew Lot: A Biblical Portrait," *Tradition* 25:1 (Fall 1989), pp. 31–41.

Leah Himmelfarb, "The *Seraph* Serpents," Bar-Ilan University, Hukkat 5760/2000, at http://www.biu.ac.il/JH/Parasha/eng/chukath/him.html.

Greta Hort, "The Plagues of Egypt," *ZAW* 69 (1957), pp. 84–103; 70 (1958), pp. 48–59.

Steven Kepnes, "Holiness: The Unique Form of Jewish Spirituality," *Conversations* 9 (Winter 2011), pp. 30–44.

Rabbi Menachem Leibtag, Tanach Study Center, Kedoshim, at http://www.tanach.org/vayikra/kdosh/kdoshs1.htm.

Curt Leviant, "Ishmael and Hagar in the Wilderness: A Parallel *Akedah*," *Midstream* 43:8 (1997), pp. 17–19.

Meshullam Margaliot, "What Was Written on the Two Tablets?" Bar-Ilan, Ki Thisa, 5758, at http://www.biu.ac.il/JH/Parasha/eng/kitisa/mar.html.

Rabbi Eitan Mayer, Parsha Themes, Tetzaveh, Tazria-Metzora, and Shelah at http://www.parshathemes.blogspot.co.il.

Rabbi Yaakov Medan, "*'Ba-Makom she-Ba'alei Teshuva Omedim' (Parshat Yosef ve-Ehav)"* (Hebrew), *Megadim* 2 (1986), pp. 54–78.

Rabbi Francis Nataf, *Redeeming Relevance in the Book of Exodus: Explorations in Text and Meaning* (Jerusalem: Urim, 2009), pp. 21–36.

Reinhard Neudecker, "'And You Shall Love Your Neighbor as Yourself—I Am the Lord' (Lev 19,18) in Jewish Interpretation," *Biblica* 73 (1992), pp. 496–517.

Uzi Paz, "The Sin of Moses and Aaron at Mei Meribah: A Close Reading of Numbers 20:1–13" (Hebrew), *Megadim* 53 (2012), pp. 75–89.

Rabbi David Sabato, "The Land Belonged to Pharaoh: The Root of the Egyptian Slavery" (Hebrew), *Megadim* 52 (2011), pp. 41–57.

Rabbi Haim Sabato, *Ahavat Torah* (Hebrew) (Tel Aviv: Mesorah la-Am, Sifrei Aliyat ha-Gag, 2000), pp. 15–20.

Meir Seidler, "Forgive Us: The Difference Between Sins and Crimes," Bar-Ilan University, Yom Kippur 2001, at http://www.biu.ac.il/JH/Parasha/eng/yomk/suc.html.

Rabbi Moshe Shamah, "At the Burning Bush," *Intersession Reader* (New York: Tebah, 2009), pp. 14–36.

Rabbi Yehudah Shaviv, "The Location of the Laws of *Arakhin* in the Torah and Its Significance" (Hebrew), *Megadim* 6 (1988), pp. 12–16.

Ernst Simon, "The Neighbor (*Re'a*) Whom We Shall Love," (and response of Harold Fisch) in *Modern Jewish Ethics: Theory and Practice*, ed. Marvin Fox (Ohio: Ohio State University Press, 1975), pp. 29–61.

Uriel Simon, "The Exegete Is Recognized Not Only Through His Approach but Also Through His Questions" (Hebrew), in *Pirkei Nehama: Nehama Leibowitz Memorial Volume*, ed. Moses Ahrend, Ruth Ben-Meir & Gavriel H. Cohn (Jerusalem: Eliner Library, 2001), pp. 241–261.

Shlomo Spiro, "On Rationalizing Biblical *Tum'a*," *Tradition* 43:1 (Spring 2010), pp. 23–37.

Rabbi Yaacov Steinman, "Camel-flage," Yeshivat Har Etzion Virtual Beit Midrash, Hayyei Sarah 5765, at http://www.vbm-torah.org/parsha.61/05chayei.htm.

Elazar Touitou, "Between 'The Plain Sense of the Text' and 'The Spirit of the Text': Nehama Leibowitz's Relationship with Rashbam's Commentary on the Torah," (Hebrew), in *Pirkei Nehama: Nehama Leibowitz Memorial Volume*, ed. Moses Ahrend, Ruth Ben-Meir & Gavriel H. Cohn (Jerusalem: Eliner Library, 2001), pp. 221–240.

Rabbi Chanoch Waxman, "Survival and Revival: On the Righteousness of Noach," Yeshivat Har Etzion Virtual Beit Midrash, Noah 5762, at http://www.vbm-torah.org/parsha.62/02noach.htm.

Rabbi Chanoch Waxman, "But My Covenant I will Establish with Yitzchak," Yeshivat Har Etzion Virtual Beit Midrash, Vayera 5762, at http://www.vbm-torah.org/parsha.62/04vayeira.htm.

Steven Wilf, *The Law Before the Law* (Lanham: Lexington Books, 2008).

Yair Zakovitch, "Juxtaposition in the Abraham Cycle," in *Pomegranates and Golden Bells: Studies in Biblical, Jewish, and Near Eastern Ritual, Law, and Literature in Honor of Jacob Milgrom*, ed. David P. Wright, David Noel Freedman & Avi Hurvitz (Winona Lake, IN: Eisenbrauns, 1995), pp. 509–524.

Adrian Ziderman, "On Bringing Up Children," Bar-Ilan University, Yithro 5760/2000, at http://www.biu.ac.il/JH/Parasha/eng/ytro/zid.html.

~

הפטרות

Haftarot

Introduction

On Shabbat and holidays we read Haftarot, the prophetic passages that generally reflect themes from the Parashah or holiday seasons. Why? The most frequently quoted explanation is that this practice began in the Maccabean period, when King Antiochus forbade Torah reading. The fourteenth-century commentator Rabbi David Avudaraham states that consequently, Jews recited prophetic passages that reminded them of the Torah readings they could not read publically.

Although this explanation is popular, it leaves us with a number of questions: First, if Antiochus were trying to disengage Jews from Torah study, why would he have permitted them to read from the books of the Prophets, which are extensions of the Torah itself? Second, this theory first appeared in the fourteenth century. Why did it take so long for the explanation to surface? These questions have led several rabbinic scholars to suggest alternate hypotheses regarding the origin of the weekly Haftarah reading.

Rabbi Samson Raphael Hirsch and Rabbi Reuven Margaliot offer a Historical Hypothesis: Haftarot were instituted to combat the erroneous beliefs of the Samaritans, who denied the sanctity of the Prophets. However, several Haftarot draw from the Book of Joshua, whose sanctity was accepted by the Samaritans, so this argument is flawed.

Zekukin de-Nura and Tosafot Ben Yehiel suggest a General Learning Hypothesis: Haftarot were instituted in order to promote Torah study. However, this theory does not adequately justify the specificity of our Haftarah-reading tradition. Any prophetic selection would have sufficed.

Rabbi Joseph Soloveitchik and Rabbi Haim David Halevi provide a Consolation Hypothesis: Haftarot were instituted to instill messianic hope in the community. But although it is true that many Haftarot contain elements of consolation, the thematic connections between the weekly Torah portions and their Haftarot demonstrate that the originators of the Haftarah-reading custom were interested in more than just consolation.

Rabbis Hai Gaon, Yitzhak Palache, and Haim David Halevi offer a Sermon Hypothesis: The practice of Haftarah reading predates the Maccabean period, and possibly extends back to the time of the prophets or to Ezra. The purpose of the Haftarot was to serve as a sermon on the Parashah, applying and extending themes and messages from each Torah reading to religious life.

The attractiveness of this theory lies in the fact that it accounts for the information we know about Haftarot. Furthermore, it explains how reading Haftarot became such a universal Jewish practice and why the Antiochus hypothesis is absent before the fourteenth century. Most importantly, it accounts for the specific connections between each Haftarah and its Parashah.

Prophets were the first to make the Torah "relevant" by playing off major themes and applying them to real-life situations. By exploring the annual Haftarah cycle, we are afforded the opportunity to survey most of the prophetic books and consider some of their most important teachings. The brief essays in this section focus on meaningful lessons from the Haftarot or broader themes from those prophetic books, without necessarily relating them to their respective Parshiyot. In this manner, we continue in the spirit of understanding the prophetic *derashot* as a method of applying the Torah's values to contemporary society—both to that of the prophet and to our own.

From Bereishit until Pinehas, the Haftarot correspond to the Parashah. After Pinehas, we begin the three weeks of calamity (from 17 Tammuz until 9 Av), and then the seven weeks of consolation, followed by the High Holiday season.

In his *Kesef Mishneh* commentary on Rambam (*Laws of Prayer,* 12:12), Rabbi Yosef Karo explains that in the time of the Gemara, Haftarot for regular Shabbatot were not standardized. Each community selected prophetic passages it felt were relevant to the Parashah. As a result, a great variety of Haftarot were chosen throughout the ages (a comprehensive list of which can be found at the end of volume ten of *Encyclopedia Talmudit*).

By now, the customs have been significantly streamlined, and most communities follow a shared Haftarah schedule. Nonetheless, there still are differences between Sephardim, Ashkenazim, and other communities for several Haftarot during the year. For the sake of convenience, I have used the Sephardic and Ashkenazic Haftarah readings in the Joseph Hertz edition of the Humash.

Additionally, there are many recurring themes in the Haftarot during the year. I tried to avoid repeating themes, and so the various prophetic passages that relate to Solomon's building of the Temple, Ezekiel's Temple Vision, or Hosea's prophecies pertaining to the symbolic marriage between God and Israel, are not addressed each time we read those Haftarot. For the subjects covered multiple times, I refer to the location where there is an essay on that topic.

הַפְטָרוֹת
לְשַׁבָּת

Shabbat
Haftarot

BEREISHIT

(Sephardim read Isaiah 42:5–21; Ashkenazim continue until 43:10)

Thus said God the Lord, Who created the heavens and stretched them out,
Who spread out the earth and what it brings forth, Who gave breath to the
people upon it and life to those who walk thereon: I the Lord, in My grace,
have summoned you, and I have grasped you by the hand. I created you, and
appointed you a covenant people, a light unto the nations.

(Isaiah 42:5–6)

God created the world, and therefore has the ability to act in history and redeem Israel from exile. The theme of God as the Creator Who enacts justice and ultimate redemption in the world is prevalent in Tanakh, and it plays a prominent role in the Haftarah.

Commenting on the Torah, Professor Yeshayahu Leibowitz observes that there are only 34 verses describing the creation of the world (Genesis 1:1–2:3). In contrast, the Torah devotes no fewer than 400 verses to the construction of the Tabernacle in the desert. The Torah is not a science textbook that describes how the world was created. Rather, it focuses on the obligation of people to follow God's commandments. When people build a house of God, then God's Presence can dwell among them (*Accepting the Yoke of Heaven*, pp. 79–81).

Sephardim and Ashkenazim alike use Isaiah's prophecy to draw relevant lessons from God's creation of the world, and each community highlights a different aspect of creation. The Sephardic Haftarah reading concludes with the glory of the Torah as a central purpose of the creation: "The Lord desires His [servant's] vindication, that he may magnify and glorify [His] Torah" (Isaiah 42:21).

The Ashkenazic Haftarah reading continues further in the passage and concludes: "My witnesses are you—declares the Lord—My servant, whom I have chosen. To the end that you may take thought, and believe in Me, and understand that I am He: before Me no god was formed, and after Me none shall exist" (Isaiah 43:10). Rabbi Shimon bar Yohai (*Sifrei Devarim* 346) drew a shocking inference from this verse: When Israel attests to

God's Presence, God is God. When Israel does not attest to God's Presence, it is as though God is not God. God depends on Israel to testify to His acting in history.

Thus, the Haftarah teaches that God as Creator works toward improving this world. Furthermore, it reminds us that Israel's role is to be a light unto the nations, attest to God's Presence, and create holiness on earth.

—

NOAH

(Isaiah 54:1–55:5)

For this to Me is like the waters of Noah: as I swore that the waters of Noah nevermore would flood the earth, so I swear that I will not be angry with you or rebuke you. For the mountains may move and the hills be shaken, but my loyalty shall never move from you, nor My covenant of friendship be shaken—said the Lord, who takes you back in love.

(Isaiah 54:9–10)

*I*n this prophecy of comfort to the Babylonian exiles, God invokes His oath to Noah that He never again would flood the earth. Similarly, Israel never will be destroyed but rather will be redeemed and return to her Land. Most Jews believed that after the destruction of the First Temple, their relationship with God had terminated. Similarly, the cessation of the Davidic monarchy appeared to them as an abrogation of God's covenant (see, for example, Psalm 89).

The prophets therefore stressed the eternality of God's covenant with Israel (Isaiah 54:9–10) and with the House of David (Isaiah 55:2–3). In a similar vein, Jeremiah prophesied that just as the laws of nature are eternal, so too are Israel and the House of David (Jeremiah 33:15–26).

Dr. Joseph Hertz suggested an interesting link between the Parashah and Haftarah. Like the Flood, which was destructive but also intended to purify humanity with a fresh beginning; so too Israel's exile served the positive end of both purifying and enabling them to build a better future (*Hertz Humash*, p. 41).

Much of Jewish history gives the impression that the Jewish people are existentially endangered. Thank God, we continue to flourish as per the divine promise in this Haftarah. The choice remains though: Will we adopt a lifestyle that enables our families to be part of a Jewish future, or will we leave that noble calling to others? The prophetic consolation for Israel challenges every individual to play an active role in building a community of continuity.

LEKH LEKHA

(Isaiah 40:27–41:16)

*A*s with the Haftarot of Bereishit and Noah, the Haftarah of Lekh Lekha was selected from the prophecies of consolation in Isaiah, chapters 40–66. The prophet addresses the Jews in exile who believed that God had abandoned them. He reminds Israel of God's eternal covenant with Abraham and his descendants.

The prophet also predicts the rise of Cyrus the Great of Persia, who would defeat the Babylonians and allow the Jews to return to their Land: "Who has roused a victor from the East, summoned him to His service? Has delivered up nations to him, and trodden sovereigns down? Has rendered their swords like dust, their bows like wind-blown straw?" (Isaiah 41:2).

Later in this block of prophecies, the prophet explicitly refers to Cyrus as God's agent: "Thus said the Lord to Cyrus, His anointed one—whose right hand He has grasped, treading down nations before him, ungirding the loins of kings, opening doors before him and letting no gate stay shut" (Isaiah 45:1).

Although Cyrus could function as God's agent in history, his central role in the defeat of Babylonia and the restoration of Israel raised a new problem. Cyrus was a pagan—and the messianic redemption was supposed to include the downfall of paganism. Amos Hakham (*Da'at Mikra: Isaiah*) explains that this prophecy addresses a religious audience. Many did not believe that a pagan king could be involved in the process of redemption. The prophet goes on to quote God saying that nobody should question God's choice of redeemer.

In modern times, many in the religious establishment opposed Zionism on the grounds that most of the founders and leaders of the Zionist movement were not religious Jews in the traditional sense. In contrast, Religious Zionist leaders and rabbis recognized and applauded the positive role of these secular Zionists in the rebuilding of the Land of Israel. Some quoted from Isaiah 40–48 as a precedent for their arguments. If Cyrus the Great advanced God's process of redemption in the Persian period, non-observant Jews could play a positive role in Israel's redemption in the modern era.

However, Cyrus still was expected to ultimately accept God and bow to the words of the prophet (see Isaiah 49:7). He was not meant to remain a pagan king. Otherwise, the full redemption could not be achieved. Similarly, we hope and pray that those who heroically dedicate themselves to building the modern State of Israel commit themselves fully to the Torah so that the process of redemption can proceed further.

VAYERA

(Sephardim read II Kings 4:1–23;
Ashkenazim continue reading until 4:37)

The Haftarah of Vayera is one of several Haftarot where different communities read from the same biblical passage but begin or end in disparate places within that passage. Although there are exceptions to this rule, Sephardim generally read a shorter Haftarah than Ashkenazim when this occurs.

II Kings, chapter 4 relates the story of the prophet Elisha and a woman who offered him hospitality. Elisha predicted that this woman would give birth to a son as a reward for her kindness, and indeed she did. These themes directly parallel elements of the Parashah: angelic guests visit Abraham and Sarah; Abraham and Sarah offer their guests hospitality; and the angels promise them the birth of Isaac.

After these initial parallels to the Parashah, the story in the Haftarah takes a tragic turn in verses 18–23. The son dies of sunstroke, and the woman goes to find Elisha. As she left her home, the woman's husband asks why she was going out if it was not a special occasion, and she replies, "*Shalom.*" This is where Sephardim, Italians, and Yemenites end the Haftarah. Ashkenazim read the continuation of the narrative in verses 24–37, which relate how the woman finds Elisha who rushes back to her house, spends time with the boy, and miraculously revives the child. It appears jarring that Sephardim, Italians, and Yemenites would conclude the Haftarah at a point where the child still is lifeless rather than proceeding to the happy and miraculous ending of the story.

Rabbi Elhanan Samet explains the surprising discrepancy by noting that the entire story becomes inordinately long for a congregational setting (37 verses). Sephardim, Italians, and Yemenites therefore abridged the Haftarah to 23 verses at the expense of reading its happy ending. They conclude with the word "*Shalom*" to strike at least some positive note (*Pirkei Elisha*, pp. 281–284).

In the final analysis, Sephardim, Italians, and Yemenites did not want to burden the community with too long a Haftarah reading. Ashkenazim favored completing the story even though that meant reading a lengthy Haftarah. Perhaps the best solution would be to read the shorter Haftarah in synagogue and then to learn the story in its entirety.

HAYYEI SARAH

(I Kings 1:1–31)

he Haftarah of Hayyei Sarah opens with an old, frail David, and his son Adonijah (Solomon's older half-brother) who declares himself David's successor. David's general Joab supports Adonijah, while Solomon's mother Bathsheba and Nathan the prophet support Solomon for kingship.

Nathan suggests a plan: "Go immediately to King David and say to him, Did not you, O lord king, swear to your maidservant: Your son

Solomon shall succeed me as king, and he shall sit upon my throne? Then why has Adonijah become king?" (I Kings 1:11). Bathsheba follows Nathan's counsel and by the end of the Haftarah David affirms his oath that Solomon will succeed him: "The oath I swore to you by the Lord, the God of Israel, that your son Solomon should succeed me as king and that he should sit upon my throne in my stead, I will fulfill this very day!" (I Kings 1:30).

Curiously, there is no trace of David's earlier oath that Solomon would be king in Tanakh. Radak (on II Samuel 12:24) quotes a midrash that takes Nathan and Bathsheba at their word. When Bathsheba's son from her original affair with David died in infancy, she told David that were she to have another son, everyone would despise him. She made David swear that her son would be king. This midrash answers the textual problem of there being no record of David's oath.

It also is possible that David never made this oath, and the plan of Nathan and Bathsheba was a ruse, similar to the way Jacob and Rebecca tricked Isaac for Esau's birthright. Should this be the case, then the story of Solomon's rise to power would parallel the deception of Isaac by Rebecca and Jacob. The narrative begins with David in a frail state, yet he responded strongly to Nathan and Bathsheba's request. This detail is similar to the frail Isaac sounding more aware and powerful as he bequeathed the rights of the first born to Jacob.

In the end, the fitting successor won in both cases. Jacob became the founder of the Jewish nation, and Solomon built the Temple in Jerusalem. However, the beginnings of Solomon's dynasty were shaky, not unlike Jacob's difficult life after he received the blessing of the birthright (see further discussion in the Haftarah of Vayhi).

TOLEDOT

(Malachi 1:1–2:7)

*I*n 540 BCE, Cyrus the Great of Persia dealt a stunning defeat to Babylonia, bringing a sudden end to their mighty empire. In 538, he issued a proclamation to the Jews: "Anyone who wishes to return to rebuild the Temple may do so" (Ezra 1:1–2). The prophets of that era, notably Haggai and Zechariah, saw this offer as a potential herald of a messianic age (see further discussion in the Haftarah of the first Shabbat of Hanukkah).

However, this potential for redemption ended largely in failure. Despite the great miracles of history that were transpiring, only 42,360 Jews returned to the Holy Land (Ezra 2:64). Even after the Temple was rebuilt, most Jews chose to remain in their comfortable Diaspora homes. The original generation of idealists eventually died out, and their children began to lose hope in the dream of redemption that had inspired their parents to return to Israel.

According to tradition, Malachi was the last of the prophets. During his leadership, Malachi offered one final message of hope to the people of Israel. "I have shown you love, said the Lord. But you ask, how have You shown us love?" (Malachi 1:2). The trials and tribulations the people experienced made them feel that God had rejected them. Malachi reminds them that God always will love Israel and that the simple fact of Israel's survival demonstrates this enduring love.

Malachi continues his prophetic message by condemning the priests. Some of them watered down Judaism, while others overemphasized ritual service in the Temple to the exclusion of leading moral personal lives. Malachi also criticizes the alarmingly high intermarriage rate among the people and points out that the extensive spiritual decay was threatening the Jewish community as a whole.

Malachi concludes with a final exhortation: "Remember the Torah of my servant Moses, whom I charged at Horeb with laws and rules for all Israel. Behold, I will send the prophet Elijah to you before the coming of the awesome day of the Lord. He shall reconcile parents with children, and children with their parents. . ." (Malachi 3:22–24).

Several commentators maintain that Malachi was conscious that prophecy would cease with him. The word of God would henceforth be available only through the written word of Tanakh. Malbim further links Malachi's exhortation to observe the Torah with the prediction of Elijah's future coming. With the end of prophecy, the Torah would sustain the people of Israel until the messianic era, at which time prophecy will resume.

VAYETZEI (SEPHARDIM)

VAYISHLAH (ASHKENAZIM)

(Hosea 11:7–12:12)

VAYETZEI (ASHKENAZIM)

(Hosea 12:13–14:10)

*H*osea was the last prophet of the Northern Kingdom of Israel before it was exiled by the Assyrians in 722–720 BCE. His book opens with a shocking prophecy. God orders Hosea to marry a woman named Gomer and have children with her. Gomer would then cheat on her marriage with Hosea. This bizarre sequence of events symbolized that God began a "marriage" with Israel in good faith, yet Israel went astray and cheated on this relationship with idolatry and other sins.

Hosea depicts God's extreme mood shifts as a result of Israel's betrayal. Chapter 2 portrays God's will to restore the marriage with a concurrent determination to punish, chastise, or even destroy Israel.

Hosea likens Israel both to a wife and children. Marriage is the ideal love relationship, but it can dissolve when it fails. In contrast, there is an unbreakable bond with one's children, no matter how estranged they might become. In the Book of Hosea, children represent a more permanent layer of the relationship between God and Israel.

In chapter 11, God invokes the imagery of children:

I fell in love with Israel when he was still a child; and I have called [him] My son ever since Egypt… How can I give you up, O Ephraim? How surrender you, O Israel?… I have had a change of heart, all My tenderness is stirred. I will not act on My wrath, will not turn to destroy Ephraim. For I am God, not man, the Holy One in your midst: I will not come in fury. (Hosea 11:1, 8–9)

However, God is not satisfied leaving the relationship in the realm of Father-child and wants to restore the ideal marriage:

And I will espouse you forever: I will espouse you with righteousness and justice, and with goodness and mercy, and I will espouse you with faithfulness; then you shall be devoted to the Lord. (Hosea 2:21–22)

The Book of Hosea closes with the call for repentance that we read on Shabbat Teshuvah (the Shabbat preceding Yom Kippur):

Return, O Israel, to the Lord your God, for you have fallen because of your sin. Take words with you and return to the Lord. Say to Him: Forgive all guilt and accept what is good; instead of bulls we will pay [the offering of] our lips. . . . (Hosea 14:2–3)

This prophecy is far more than a call for repentance; it is an ongoing proposal to restore the "marriage" between God and Israel.

VAYISHLAH (SEPHARDIM)

(Obadiah 1:1–21)

*T*he Book of Obadiah contains only 21 verses, pertaining to the crimes of Edom, the descendants of Esau who lived southeast of Israel at the time of the destruction of the First Temple in 586 BCE. The Edomites cheered as the Babylonians destroyed Israel, captured escapees and either killed them or turned them over to the Babylonian invaders, and drew maps to expropriate the Land of Israel in anticipation of Israel's exile. Obadiah predicts that in the future

Edom would fall; Israel would be redeemed; and God's kingdom would be complete.

We recite the final verse of Obadiah every day when we conclude the Song at the Sea: "For liberators shall march up on Mount Zion to wreak judgment on Mount Esau; and dominion shall be the Lord's" (Obadiah 1:21). God's Presence will be manifest fully in this world only with the downfall of human evil—represented by "Edom" and "Amalek."

In addition to the prominent theme of the ultimate downfall of human evil, Obadiah refers to the return of the exiles to the Land of Israel, and these references affected Jewish identity in the medieval period: "And this exiled host of the people of Israel, who are among the Canaanites, as far as Zarephath; and the exiles of Jerusalem, who are in Sepharad, shall possess the cities of the Negev" (Obadiah 1:20). Which countries was Obadiah referring to?

Many medieval commentators, including Rashi, Ibn Ezra, and Rambam, maintain that Obadiah was referring to France and Spain. Zarephath and Sepharad are the Hebrew words used in the medieval period (and today) for those countries. Many Sephardic Jews believed that the Spanish Jewish community began in the biblical period based on this verse in Obadiah.

However, Zarephath is referenced elsewhere in Tanakh (I Kings 17:9). It is near Sidon (Phoenicia) north of Israel. It is likely that Obadiah was referring to that location rather than France.

While there are no other biblical references to "Sepharad," the Talmud and other early midrashim refer to Spain as "Aspamya" (like España), not Sepharad. Only in the medieval period do we find Jews regularly referring to Spain as Sepharad. Contemporary scholars debate the location of Obadiah's Sepharad, with the most likely candidate being Sardis in Asia Minor, often called *Sard/Spard* in Aramaic inscriptions.

If Sepharad originally referred to Sardis, how did medieval Jews start calling Spain "Sepharad"? David Neiman suggests that a group of Phoenicians, who originally lived in Lydia, eventually migrated out to coastal cities in Greece. The capital city was known as Sardis, or *Sard/Spard*. Phoenicians were the early colonizers of the Iberian Peninsula. Jews living in the Iberian Peninsula were aware of the trade routes, and adopted this title for Spain named after the Phoenicians (*Journal of Near Eastern Studies* 22 [1963], pp. 128–132).

Although Obadiah likely was not referring to Spain or France, the medieval communities living in those lands drew direct solace from Obadiah's prophecy by understanding his prophecy as referring to Spain and France. Far beyond those particular localities, however, Obadiah's emphasis on the elimination of human evil and ultimate redemption remain compelling themes for any age.

VAYESHEV

(Amos 2:6–3:8)

he Haftarah of Vayeshev focuses on what happens when Jews become their own worst enemies. The eighth-century BCE prophet Amos prophesied in the Northern Kingdom of Israel shortly before the exile of the Ten (Lost) Tribes. His was a period of prosperity and peace. Tragically, the wealthy citizens abused their prosperity and oppressed the poor, even selling them into slavery. Despite their immoral behavior, they thought they were righteous because they brought sacrifices and were wealthy. These facts proved divine favor, in their misguided view.

This passage was selected as the Haftarah of Vayeshev based on its opening verse: "Because they have sold for silver those whose cause was just (*tzaddik*), and the needy for a pair of sandals" (Amos 2:6). Several midrashic traditions identify this *tzaddik* as Joseph, who was sold into slavery by his brothers. Now in Amos' time, Joseph's descendants were selling their own brethren into slavery.

To counter the shallow theological attitudes prevalent in his generation, Amos links poverty and righteousness by referring to poor people as righteous and humble. Although it is possible that some poor people could be wicked and some rich people could be righteous, Amos used this extreme formulation to refute the dangerous theology of his wealthy contemporaries, who wrongly believed that wealth itself proved divine favor. Additionally, Amos condemns the citizens' use of their service of God as a cover for their immorality (see further discussion in the Haftarah of Parashat Tzav).

Finally, Amos deflates his generation's wrongful application of the "Chosen People" concept. They believed that since God chose Israel they could do whatever they wanted. Amos countered that God's unique relationship with Israel implies that Israel has an even greater moral responsibility: "Hear this word, O people of Israel, that the Lord has spoken concerning you, concerning the whole family that I brought up from the land of Egypt: You alone have I singled out of all the families of the earth—that is why I will call you to account for all your iniquities" (Amos 3:1–2).

Upholding one of the central messages of the Torah, Amos advocates morality and accountability as necessary ingredients to being God-fearing. He tells his people that they must lead religious-ethical lifestyles that exemplify being the Chosen People.

Mikketz

(I Kings 3:15–4:1)

*T*he Haftarah of Mikketz focuses on the celebrated narrative of King Solomon and his clever resolution of the dispute between two harlots who each claimed to be the mother of the same child. By producing a sword to solve the case by "dividing the child in two," Solomon gained national fame and royal authority. Many commentators ask: True, his solution to a difficult situation was clever, but does this story demonstrate that he was the wisest person of all time?

It is likely that the litigants' being harlots carries significance in uncovering the meaning of this story. During his encounter with God while requesting wisdom (I Kings 3:5–15) Solomon is identified by his name, but never as "king." Conversely, when rendering judgment to the harlots (3:16–28), Solomon is referred to as "the king" and never by his name.

Part of the reason behind this shift in titles is to teach that before God, all people are equal. No one else may be called "king" except God. In the episode with the harlots, Solomon fulfilled one of his most important roles as a king, namely, serving as the highest judge in the land. Therefore, the text repeatedly refers to him as "the king" before whom all citizens stand in judgment.

Biblical "wisdom" does not refer exclusively to having a high IQ or superior problem-solving abilities. It also includes the skill to judge fairly and live righteously in accordance with Torah wisdom. Just as all people stand as equals before the true King; so too a human king's divine wisdom means that all people would receive a fair hearing before him. It appears that a primary message of this narrative is that *anyone*—including the lowest members of society—could gain an audience before Solomon. He thus exemplified divine wisdom.

One of Isaiah's visions of redemption appears to model the ideal king after Solomon in this narrative. He will render justice without witnesses and judge the poor: "He shall sense the truth by his reverence for the Lord: he shall not judge by what his eyes behold, nor decide by what his ears perceive. Thus he shall judge the poor with equity and decide with justice for the lowly of the land. . ." (Isaiah 11:3–4).

Solomon solved a difficult case between two harlots, giving them as serious a hearing as he would to anyone else in the kingdom. All stood to be heard fairly by the king who judged with divine wisdom.

(Adapted from Hayyim Angel, "Cut the Baby in Half: Understanding Solomon's Divine Wisdom," *Jewish Bible Quarterly* 39:3 [2011], pp. 189–194.)

VAYIGASH

(Ezekiel 37:15–28)

At the time of the destruction of the First Temple in 586 BCE, many Jews wrongly thought their nation had permanently been disbanded and that their covenant with God was over. Living in the Babylonian exile, the prophet Ezekiel offered a message of consolation that instilled newfound faith for a people in despair.

Most famous among Ezekiel's visions is the dramatic revival of the Dry Bones (Ezekiel 37:1–14, read as the Haftarah of Shabbat Hol ha-Mo'ed Pesah). Both people *and* the prophet were stunned by God's bringing dry bones to life. This vision was intended as a parable to Israel. Like dead bones, the Israelites felt hopeless. With this vision, God indicated that He would restore life to the nation and bring them back to their beloved land.

Following the restoration vision of the Judean exiles, Ezekiel prophesies that the Ten Lost Tribes from the Assyrian invasions will return to Israel as well. We read this prophecy as the Haftarah of Vayigash, the Parashah in which Judah leads the brothers to reconciliation with Joseph. Ezekiel similarly predicts the restoration of the two nations, Judah and Joseph, united under one Davidic king.

These prophecies of restoration are so powerful that the writers of the Hatikvah drew from it when composing what would become Israel's national anthem. Ezekiel speaks of the exiles saying that "our hope is gone"—*avedah tikvatenu*. The anthem triumphantly responds, *od lo avedah tikvatenu*! We have not yet lost our hope! What a fitting response to Ezekiel's monumental prophecy of Israel's return to her Land!

We are witnesses to the unfolding miracle of the State of Israel today. We hope and pray that the second part of Ezekiel's vision, Jewish unity and harmony, will be fulfilled speedily.

VAYHI

(I Kings 2:1–12)

The Book of Kings opens with instability in the monarchy. David is frail, and his son Adonijah attempts to usurp the throne. In his dying words, David commands Solomon to eliminate individuals who are dangerous to the kingdom, and Solomon follows that advice (I Kings, chapters 1–2). Solomon then creates an ideal kingdom through his faithfulness to God and His commandments (I Kings, chapters 3–10). That state of affairs came to an abrupt collapse when he turned to idolatry at the end of his life (I Kings, chapter 11). Shortly after

Solomon's death, the nation split into two, and the seeds for destruction of the Temple were planted.

The Solomon narratives are valuable and powerful in their own right, but they also play an important role in the broader biblical narrative. The Book of Kings completes the first nine biblical books. The world began with instability (*tohu va-bohu*). Adam and Eve were placed in the Garden of Eden, conditional on their faithfulness to God's command. Sin undermined the fabric of creation by leading to exile from Eden and ultimately the flood.

In the Book of Kings, the monarchy also started with instability. Through faithfulness to God, Solomon built a kingdom and a Temple. Sin then undermined that stability and led ultimately to destruction and exile. The surviving Jews were exiled either to Babylonia—the homeland of Abraham—or to Egypt (II Kings 25:26), thus effecting a complete reversal of the earliest biblical narratives.

Living at the time of these disasters, the prophet Jeremiah laments the reversal of creation to its primeval state of desolation: "I look at the earth, it is unformed and void (*tohu va-bohu*); at the skies, and their light is gone" (Jeremiah 4:23).

From the earliest narratives in the Torah until the conclusion of the Book of Kings, Tanakh teaches that the world was created with the need of people's morality and faithfulness to bring it stability. When people act as faithful partners with God, there is peace and harmony. When they fail in this task, the world reverts to chaos and instability. Creation and history thus generate the ultimate religious-moral challenge to humanity.

(Adapted from Hayyim Angel, "Seeking Prophecy in Historical Narratives: Manasseh and Josiah in Kings and Chronicles," *Milin Havivin: Beloved Words* 3 (2007), pp. 110–121; reprinted in Angel, *Revealed Texts, Hidden Meanings: Finding the Religious Significance in Tanakh* [Jersey City, NJ: Ktav-Sephardic Publication Foundation, 2009], pp. 245–261.)

SHEMOT

(Sephardim read Jeremiah 1:1–2:3;
Ashkenazim read Isaiah 27:6–28:13 and 29:22–23)

*A*lthough the Sages of the Talmud codified the prophetic passages to be read as Haftarot for holidays, they left the choice of regular Shabbat Haftarot to the discretion of individual communities (R. Yosef Karo, *Kesef Mishneh* on Rambam, *Laws of Prayer*, 12:12). Consequently, several Haftarah reading traditions have arisen. Parashat Shemot is an example where Sephardim, Ashkenazim, and Yemenites adopted passages from different prophetic books to highlight different themes from the Parashah.

Sephardim read the beginning of the Book of Jeremiah (1:1–2:3). In this passage, God selects Jeremiah as a prophet. Jeremiah expresses reluctance only to be rebuffed by God: "I replied: Ah, Lord God! I don't know how to speak, For I am still a boy. And the Lord said to me: Do not say, I am still a boy, but go wherever I send you and speak whatever I command you" (Jeremiah 1:6–7). This choice of Haftarah focuses on the parallels between Jeremiah's initiation and ensuing reluctance, and Moses' hesitations in accepting his prophetic mission in the Parashah.

Ashkenazim read from Isaiah, focusing primarily on the theme of national redemption: "[In days] to come Jacob shall strike root, Israel shall sprout and blossom, and the face of the world shall be covered with fruit" (Isaiah 27:6). "For when he—that is, his children—behold what My hands have wrought in his midst, they will hallow My name. Men will hallow the Holy One of Jacob and stand in awe of the God of Israel" (Isaiah 29:23). Although there is rebuke in the middle of the Haftarah, the passage begins and ends with redemption.

Yemenites read one of Ezekiel's harshest diatribes against the Jews for their infidelity to God since their inception as a nation. He compares them to an unfaithful woman who has cheated on God by turning to idolatry and the allures of pagan nations: "O mortal, proclaim Jerusalem's abominations to her" (Ezekiel 16:2).

Ashkenazim highlight the link between the national exile and redemption. Yemenites selected Ezekiel's caustic condemnation of the Israelites, implying that the Israelites *deserved* slavery as a punishment for having assimilated in Egypt. It likely was used as an exhortation to contemporary Jews to remain faithful to the Torah. Sephardim chose to highlight the development of the outstanding individual figure of the Parashah—Moses.

———

VAERA

(Ezekiel 28:25–29:21)

*T*he Haftarah of Vaera features Ezekiel's condemnation of Egypt's arrogance: "Thus said the Lord God: I am going to deal with you, O Pharaoh king of Egypt, mighty monster (*ha-tannim ha-gadol*), sprawling in your channels, who said, my Nile is my own; I made it for myself" (Ezekiel 29:3).

The *tannin* was a mythical monster of chaos found in ancient pagan literature. Professor Moshe David (Umberto) Cassuto (1883–1951) explains that pagan myths spoke of demonic forces of chaos, and the gods had to defeat them in order to create order in the world. In contrast, the Torah relates that God was present from the beginning, and there was a harmonious process of creation. The Torah names only one creature besides humankind in the creation narrative: the great sea monsters (*ha-tanninim ha-gedolim*) (Genesis 1:21). Cassuto interprets this reference as an anti-pagan polemic. God created *tanninim* well into the process of creation, along with all the regular animals. There were no primeval conflicts or cosmic battles.

While the Torah is silent about mythical monsters (since people might take those references literally), the prophets and psalmists poetically referred to them later in Tanakh. "In that day the Lord will punish, with His great, cruel, mighty sword Leviathan the Elusive Serpent—Leviathan the Twisting Serpent; He will slay the Dragon (*tannin*) of the sea" (Isaiah 27:1). This verse refers to the messianic redemption, which will restore the original purpose of creation.

Prophets and Psalmists employed these mythical references to depict God's battle against human evil. There is a profound transition in Tanakh from the surrounding pagan world. The only "demonic" forces are human. Human injustice and immorality—and not mythical beings—are the "monsters" that undermine the fabric of creation. In contrast, righteous, ethical behavior fulfills and upholds creation. For the prophets, God defeating "monsters" refers to His intervening in history to uphold justice and bring redemption.

(Moshe David Cassuto, "Epic Poetry in Israel," in *Biblical and Canaanite Literatures*, vol. 1, pp. 62–90).

BO

(Jeremiah 46:13–28)

*I*n the Haftarah of Bo, Jeremiah predicts the downfall of the Egyptians by the rising Babylonian power in the sixth century BCE. Jeremiah strongly opposed Israel's alliance with Egypt and preached submission to Babylonia by becoming a taxpaying vassal state.

Prophets often opposed alliances with other nations, mainly because (1) they viewed excessive dependence on these alliances as symptomatic of a decreased faith in God; (2) alliances generally led to cultural influence as well; and (3) alliances often were politically unsound—nations would help one another only when it served their own best interests, not because they genuinely cared about Israel.

Within Tanakh, there is a conflict regarding the religious status of making alliances with foreign powers. The prophetic narratives in the Books of Kings (chapters 18–20) and Isaiah (chapters 36–39) indicate that the righteous King Hezekiah forged an alliance with Egypt. These texts do not ascribe any lack of faith to Hezekiah; on the contrary, they extol his faith in God. In contrast, the prophet Isaiah explicitly articulates opposition to Hezekiah's alliance with Egypt (Isaiah 30:1–3; 31:1–3).

This clash in prophetic texts speaks to the broader issue of what it means to "have faith." According to the prophetic narratives, one must believe in God and simultaneously make every effort to help oneself and one's country. According to the prophecies of Isaiah and Jeremiah, one must place all trust in God and not depend on human efforts.

A direct application of this ancient prophetic debate is manifest in the religious communities living in the modern State of Israel. Religious Zionists believe that God governs the world, but Israel also needs an army to protect its citizens from its many enemies. Consequently, students in Yeshivot Hesder of the Religious Zionist movement study Torah and also serve in the Israel Defense Forces. In contrast, some who learn Torah all day sincerely believe that God will protect the Land of Israel through the merit of their learning. They follow the preaching of Isaiah and Jeremiah.

In practice, Jewish tradition firmly espouses the first view, adopting the principle of *en somekhin al ha-nes*, one is not permitted to rely on supernatural miracles, as halakhah. Although the idealism of those who believe in supernatural protection is admirable when sincerely held, it is a potentially suicidal belief when unaccompanied by prophetic assurances of divine protection.

BESHALLAH

(Sephardim read Judges 5:1–31; Ashkenazim also read chapter 4)

*T*he period of the Judges was generally a "Dark Age" between the stellar leadership of the period of Moses-Joshua and that of Samuel. One of the brightest stars in Judges is Deborah, the only leader in the Book of Judges explicitly called a prophet. Unlike the other leaders of that period, Deborah is said to have judged before there was any military crisis (Judges 4:4). Most judges were ad hoc military saviors who arose to rescue Israel from its oppressors.

The victory song that Deborah and her general Barak sang is a beautiful accompaniment to the Song at the Sea from the Parashah. Although there are many parallels between the two songs, some midrashim detect intriguing differences.

> On that day Deborah and Barak son of Abinoam sang: When locks go untrimmed in Israel, when people dedicate themselves—bless the Lord!

Hear, O kings! Give ear, O potentates! I will sing, will sing to the Lord, will hymn the Lord, the God of Israel. (Judges 5:1–3)

At the Red Sea, God did everything for Israel. In contrast, people played an active role in the victory of Deborah-Barak, so the volunteers deserve credit. But was it appropriate to thank them in a religious song dedicated to God? Even if it were fitting, perhaps Deborah and Barak should have started their song with praises to God and then turned to blessing the volunteers for their heroism.

"Deliverance ceased, ceased in Israel, till I arose, O Deborah, arose, O mother, in Israel!" (Judges 5:7). In this verse, Deborah casts herself as a mother figure. However, one talmudic Sage also criticizes her for giving herself too much credit in a song of praise to God (*Pesahim* 66b).

In the Song at the Sea, all credit goes to God. We read this song every day in our morning prayers. However, the Song at the Sea may leave us missing something, since the splitting of the Red Sea did not involve any human participation. It sets a tone for awe of God, but not for an active mutual relationship.

Deborah's song blesses God and also credits the army and her own inspired leadership. It captures the realities of religious human experience. It blends the heights of prophetic ecstasy with the human desire for affirmation. It causes us to rejoice with Deborah and Barak, and at the same time encourages introspection about striking the proper balance between thanking God and crediting people.

Thus the Parashah and Haftarah complement one another. Each offers a different perspective on how to most effectively build a relationship with God.

YITRO

(Sephardim read Isaiah 6:1–13;
Ashkenazim continue reading until 7:6, and add 9:5–6)

*I*n the Haftarah of Yitro we read Isaiah's exalted vision of God on His throne surrounded by the angelic host: "In the year that King Uzziah died, I beheld my Lord seated on a high and lofty throne; and the skirts of His robe filled the Temple" (Isaiah 6:1).

Though deeply inspired by this vision, our Sages detected a difficulty with it. God had told Moses: "for man may not see Me and live" (Exodus 33:20). How could Isaiah perceive God in a prophetic vision and live to tell about it?

The Talmud offers a remarkable answer: "All the prophets looked through a dim glass, but Moses looked through a clear glass" (*Yevamot* 49b). In other words, Isaiah believed that he saw God, but his vision was not fully accurate—and he did not perceive this distortion. Because Moses' prophecy was of a different order, he understood that he could not see God.

Rabbenu Bahya (fourteenth-century Spain) adds another dimension to the talmudic passage by referring to God's distinction between Moses' prophecy and that of all other prophets:

> He said, Hear these My words: When a prophet of the Lord arises among you, I make Myself known to him in a vision (*ba-mar'ah*), I speak with him in a dream. Not so with My servant Moses; he is trusted throughout My household. With him I speak mouth to mouth, plainly (*ba-mar'eh*) and not in riddles, and he beholds the likeness of the Lord. (Numbers 12:6–7)

Moses perceived God through a *mar'eh*, a clear vision. However, all other prophets saw through a *mar'ah*, a mirror. They perceived a combination of objective divine truth and a reflection of their subjective personalities.

In contrast, Moses was unique in his perception of objective truth. God's praise of Moses' unparalleled prophecy appears alongside the Torah's praise of his matchless humility (Numbers 12:3). It appears that humility and prophecy are linked. The extent of one's humility is the extent that God's Presence is welcomed within.

(Adapted from Hayyim Angel, "Through an Opaque Lens: Non-Moshe Prophecy and Some Religious Implications," in *Through an Opaque Lens* [New York: Sephardic Publication Foundation, 2006], pp. 15–20.)

———

MISHPATIM

(Jeremiah 34:8–22; and 33:25–26)

*T*he Haftarah of Mishpatim describes a failure of the Jews immediately preceding the destruction of the First Temple by the Babylonians. Under siege, King Zedekiah orders that all slaves be freed—perhaps in an effort to obtain divine favor, or perhaps in an effort to increase the number of available soldiers to battle against Babylonia. The Judeans took a solemn oath to free their slaves. However, when the siege temporarily broke, the Judeans immediately re-enslaved those they had emancipated.

God condemns their hypocrisy. Within a few years, the Judeans themselves were dragged off as slaves to Babylonia. This Haftarah relates to the beginning of the Parashah, which teaches that the Hebrew servant should not remain permanently in a state of slavery but rather should be set free after a set term.

This Haftarah is the only time in Tanakh outside of Genesis chapter 15 where the "covenant between the halves" is explicitly mentioned. Earlier commentators speculated to explain the significance of splitting animals in half and then having the parties of the covenant walk in between them. Rabbi Shemuel David Luzzatto (nineteenth-century Italy) suggested that this type of covenant symbolized that only death should separate between the parties of the covenant. They solemnly agreed that they would remain committed to their treaty throughout their lifetimes. Rashi maintained that the covenant was more menacing and threatened dire consequences to anyone who broke the treaty. Just as the animal has been cut up, so too one who breaks the treaty would face doom.

In the previous two centuries, archaeologists have uncovered ancient Near Eastern parallels to this form of covenant. The nature of the treaty was indeed ominous, as Rashi had suggested. Here are two such texts:

If Matti'el, the son of Attarsamak, kin[g of Arpad,] is false to [the gods of this treaty . . .] . . . [As] this calf is cut up, thus Matti'el and his nobles shall be cut up.

If Mati'ilu sins against (this) treaty made under oath by the gods, then, just as this spring lamb, brought from its fold, will not return to its fold . . . alas, Mati'ilu, together with his sons, daughters, officials, and the people of his land [will be ousted] from his country. . . . This head is not the head of a lamb, it is the head of Mati'ilu, it is the head of his sons, his officials, and the people of his land. If Mati'ilu sins against this treaty, so may, just as the head of this spring lamb is torn off, and its knuckle placed in its mouth... the head of Mati'ilu be torn off, and his sons. . . .

(Translations from James B. Pritchard, *Ancient Near Eastern Texts*, pp. 532, 659–660)

The discoveries of ancient Near Eastern analogues to this form of treaty making enables us to understand the solemnity of the covenant. In the case mentioned in the Haftarah, the people should have been more faithful to the Torah and to their own oath in letting their slaves go free.

——

TERUMAH

(I Kings 5:26–6:13)

*I*n chapters 6–8 of I Kings, we find the description of the building of the Temple and Solomon's palace in loving detail. "In the four hundred and eightieth year after the Israelites left the land of Egypt, in the month of Ziv—that is, the second month—in the fourth year of his reign over Israel, Solomon began to build the House of the Lord" (I Kings 6:1).

The Jerusalem Talmud (*Rosh Ha-Shanah* 1:8) observes that this verse uses the exodus as its chronological point of reference. In I Kings 9:10, however, Tanakh counts time from the building of the Temple: "At the end of the twenty years during which Solomon constructed the two buildings, the Lord's House and the royal palace. . . ." Thus the Temple construction was a watershed in Israel's history and became a new beginning, a new point of reference.

The literary intertwining of the construction projects of the Temple and Solomon's palace intimates that Jerusalem is the political capital of Israel and also the capital of God's Kingdom. The Temple represents the place where Heaven meets earth. From its inception, it was available to all God-fearing people, not only Israelites. Solomon mentions this in his inaugural prayer: "Or if a foreigner who is not of Your people Israel comes from a distant land for the sake of Your name—for they shall hear about Your great name and Your mighty hand and Your outstretched arm—when he comes to pray toward this House, oh, hear in Your heavenly abode and grant all that the foreigner asks You for. Thus all the peoples of the earth will know Your name and revere You, as does Your people Israel; and they will recognize that Your name is attached to this House that I have built" (I Kings 8:41–43).

Ultimately, the Temple represents the Garden of Eden, an opportunity for a perfected, harmonious humanity to serve God and live in peace. We mourn its absence and pray for its rebuilding speedily in our days.

TETZAVVEH

(Ezekiel 43:10–27)

*I*n Ezekiel's final vision (chapters 40–48), an angel gives the prophet a virtual tour of the future Temple, and God reveals the laws of the dedication ceremony for that Temple. The climactic moment of the vision occurs in chapter 43, when God's Presence returns from the Babylonian exile to reoccupy the rebuilt Temple.

Some commentators argue that Ezekiel's vision must refer to the future Third Temple, since several aspects of the prophecy went unfulfilled during the Second Temple period. However, this view is beset with difficulties. At the time of Ezekiel's vision, the Second Temple had not yet been rebuilt. Of what relevance would a Third Temple be to Ezekiel's audience? Moreover, God instructs Ezekiel to teach the plan and laws of the Temple to his generation (Ezekiel 43:11, 19). If Ezekiel's contemporaries were intended to build the Temple, then the prophecy must refer to the

Second Temple. Radak—who insists that Ezekiel is predicting the Third Temple—is forced to say that these verses refer to the resurrection of the dead that will occur during the messianic age.

A better resolution is that Ezekiel's vision was intended for the Second Temple, which he and his contemporaries were supposed to build. However, the fulfillment of that vision depended on the full participation of that generation. It was miraculous that Cyrus the Great permitted the Jews to return to their land and rebuild the Temple, and the Second Temple was indeed built. However, most Jews did not return to Israel when Cyrus the Great gave them permission, and there was a scourge of intermarriage and assimilation. Whereas some aspects of Ezekiel's prophecies were realized, the full messianic dream remained unfulfilled (Rashi, Malbim; cf. *Berakhot* 4a; *Yoma* 9b).

Thus Ezekiel was envisioning the *last* Temple, where God's Presence would be fully manifest. This prophecy *should* have been completely fulfilled in the Second Temple Period, but we now still wait for it to be fulfilled when the Third Temple is built.

KI TISSA

(Sephardim read I Kings 18:20–39; Ashkenazim add 18:1–19)

lijah the prophet was one of the most fiery and exciting characters in Tanakh. He served during the reign of Israel's most wicked king, Ahab (873–852 BCE). Ahab's wife Jezebel introduced the Baal cult into the Northern Kingdom of Israel and made it into the state religion. Consequently, she persecuted and murdered God-fearing individuals. Elijah used dramatic force to combat Ahab, Jezebel, and the Baal cult.

Elijah felt that God's honor demanded emergency measures, and he decreed a drought that would last for three years. Although God acceded and brought the drought, the Elijah narratives revolve around God's attempts to teach Elijah that this level of rebuke was too severe. God brought Elijah to a starving woman in Zarephath (north of Israel), so that the prophet could see firsthand what his drought had caused. Elijah helped the woman but failed to learn the lesson or retract his decree.

Rabbis Yehoshua Bachrach (*Yonah ben Amitai ve-Eliyahu*) and Elhanan Samet (*Pirkei Eliyahu*) explain that God supported Elijah because he was correct in his assessment that the people were in a terrible spiritual state. Nonetheless, God attempted to teach Elijah that brute force against the nation would not achieve his goal of lasting repentance.

The Haftarah of Ki Tissa relates the pinnacle of Elijah's struggle—his challenge to the Baal cult at Mount Carmel. God answered Elijah with fire and the people all declared, "The Lord alone is God, the Lord alone is God!" (I Kings 18:39). Our Haftarah concludes with this verse, thus proclaiming Elijah victorious in winning the hearts of the people.

However, the ensuing narrative relates that this victory was short-lived. Elijah died miserable after realizing that his dramatic approach did not achieve the lasting repentance he so desperately desired. Similar to the Torah's account of the Golden Calf so soon after the Revelation at Sinai, the Elijah narratives teach that dramatic miracles do not create an enduring believing society. Only constant day-to-day commitment can. (See further discussion in the Haftarah of Pinehas.)

VAYAKHEL-PEKUDEI

(Sephardim read I Kings 7:13–26 for Vayakhel;
I Kings 7:40–50 for Pekudei. Ashkenazim read I Kings 7:40–50 for
Vayakhel; 7:51–8:21 for Pekudei. I Kings 7:40–50 is also read
on the second Shabbat of Hanukkah.)

These passages pertain to King Solomon's building of the Temple. See the discussions in the Haftarah of Terumah, and the second Shabbat of Hanukkah.

VAYIKRA

(Isaiah 43:21–44:23)

$\mathcal{T}$he Haftarah of Vayikra contains one of the most sustained criticisms of idolatry in all of Tanakh. Contact with the height of world culture in the Babylonian exile must have raised religious doubts in many Jews' minds. The prophet's rebuke was intended to deter Jews from assimilating into the dominant pagan civilization.

The prophets and Sages identify several motivations for why the Israelites pursued idolatry. Hosea (chapter 2) laments the fact that the Israelites worshipped both God and Baal, the Canaanite storm god. Given Israel's dependence on rainfall, many farmers served several deities with the hopes that one would provide that rain. This was a practical consideration, rather than a result of serious religious reflection.

Of course, the Torah does not allow for this sort of theological hedging. Elijah addressed this paradox as he battled the prophets of Baal for the hearts of the people: "Elijah approached all the people and said, 'How long will you keep hopping between two opinions? If the Lord is God, follow Him; and if Baal, follow him!'" (I Kings 18:21).

Archaeologists have uncovered a fascinating ostracon (piece of pottery) dated to the ninth century BCE in Kuntilet Ajrud in Northern Israel. On it there is a depiction of two humanlike figures with an inscription that reads, "I bless you by Y-H-W-H of Samaria and by his (or its) Asherah." The confusion of the Israelites is reflected poignantly in this picture and inscription. They accepted God, but also incorporated pagan beliefs and practices into their worldview.

Alternatively, one talmudic passage suggests that the Israelites knew that idolatry was nonsensical, but they engaged in its worship so that they could be promiscuous (*Sanhedrin* 63b). Paganism does not make moral demands on people as does the Torah. The lure to paganism was the libertine existence it promoted.

Another talmudic passage suggests that we are unable to understand the deep appeal of paganism. The great biblical idolater King Manasseh (II Kings, chapter 21) appeared to Rabbi Ashi and told him: "Were you there, you would have picked up the skirt of your garment and sped after me [to worship idols]" (*Sanhedrin* 102b). According to this passage, there was some temptation to idolatry in the biblical era that we no longer can fathom (cf. *Yoma* 69b).

"Idolatry" today takes on different forms from the paganism of the ancient world. However, the three root causes for making wrong choices are as strong as ever: (1) genuine confusion and the inability to distinguish between right and wrong; (2) the desire, whether conscious or unconscious, to reduce moral responsibility; and (3) irrational desire despite knowledge that one is making the wrong choice. Biblical and rabbinic analysis of idolatry, then, remains critically relevant in the modern world.

TZAV

(Jeremiah 7:21–8:3; 9:22–23)

Many prophets lament how many Israelites wrongly believed that to be "religious" meant to serve God in the Temple regardless of how they behaved outside of the Temple. Even if they were immoral, they felt that they had God's favor so long as they came to the Temple and offered sacrifices. The Torah and prophets categorically repudiate this misguided viewpoint. Fear of God in the Torah necessarily includes living a morally upright life.

When Jeremiah first prophesied the destruction of the Temple in 609 BCE, exhorting the people to live moral lives to accompany their Temple service, the people were outraged and even tried him as a false prophet. Only the heroic intervention of several elders saved Jeremiah from death (Jeremiah chapters 7, 26).

How could the people execute Jeremiah as a false prophet without knowing if his predictions were true or false? The simplest answer is that they were wicked people who had no interest in repenting. Therefore, they opposed Jeremiah because he criticized them—and most people are averse to criticism. From this vantage point, they used the trial merely as a pretext to murder him.

However, the people could have had nobler motivations as well. Most people in that society believed that no deity would destroy his own

Temple. Although this was essentially a pagan belief, many Judeans had adopted a monotheistic version of this conviction and therefore refused to imagine that God ever would allow His Temple to be destroyed.

The people also had a recent historical precedent to support their view. Less than a century earlier—in 701 BCE—God had miraculously saved Jerusalem from the Assyrian siege (see Isaiah, chapter 37). The people of Jeremiah's generation mistakenly concluded that this remarkable event proved that God would *never* allow Jerusalem to fall. Jeremiah attempted to change their beliefs, but only the actual destruction of the Temple in 586 BCE finally made them realize that Jeremiah had been right all along.

The Haftarah of Tzav focuses on sincerity of worship, rather than the empty veneration of the Temple, offerings, and the Ark. For the Haftarah of Yom Kippur morning, we read a similar theme in Isaiah, chapter 58, where the prophet condemns those who fasted on Yom Kippur but then acted immorally when they left the Temple precincts.

To this day, many speak of "religious" people who commit immoral acts. We need the prophetic message as much as ever, which teaches that the Torah defines religious people as those who develop an ongoing relationship with God and who live by the high ethical standards established by the Torah. By the Torah's definition, an unethical person cannot be called "religious."

SHEMINI

(Sephardim read II Samuel 6:1–19;
Ashkenazim continue reading to 7:17)

The Haftarah of Tzav addresses fraudulence in worship: serving God with apparent fervor while living immorally. The Haftarah of Shemini addresses a subtler spiritual hazard: serving God sincerely but becoming overzealous, thereby not following God's laws as prescribed.

Parashat Shemini describes the tragic episode of Aaron's sons Nadab and Abihu who offered an "alien incense," a non-mandated offering. After their deaths, Moses said to Aaron, "This is what the Lord meant when He said: Through those near to Me I show Myself holy, and gain glory before all the people" (Leviticus 10:3). Although they had sinned and died for that sin, God considered them among those who were near to God.

The last words of the first generation in the desert reflect a similar fear. Although Korah and his associates were rebels, many Israelites concluded after their deaths that God is dangerous: "But the Israelites said to Moses, Lo, we perish! We are lost, all of us lost! Everyone who so much as ventures near the Lord's Tabernacle must die. Alas, we are doomed to perish!" (Numbers 17:27–28).

The Torah responds to these concerns by prescribing boundaries for approaching God properly. The Yom Kippur ceremony (Leviticus, chapter 16) and how the priests must guard the sacred precincts (Numbers, chapter 18), are direct responses to the people's concerns.

Nonetheless, we find later biblical examples where righteous individuals attempted to come closer to God than permitted. The otherwise righteous King Uzziah entered an area of the Temple reserved only for priests. Although the priests attempted to stop him, he forcefully tried to enter until he was stricken with the skin affliction *tzara'at* (II Chronicles, chapter 26).

The Haftarah of Shemini records another example. As David was moving the Ark to Jerusalem, which would become the nation's capital and home of the future Temple, the Ark began to totter and Uzzah straightened the Ark. Although Uzzah's motivation to protect the honor of the Ark was sincere, touching the Ark tragically cost Uzzah his life.

Of course, these cases are extreme—the individuals who crossed boundaries to God's most sacred spaces lost their lives or were stricken with *tzara'at*. These dramatic examples teach that our efforts to approach God must follow the prescribed methods of the Torah with proper reverence. Feelings of spontaneous spirituality and desire to get closer to God are best channeled through the laws and teachings of the Torah. There is a wide range of valid halakhic practices, but those guidelines remain the hallmarks of traditional Jewish behavior in one's relationship with God.

TAZRIA

(II Kings 4:42–5:19)

METZORA

(II Kings 7:3–20)

*T*he Haftarot of Tazria and Metzora contain prophetic narratives involving people afflicted with the biblical skin disease *tzara'at*. Although *tzara'at* commonly is translated as "leprosy," it is clear from its symptoms listed in the Torah that this was a different disease or perhaps even a range of ailments.

Abarbanel suggests that the *metzora* (the person afflicted with *tzara'at*) was quarantined to avoid contagion. However, Shemuel David Luzzatto (nineteenth-century Italy) correctly observes that the Torah never discusses contagious diseases. In the Oral Law, the laws of quarantine were suspended during the pilgrimage festivals. If the *metzora* were indeed contagious, the Sages never would have disregarded quarantine.

Rabbi Samson Raphael Hirsch (nineteenth-century Germany) further observes that if a person is completely covered with the symptoms of *tzara'at*, doctors would consider these symptoms to be the worst form of the disease, whereas according to the law such an individual is ritually pure. It is clear that the Torah views *tzara'at*, not as a contagious disease, but rather as a spiritual affliction. To highlight this point, the potential *metzora* goes to a priest, not a doctor, to determine his or her status.

The Torah prescribes that those declared a *metzora* must tear their clothing like mourners, loosen their hair, and cry out *tamei, tamei* (impure! impure!) (13:45). Crying out serves as warning for others to stay away from them. The *metzora* also covers his or her face with a cloak down to the upper lip, thereby hiding from the rest of world.

Tzara'at comes as result of sin. It is connected with death and mourning. In this remarkable case, the mourner and "deceased" are the same person. Conceptually, the *metzora* is viewed as dead and must mourn for him or herself. The isolation of the *metzora* is a catalyst for introspection. The ritual purification process is then a rehabilitation, where the *metzora* can mourn and then return to society.

AHAREI MOT

(Ezekiel 22:1–19)

*E*zekiel prophesied in the Babylonian exile during the period surrounding the destruction of the First Temple in 586 BCE. The first half of his book contains some of the most scathing prophecies in Tanakh.

The Haftarah of Aharei Mot contains one such prophecy: "Further, O mortal, arraign, arraign the city of bloodshed; declare to her all her abhorrent deeds! ... You stand guilty of the blood you have shed, defiled by the fetishes you have made..." (Ezekiel 22:2–4). Rather than serving as a light unto the nations, Jerusalem had become a model of immorality.

In the eighth century BCE, the prophet Isaiah used smelter's pot imagery to describe how God would refine Israel so that the wicked would vanish and the righteous would remain as a pure foundation (Isaiah 1:18–20). Ezekiel offers a harsher prophecy by stating that *all* Israel had become dross and therefore deserved to be destroyed (Ezekiel 22:18–22).

In a similar vein, the eighth-century BCE prophets Amos, Hosea, and Isaiah likened Israel to Sodom when describing Israel's wickedness or destruction. Ezekiel one-upped them by stating that Israel is *worse* than Sodom:

> As I live—declares the Lord God—your sister Sodom and her daughters did not do what you and your daughters did...Since you have sinned more abominably than they, they appear righteous in comparison. So be ashamed and bear your disgrace, because you have made your sisters look righteous. (Ezekiel 16:48–52)

Ezekiel wanted to vindicate God for the destruction of the Temple. The people claimed that God had abandoned them and had unfairly brought destruction and exile upon them. The prophet retorted that God loved the people—but they drove Him away with their idolatry and immorality. Were the people to become ashamed of their past deeds and repent, they could restore a good relationship with God. Ezekiel's harsh criticisms, then, were part of a larger message of hope that helped the Jews through the most difficult period in biblical history.

KEDOSHIM (SEPHARDIM)

(Ezekiel 20:2–20)

*T*he Torah teaches that Israelites are not inherently superior to Canaanites. Their continued settlement in the Land of Israel is contingent on their good behavior and fidelity to their covenant with God. Just as the Canaanites were expelled for their evils, so Israel would be cast out of their land if they are unfaithful (Leviticus 18:24–28).

Living at the time of the destruction of the Temple and Babylonian exile, the prophet Ezekiel tells the people that God chose Israel in Egypt and told them to renounce idolatry (Ezekiel 20:5–7). That generation failed. God wanted to destroy them while they were yet in Egypt, but refrained from doing so in order to avoid desecrating His Name. After God redeemed them, they sinned in the desert. God again spared them in order to avoid the desecration of His Name, but also prevented that generation from entering the Land of Israel (Ezekiel 20:10–17). Ezekiel proceeds to a remarkable prophecy of redemption:

> With a strong hand and an outstretched arm and overflowing fury I will bring you out from the peoples and gather you from the lands where you are scattered, and I will bring you into the wilderness of the peoples; and there I will enter into judgment with you face to face. . . . I will remove from you those who rebel and transgress against Me; I will take them out of the countries where they sojourn, but they shall not enter the land of Israel. Then you shall know that I am the Lord. (Ezekiel 20:34–38)

Strikingly, this prophecy casts redemption as a punishment! God will redeem Israel because He wants to avoid the desecration of His Name, not for Israel's sake. This unique prophetic viewpoint is rooted in Ezekiel's focus on God as the "primary Character" in exile Who will be redeemed.

In addition to stressing a God-centric redemption, Ezekiel's prophecy features another surprising dimension. Ezekiel avoids reference to a Babylonian downfall in this prophecy, and for that matter in his entire book. Babylonia is not the Pharaoh in Ezekiel's exile-redemption model. Israel has replaced Pharaoh, and God therefore must rescue Israel from herself and her own hardened heart of stone.

On Shabbat Parah, we read the prophecy of redemptive purification in Ezekiel, chapter 36, which is directly linked to chapter 20 in content and theme. It continues the narrative but shifts focus to Israel's purification process during the final redemption. Israel will return to her Land and be given a new heart, one that is open to serving God (Ezekiel 36:26).

KEDOSHIM (ASHKENAZIM)

(Amos 9:7–15)

*I*n the Haftarah of Vayeshev, Amos condemns the Northern Kingdom of Israel for crimes of immorality. Although the Israelites served God through sacrifices, they failed to live the requisite moral life that the Torah demands. Israel's relationship with God necessitates moral responsibility and accountability.

The Haftarah of Kedoshim read by Ashkenazim opens with the same premise. Amos states that even the exodus from Egypt need not be considered a unique historical event if the Israelites violate their covenant with God: "To Me, O Israelites, you are just like the Ethiopians—declares the Lord. True, I brought Israel up from the land of Egypt, but also the Philistines from Caphtor and the Arameans from Kir" (Amos 9:7).

Lest one conclude that the Israelite exile would be permanent, Amos envisions Israel's future return to her Land. The doors of repentance always remain open. This Haftarah teaches that God's choosing Israel comes with a promise of Israel's eternality.

Amos' contemporary Hosea presented a similar idea of Israel's chosenness. On the one hand, the Israelites had fallen into a state of spiritual decrepitude to the point where they needed to be exiled to purify themselves and restore their relationship with God. God initially refers to them as rejected: "He said, 'Name him *Lo-ammi*; for you are not My people, and I will not be your [God]'" (Hosea 1:9).

However, after rehabilitation in exile, God would restore the special relationship with Israel: "The number of the people of Israel shall be like that of the sands of the sea, which cannot be measured or counted; and instead of being told, 'You are Not-My-People,' they shall be called Children-of-the-Living-God'" (Hosea 2:1). "I will sow her in the land as My own . . . and I will say to Lo-ammi, 'You are My people,' and he will respond, '[You are] my God'" (Hosea 2:25).

Both Amos and Hosea emphasize that Israel's relationship with God never is an excuse for Israel to be unfaithful. When Israel breaks their covenant with God they damage the relationship. Simultaneously, they teach that God's arms are always open for a renewal of the relationship through repentance and faithfulness to the covenant.

EMOR

(Ezekiel 44:15–31)

zekiel's vision of the Temple (chapters 40–48) is the only time in Tanakh that God reveals legislation to a prophet after Moses. Not only does Ezekiel legislate prophetically, but several laws in this section actually differ from those presented in the Torah! For example, the Torah prohibits regular priests from marrying divorcees, but allows them to marry widows. However, Ezekiel states that they may not marry widows, either!

The Sages considered banning the Book of Ezekiel as a result of these discrepancies:

> Rab Judah said in the name of Rab, That man is to be remembered for good, and Hanina b. Hezekiah is his name; for were it not for him the Book of Ezekiel would have been suppressed, since its sayings contradicted the words of the Torah. What did he do? He took up with him three hundred barrels of oil and remained there in the upper chamber until he had explained away everything. (*Shabbat* 13b; *Hagigah* 13a; *Menahot* 45a)

Staying awake into the wee hours of the morning, Hanina b. Hezekiah somehow found a means of harmonizing the conflicts. Unfortunately, we have no record of these resolutions. Several commentators suggest the alternative solution that Ezekiel is not eliminating any laws of the Torah, but rather is prescribing higher standards.

In addition to the discrepancies between Ezekiel's prophetic legislation and the Torah, the Sages were troubled by the fact that Ezekiel received laws through prophecy altogether. This contradicted their dictum, "'These are the commandments' (Leviticus 27:34), which implies that no prophet is at liberty to introduce anything new henceforward" (*Sifra Behukkotai* 8:13).

Rather than looking to Ezekiel as a second Moses, some Sages turned to Ezra—a non-prophetic Sage—to fill that role: "Rabbi Yosei said: Had Moses not preceded him, Ezra would have been worthy of receiving the Torah for Israel" (*Sanhedrin* 21b).

However, the Book of Ezekiel appears to be linking Ezekiel to Moses. Rabbi Eliezer of Beaugency (twelfth-century France) observed this as well:

> You will not find a prophet exhorting his generation about Torah and the commandments except for [Ezekiel]. Most of [Ezekiel's] words echo the style of the Torah, and he repeated nearly the entire Torah to them . . . as though he were giving the Torah to them anew (Introduction to Ezekiel).

━

BEHAR

(Jeremiah 32:6–27)

The Haftarah of Behar relates Jeremiah's prophecy of redemption that shocked even the prophet himself. Immediately preceding the destruction of the Temple, God ordered Jeremiah to redeem a field of one of his relatives (the laws of field redemption are found in Parashat Behar). Jeremiah was stunned. Why spend money to redeem a relative's field if Israel was about to go into exile? God responded that Israel would indeed be exiled, but then ultimately would be redeemed. Jeremiah's effort at keeping the ancestral field in the family was a sign of Israel's future return.

In the course of his prayer, Jeremiah addresses God with respectful epithets: "O *great* and *mighty* God whose name is Lord of Hosts" (Jeremiah 32:18). Ever sensitive to minor nuances, the Talmud compares this verse with similar verses scattered throughout the Bible: "For the Lord your God is God supreme and Lord supreme, the *great*, the *mighty*, and the *awesome* God" (Deuteronomy 10:17). "O Lord, *great* and *awesome* God, who stays faithful to His covenant with those who love Him and keep His commandments!" (Daniel 9:4). "And now, our God, *great*, *mighty*, and *awesome* God, who stays faithful to His covenant" (Nehemiah 9:32).

Focusing on the fact that Moses had used a fuller formula, "the great, the mighty, and the awesome God," the Sages observed that Jeremiah and Daniel used only parts of that formulation, and that the leaders of the prayer in Nehemiah, chapter 9 returned to Moses' complete formula. They posited the following reasoning behind this development:

> Jeremiah said, "Foreigners are destroying His Temple! Where are His awesome deeds?" Therefore he omitted awesome. Daniel said, "Aliens are enslaving His sons. Where are His mighty deeds?" Therefore he omitted mighty. But [the Men of the Great Assembly] came and said, "On the contrary! He performs mighty deeds by suppressing His wrath.... He performs awesome deeds, since were it not for the fear of Him, how could one nation persist among the nations!" But how could [Jeremiah and Daniel] abolish something established by Moses? R. Eleazar said: Since they know that the Holy One, blessed be He, insists on truth, they would not ascribe false [things] to Him. (*Yoma* 69b)

The Talmud praises the Men of the Great Assembly for their optimism and for restoring the list of God's attributes to its original form. The Talmud gives them the final word, and the first benediction of the Amidah contains this complete formulation: *ha-gadol, ha-gibor, ve-ha-nora*.

At the same time, however, the Talmud applauds the religious integrity of Jeremiah and Daniel. Living at the time of destruction and exile, they could not bring themselves to recite the full litany of God's praises. We learn from them that we should approach God from the depths of our souls, speaking our heart regardless of circumstances. In this manner, our relationship with God is genuine and true.

Tradition balances these poles by suggesting that only the most righteous of individuals can fully speak their heart. The community, on the other hand, follows the legislation of the Men of the Great Assembly and recites the full litany of praises in the Amidah, regardless of circumstances. The tension within this talmudic passage prods all members of the community to develop an increasingly honest personal relationship with God.

—

BEHUKKOTAI

(Jeremiah 16:19–17:14)

*P*arashat Behukkotai contains the blessings for faithfulness to the Torah and curses for infidelity to the Torah. The Haftarah teaches a similar outcome:

> Thus said the Lord: Cursed is he who trusts in man, who makes mere flesh his strength, and turns his thoughts from the Lord. He shall be like a bush in the desert, which does not sense the coming of good: It is set in the scorched places of the wilderness, in a barren land without inhabitant. Blessed is he who trusts in the Lord, whose trust is the Lord alone. He shall be like a tree planted by waters, sending forth its roots by a stream: It does not sense the coming of heat, its leaves are ever fresh; it has no care in a year of drought, it does not cease to yield fruit. (Jeremiah 17:5–8)

There are related biblical passages in the Books of Joshua and Psalms. God exhorted Joshua with a similar message at the outset of his career: "Let not this Book of the Torah cease from your lips, but recite it day and night, so that you may observe faithfully all that is written in it. Only then will you prosper in your undertakings and only then will you be success-ful" (Joshua 1:8). To Joshua, God emphasized commitment to the Torah; in contrast, Jeremiah emphasizes faith in God and not in people.

Psalm 1 weaves together the language of these two passages:

> Happy is the man who has not followed the counsel of the wicked, or taken the path of sinners, or joined the company of the insolent; rather, the teach-ing of the Lord is his delight, and he studies that teaching day and night. He is like a tree planted beside streams of water, which yields its fruit in sea-son, whose foliage never fades, and whatever it produces thrives. Not so the wicked; rather, they are like chaff that wind blows away. Therefore the wicked will not survive judgment, nor will sinners, in the assembly of the righteous. For the Lord cherishes the way of the righteous, but the way of the wicked is doomed. (Psalm 1)

All three passages emphasize righteousness as the proper path. God exhorted Joshua to be faithful to the Torah in order to be successful. Jeremiah stressed having faith in God and not placing faith in people. Psalm 1 mentions righteous behavior and then shifts focus to Torah study as the keys to living a rooted religious life. Together, these passages present the key aspects of religious life—faithfulness to the Torah, faith in God, and righteous action.

BEMIDBAR

(Hosea 2:1–22)

*T*his passage contains one of Hosea's prophecies regarding the relationship between God and Israel. See the discussion in the Haftarah of Vayetzei.

NASO

(Judges 13:2–25)

*S*amson's hair as the secret to his superhuman strength has long baffled interpreters. Why should his hair represent his strength? A fuller consideration of the Samson narrative in Judges, chapters 13–16 sheds light on this ancient riddle.

Following the remarkable account of the angelic heralding of Samson and his Nazirite vows, we may have expected that Samson would become a saintly leader. Instead, Samson's first recorded words express his desire to marry a Philistine woman! Samson wanted this woman because "she is the one that pleases me (*yasherah be-enai*)" (Judges 14:3). Despite his parents' protests, he married her, thereby inaugurating an ongoing series of relationships with Philistine women that led to Samson's downfall.

A broader look at the Book of Judges demonstrates that the Israelites' problem throughout this dark period is that they intermarried with pagans, which led to widespread acculturation and practice of idolatry. This decline is a running theme in Judges, but is particularly pronounced in the two episodes in chapters 17–21 (positioned after the Samson narrative). Chapters 17–18 describe Micah's building of an illegal shrine and the moral corruption of his society. Chapters 19–21 describe the horrifying story of the "Concubine at Gibeah" that led to national civil war and the near extermination of the Tribe of Benjamin. The refrain of these two stories—including the last verse of the Book of Judges—is that "in those days there was no king in Israel; everyone did as he pleased (*ish ha-yashar be-enav ya'aseh*)" (Judges 21:25).

Samson's hair represented that which distinguished him from everyone else. Samson's hair symbolized his special relationship with God. By intermarrying with a pagan woman who was "pleasing to him (*yasherah be-enai*)" (Judges 14:3), and erasing his distinction so he was like everyone else by cutting his hair, Samson becomes a microcosm for all Israel. The people also intermarried and did as they pleased. By forsaking the covenant with God that had made them unique, the Israelites forfeited their special divine protection and consequently were invaded time and again by stronger oppressors. Samson survived only by being distinctive, represented by his hair. When he removed his distinctiveness, he reverted to being a normal man among many hostile enemies, and was easily defeated by the Philistines.

In contrast, the prophet Samuel also was consecrated as a Nazirite prior to his birth. He taught that righteous behavior and communal involvement form the basis of the ideal society in Israel.

BEHA'ALOTEKHA

(Zechariah 2:14–4:7)

*T*his Haftarah also is read on the first Shabbat of Hanukkah. See the discussion there.

SHELAH

(Joshua 2:1–24)

*T*he Haftarah of Shelah relates the story of Joshua's sending two spies to Jericho in anticipation of the Israelite crossing into the Promised Land. The spies went to the inn of a harlot named Rahab, who saved them from the king of Jericho in exchange for her life and the lives of her family members.

In addition to her prudent measures, she also used religious language: "I know that the Lord has given the country to you, because dread of you has fallen upon us, and all the inhabitants of the land are quaking before you...for the Lord your God is the only God in heaven above and on earth below" (Joshua 2:11–13).

Ralbag maintains that Rahab used this formulation in order to flatter the spies to commit to the deal she would make with them. Several midrashim, on the other hand, take Rahab at her word and assume that she genuinely accepted God and even converted (*Mekhilta Yitro* 1; *Deuteronomy Rabbah* 2:28). One rabbinic tradition asserts further that Rahab eventually married Joshua (*Megillah* 14b). Regardless of the historical factuality of this rabbinic tradition, our Sages make a remarkable point: Someone from the lowest echelon of the most depraved society can convert sincerely and marry a prophet.

Rahab used a scarlet cord to lower the spies out her window in their escape, and intended to use that cord to identify her home during the

Israelite conquest. Following midrashic traditions, Rashi explains that Rahab's use of this cord was an act of repentance. Previously she had used this cord to allow customers to climb into her home for harlotry. Now, she would use the same cord to assist the Israelites.

One final message can be drawn by the juxtaposition of Rahab's being saved with the following narrative of Achan's sin and Israel's defeat at the Ai. Whereas Rahab was accepted into the Israelite people (Joshua 6:25), the well-pedigreed Achan from the Tribe of Judah was executed for plundering the city of Jericho against Joshua's religious ban (Joshua, chapter 7). This juxtaposition teaches an important point regarding the battle against Canaan: It was not ethnic, but rather ethical. Canaanites such as Rahab who acted righteously were accepted, whereas Israelites who acted wickedly such as Achan were not accepted.

KORAH

(I Samuel 11:14–12:22)

When the Israelites first requested a king as a new form of government, the prophet Samuel opposed them. He believed that a human monarchy would impede on God's reign. God expressed chagrin over the request for a monarchy, even likening it to idolatry. Nevertheless, God acceded to the people's request:

> Samuel was displeased that they said Give us a king to govern us.

> Samuel prayed to the Lord, and the Lord replied to Samuel, "Heed the demand of the people in everything they say to you. For it is not you that they have rejected; it is Me they have rejected as their king." (I Samuel 8:6–7)

While Samuel fully opposed the institution of monarchy, God espoused a complex view that kingship was dangerous yet necessary. Therefore, God incorporated both diametrically opposed sides of the human debate. It appears that Samuel combined genuine religious concerns with personal feelings of rejection. Additionally, he hoped that his sons would succeed him (12:2–4). These subjective feelings prevented him from being fully in sync with God's will.

At Saul's second coronation, Samuel condemned the people for requesting a king. He concluded his censure by successfully praying for a storm:

> "I will pray to the Lord and He will send thunder and rain; then you will take thought and realize what a wicked thing you did in the sight of the Lord when you asked for a king." Samuel prayed to the Lord, and the Lord sent thunder and rain that day, and the people stood in awe of the Lord and of Samuel. (I Samuel 12:17–18)

The storm indicates divine support for Samuel and his absolute opposition of the monarchy. However, God upholds a complex view of monarchy by both endorsing the people's request for a king and answering Samuel's prayer for the storm. Internalizing God's composite position, the people conceded that while they still wanted a king, monarchy posed a serious spiritual hazard: "The people all said to Samuel, 'Intercede for your servants with the Lord your God that we may not die, for we have added to all our sins the wickedness of asking for a king'" (12:19).

Later prophets, on the other hand, acknowledged the positive aspect of monarchy. Yehudah Kiel (*Da'at Mikra: Samuel*) observes that later prophets tended to condemn the sinful behavior of kings but did not oppose the institution of monarchy itself. Without the feelings of personal rejection experienced by Samuel, later prophets were able to fully internalize God's complex position, namely, that monarchy poses certain religious hazards but also can be beneficial to the nation when the king is God-fearing.

(Adapted from Hayyim Angel, "'I Am the Seer': Objective and Subjective Elements of Samuel's Relationship to Saul and the Monarchy in I Samuel 8–16," *Milin Havivin: Beloved Words* 4 (2008–2010), pp. 6–18; reprinted in Angel, *Creating Space Between Peshat and Derash: A Collection of Studies on Tanakh* [Jersey City, NJ: Ktav-Sephardic Publication Foundation, 2011], pp. 84–96.)

HUKKAT

(Judges 11:1–33)

*T*he Haftarah for Hukkat presents the judge Jephthah's political argument with the Ammonites over disputed territories. Ammon claimed that they were attacking because Israel wrongly occupied Ammonite territory. Jephthah retorted with several arguments including a historical claim from Parashat Hukkat.

The land in question *never* had belonged to Ammon. Moses captured those lands from Sihon the Amorite king (Numbers, chapter 21). Moreover, Moses did not fight a war of aggression; Sihon had attacked the Israelites. Additionally, Israel specifically avoided passing through Ammon's land when approaching the Land of Israel as per God's command in the Torah. Therefore, the claim of the Ammonites was baseless. Jephthah bolstered his argument on political grounds by noting that for some 300 years, Ammon never said anything about those lands. How could they attack on the basis of this false argument now? Since Ammon had no historical or diplomatic rebuttal, they ignored Jephthah's response and attacked Israel. Jephthah defeated them and they stopped raiding Israel.

Although Jephthah saved Israel from Ammonite oppression, he was guilty of two grievous errors. One emanated from misguided piety. As he went to the battlefront against the Ammonites, he vowed that the first creature to greet him if he would emerge victorious would be offered as a sacrifice to God. Tragically, his own daughter emerged, yet Jephthah did nothing to annul his vow and instead appears to have fulfilled it.

Additionally, the Tribe of Ephraim complained that Jephthah did not invite them to help in the battle against Ammon. Jephthah curtly responded that he had invited them but they snubbed him. In turn, the Ephraimites insulted him, enraging Jephthah to the point that he waged war and killed some 42,000 of their tribesmen.

Jephthah was a military hero by defeating an invader. At the same time, the Sages could not approve of his other actions. The Haftarah of Hukkat focuses on the positive aspect of his tenure, but Jephthah still goes down in history as one of the lowest of our biblical leaders. One talmudic Sage remarks, "Jephthah in his generation is like Samuel in his generation, to teach you that the most worthless, once he has been appointed a leader of the community, is to be accounted like the mightiest of the mighty" (*Rosh Ha-Shanah* 25b). The Talmud teaches that we should show respect to our leaders, even the lowest of them (with Jephthah being the case in point). At the same time, however, we must distance ourselves when leaders act immorally, as the Sages do regarding Jephthah. Rather than venerating leaders in their own right, Tanakh insists that religious/moral heroes are paramount.

BALAK

(Micah 5:6–6:8)

*S*everal prophets boil down aspects of the Torah into a few key principles. When recounting God's great acts toward Israel, Micah selects only two events from the Torah: the exodus from Egypt, and God's thwarting Balaam from cursing Israel:

> I brought you up from the land of Egypt, I redeemed you from the house of bondage, and I sent before you Moses, Aaron, and Miriam. My people, remember what Balak king of Moab plotted against you, and how Balaam son of Beor responded to him. [Recall your passage] from Shittim to Gilgal—and you will recognize the gracious acts of the Lord. (Micah 6:4–5)

Perhaps Micah selected these two events because they are radically different. The exodus from Egypt was done in the full view of Israelites and Egyptians. In contrast, the people of Israel were unaware of God's thwarting Balaam. Only God's revealing this story to Moses informed the Israelites of God's intervention behind the scenes. The Talmud views the Balaam passage as separate from the rest of the Torah, possibly because of its private nature: "Moses wrote his own book and the portion of Balaam" (*Bava Batra* 14b).

In this prophetic passage, Micah also condemns the Israelites for offering sacrifices while living immoral lives (see the discussion in the Haftarah of Tzav). Micah boils the Torah down to its essence: "He has told you, O man, what is good, and what the Lord requires of you: only to do justice and to love goodness, and to walk modestly with your God" (Micah 6:8).

One talmudic passage surveys prophetic portrayals of the essence of the Torah:

David came and reduced them to eleven [principles, see Psalm 15]. . . . Isaiah came and reduced them to six [see Isaiah 33:15–16]. . . . Micah came and reduced them to three [see Micah 6:8]. . . . (*Makkot* 24a)

There is something very powerful about the Talmud's statement, that the essence of the Torah and all its commandments can be thought of as Micah's "do justice and love goodness, and walk modestly with your God." These principles serve as guideposts for the validity of all religious behavior.

PINEHAS

(I Kings 18:46–19:21)

*T*he Haftarah of Pinehas continues from where the Haftarah of Ki Tissa ended (see the discussion there). Following Elijah's victory over Baal at Mount Carmel, the prophet expected that the nation would instantly repent and eliminate the Baal cult. Instead, his victory was short-lived. Ahab told his wife Jezebel about Elijah's victory, and she responded with a death warrant against the prophet. Elijah was forced to flee the Northern Kingdom to Mount Sinai.

Sensing failure, Elijah asked God to take his life: "Enough! he cried. Now, O Lord, take my life, for I am no better than my fathers" (I Kings 19:3). However, God wanted to teach Elijah a lesson:

There was a great and mighty wind, splitting mountains and shattering rocks by the power of the Lord; but the Lord was not in the wind. After the wind—an earthquake; but the Lord was not in the earthquake. After the earthquake—fire; but the Lord was not in the fire. And after the fire—a soft murmuring sound. When Elijah heard it, he wrapped his mantle about his face and went out and stood at the entrance of the cave. Then a voice addressed him: Why are you here, Elijah? (19:11–13)

God's voice was not found in the displays of power—wind, earth-quake, fire. God's voice was soft. Throughout Elijah's career, God had attempted to teach this lesson to Elijah. However, despite those divine efforts, Elijah wanted God to punish the Israelites: "He answered, I am moved by zeal for the Lord, the God of Hosts; for the Israelites have for-saken Your covenant, torn down Your altars, and have put Your prophets to the sword. I alone am left, and they are out to take my life" (19:14).

God therefore dismissed Elijah and replaced him with Elisha, who developed a much closer relationship with the people (19:15–16). Although Elijah was right that the people were wicked, a prophet must also remain by the people's side, encouraging them to improve. Once he condemned them before God, he could no longer serve as their spiritual guide. In contrast to his mentor Elijah, Elisha became a prophet of the people, learning a central lesson from Elijah's career.

—

MATTOT

(Jeremiah 1:1–2:3)
(This Haftarah also is read by Sephardim on Parashat Shemot.)

The first Haftarah of the Three Weeks between the fasts of 17 Tammuz and Tisha B'Av, is taken from the Book of Jeremiah. Jeremiah predicted and then lived through the destruction of the First Temple, and therefore his words are apt for this period of mourn-ing on the Jewish calendar.

God begins the conversation by informing the prophet, "Before I cre-ated you in the womb, I selected you; before you were born, I consecrat-ed you" (Jeremiah 1:5). Jeremiah is the only biblical prophet whose pre-birth consecration as a prophet is mentioned. Samson and Samuel were both consecrated as Nazirites—but not explicitly as prophets—prior to their births.

Rambam (*Guide for the Perplexed* II:32) extrapolates from Jeremiah's initiation prophecy that all prophets were chosen pre-birth. Today, one might suggest that the verse refers to some genetic tendency toward spiritual greatness. Rambam identified with Jeremiah in a letter he composed about himself to the rabbis of Lunel, France: "Before I was created in the womb the Torah knew me and before I was born, it consecrated me to its study, and made me cause its springs to gush forth."

Even if Rambam were correct, the question remains why Jeremiah was the only prophet that God informed of this pre-birth sanctification. Radak suggests that God wanted to encourage Jeremiah prior to what would be a very difficult prophetic career, even by prophetic standards. Menahem Boleh (Da'at Mikra: Jeremiah) further suggests that God informed Jeremiah at the outset that he had no choice but to accept his prophetic mission. Elsewhere in the Book of Jeremiah, the prophet laments God's forcing him to go:

> You enticed me, O Lord, and I was enticed; You overpowered me and You prevailed . . . I thought, I will not mention Him, No more will I speak in His name—but [His word] was like a raging fire in my heart, shut up in my bones; I could not hold it in, I was helpless. (Jeremiah 20:7–9)

Despite the bleak period in which he prophesied, Jeremiah stressed that the God-Israel relationship could always be restored to its original pristine state. The Haftarah concludes:

> Go proclaim to Jerusalem: Thus said the Lord: I accounted to your favor the devotion of your youth, your love as a bride—how you followed Me in the wilderness, in a land not sown. Israel was holy to the Lord, the first fruits of His harvest. . . . (Jeremiah 2:2–3).

For discussions of genetic tendencies to spirituality, see Dean Hamer, *The God Gene: How Faith Is Hardwired into Our Genes*, 2005. Carl Zimmer, "Faith Boosting Genes: A Search for the Genetic Basis of Spirituality," *Scientific American* (October 2004), sciam.com/article.cfm?articleID=000AD4E7-6290-1150-902F83414B7F4945.

MASEI

(Jeremiah 2:4–28; 3:4; 4:1–2)

*I*n this second Haftarah of the Three Weeks between the fasts of 17 Tammuz and Tisha B'Av, Jeremiah rebukes the people for their infidelity to God. He reserves special criticism for the spiritual leadership: "The priests never asked themselves, 'Where is the Lord?' The guardians of the Torah ignored Me; the rulers rebelled against Me, and the prophets prophesied by Baal and followed what can do no good" (Jeremiah 2:8).

Although Jeremiah here speaks about false prophets of idolatry, he suffered more as a result of false prophets who spoke in the name of God. These false prophets predicted that Babylonia would capitulate, and that the exiled Jews would return to Israel. In contrast, Jeremiah predicted that the Temple would be destroyed unless Israel repented and remained as a loyal vassal to Babylonia.

Jeremiah conceded that there was no way for the people to know in advance who was right, and therefore the nation would have to wait to see whose prediction would be fulfilled (Jeremiah 28:11). Waiting, however, was not a helpful option. The false prophets were calling for revolt against Babylonia, whereas Jeremiah was calling for loyalty to Babylonia.

To address these difficulties, Jeremiah extended the Torah's category of prophesying in the name of idolatry to include anyone who did not actively promote repentance. Since the false prophets predicted the unconditional downfall of Babylonia irrespective of any repentance on Israel's part, they must have been fraudulent (Jeremiah 23:13–14). Only those who actively encouraged repentance and faithfulness to the Torah could be trusted as true prophets.

While condemning the false prophets, Jeremiah urged the Jews not to listen to them: "For thus said the Lord of Hosts, the God of Israel: Let not the prophets and diviners in your midst deceive you, and pay no heed to the dreams they (Hebrew "you") dream" (Jeremiah 29:8). Radak explains the verse: "You [the people] cause [the false prophets] to dream, for if you did not listen to their dreams, they would not dream these things." Thus Jeremiah's critique of the false prophets includes an accusation of their being at least partially driven by a desire to please the people. These leaders were saying what their constituents wanted to hear, rather than speaking the truth. A vicious cycle was created between the false prophets, the political leadership, and the masses, leading to the destruction of Jerusalem and the Temple.

⚊

DEVARIM

(Isaiah 1:1–27)

*T*his passage pertains to false worship by serving God in the Temple but then living immorally. See the discussion in the Haftarah of Tzav.

⚊

THE SEVEN WEEKS OF CONSOLATION

(We read seven passages of redemption selected from Isaiah, chapters 40–66 during the seven Shabbatot between Tisha B'Av and Rosh Ha-Shanah.)

*R*ambam (*Laws of Kings*, 11:1) writes that one who denies that the Messiah will come denies both the words of the prophets and the Torah itself. He considers belief in the messianic redemption one of the 13 core tenets of Jewish belief.

One of the most explicit passages of redemption in the Torah is found in Deuteronomy:

> When all these things befall you—the blessing and the curse that I have set before you—and you take them to heart amidst the various nations to which the Lord your God has banished you, and you return to the Lord your God, and you and your children heed His command with all your heart and soul…then the Lord your God will restore your fortunes and take you back in love. He will bring you together again from all the peoples where the Lord your God has scattered you…And the Lord your God will bring you to the land that your fathers possessed, and you shall possess it; and He will make you more prosperous and more numerous than your

fathers. Then the Lord your God will open up your heart and the hearts of your offspring to love the Lord your God with all your heart and soul, in order that you may live. (Deuteronomy 30:1–6)

In this passage, we see the elements of a restored relationship between God and Israel: Israel's repentance, ingathering of the exiles, peace, and prosperity. These aspects of Israel's future became one of the prophets' central missions: to restore the ideal relationship between God and Israel by encouraging Israel to be faithful to God and the Torah.

The Temple represents the perfected world when humanity serves God and lives together in peace (see the Haftarot of Terumah and Rosh Hodesh). Jews will miraculously return from the exile and rebuild their land, and live together in harmony (see the Haftarah of Vayigash). They will repent and serve God with a pure heart (see the Haftarah of Kedoshim for Sephardim).

The messianic ideal is the supreme religious-ethical imperative. It requires that we take full responsibility for our actions and work tirelessly to improve ourselves and society, rather than living in isolation from the world (see the Haftarah of Tetzavveh).

HA'AZINU

II Samuel 22:1–51

We recite David's song of salvation (II Samuel, chapter 22) as a Haftarah twice during the year. On the seventh day of Pesah, there is a parallel with the Torah reading of the day. David praises God for saving him from his enemies, similar to Israel's praising God for saving them from the Egyptians at the Red Sea.

Reading David's song as the Haftarah for Ha'azinu is less thematically compelling, since the Haftarah does not seem to have anything in common with the Parashah except that both passages are instances of biblical poetry. This link enables us to explore the poetic nature of Tanakh.

At the end of Ha'azinu, there is a prose epilogue: "And Moses came and spoke all the words of this poem in the ears of the people, he, and

Hosea the son of Nun" (Deuteronomy 32:44). Given the context of the verse, most commentators reasonably understand that "this poem" refers to the Song of Ha'azinu. In contrast, the Talmud (*Nedarim* 38a) homiletically explains that "this poem" refers to the entire Torah. What is the rationale for calling the entire Torah a "poem"?

In the introduction to his commentary on the Torah, Rabbi Naftali Tzvi Yehudah Berlin (Netziv) explains that poetry is not simply characterized by features such as meter, rhyme, or alliteration. Poetry contains allusions packed into fewer, multivalent words. Similarly, the Torah contains infinite depth. One who understands only its basic prose meaning will miss many layers of the Torah's intended import.

Netziv's point is illustrated by the literary critic Erich Auerbach in his essay *Mimesis*. In Homeric literature, the thoughts and feelings of the characters are revealed either to each other or as monologues to the reader. Auerbach contrasts this phenomenon with the Binding of Isaac (Genesis, chapter 22) where the Torah deliberately keeps the characters' feelings in the background so that the story is fraught with psychological tension and is open to many types of elucidation (see also Rabbi Samson Raphael Hirsch on Exodus 2:4).

Although appreciating the poetic nature of the Torah enables us to seek its deeper meanings, one could abuse a poetic focus. "Raba expounded: Why was David punished? Because he called words of Torah 'songs,' as it is said: 'Your statutes have been my songs in the house of my pilgrimage' (Psalms 119:54)" (*Sotah* 35a). Perhaps the Talmud is concerned that some may focus on the deeper layers of the Torah but ignore its plainest prose messages. Ideal Torah study and observance requires a foundation in the basics and then a life-long pursuit of growth into the poetic reaches of the Torah.

VE-ZOT HA-BERAKHAH

(Sephardim read Joshua 1:1–9; Ashkenazim add 1:10–18)

*S*ee the discussion on the Haftarah of Simhat Torah.

הַפְטָרוֹת
לַחַגִּים
וְלַיָּמִים
מְיוּחָדִים

Haftarot
for
Holidays
& Special
Days

ROSH HODESH

(Isaiah 66:1–24)

*M*ost prophecies of consolation in the Book of Isaiah pertain specifically to Israel. Certain prophecies, however, have a more universalistic component as well:

> [The time] has come to gather all the nations and tongues; they shall come and behold My glory. . . . And from them likewise I will take some to be levitical priests, said the Lord. (Isaiah 66:18, 21)

> As for the foreigners who attach themselves to the Lord, to minister to Him, and to love the name of the Lord, to be His servants—all who keep the Sabbath and do not profane it, and who hold fast to My covenant—I will bring them to My sacred mount and let them rejoice in My house of prayer. Their burnt offerings and sacrifices shall be welcome on My altar; for My House shall be called a house of prayer for all peoples. (Isaiah 56:6–7)

This universalistic approach stems back to the Torah. The Garden of Eden was intended for everyone, not just Israel. Similarly, the prophets longed for all humanity to recognize God and accept ethical monotheism.

When dedicating the First Temple, King Solomon understood that the Temple was intended for all who seek God (I Kings 8:41–43). Isaiah likewise envisioned that

> In the days to come, the Mount of the Lord's House shall stand firm above the mountains and tower above the hills; and all the nations shall gaze on it with joy. And the many peoples shall go and say: Come, let us go up to the Mount of the Lord, to the House of the God of Jacob; that He may instruct us in His ways, and that we may walk in His paths. For instruction shall come forth from Zion, the word of the Lord from Jerusalem. (Isaiah 2:2–3)

Dr. Norman Lamm observes that "a truly religious Jew, devoted to his own people in keen attachment to both their physical and spiritual welfare, must at the same time be deeply concerned with all human beings. Paradoxically, the more particularistic a Jew is, the more universal must be his concerns" (*Shema*, p. 35).

The Torah and prophets teach that by remaining true to our traditions, we may respect the diversity of all people once they accept the morality mandated by the Torah for all people, called the Noahide laws. People need not become Jewish to serve God in the Temple, nor to attain a share in the world to come. In this manner humanity can attain peace and harmony through mutual respect and shared religious morality.

MAHAR HODESH

(I Samuel 20:18–42)

*W*e read the Haftarah of Mahar Hodesh when Rosh Hodesh falls on a Sunday, as its opening verse sets the narrative on the day preceding Rosh Hodesh. After David killed Goliath, Jonathan became enamored with David and made a pact with him (I Samuel 18:1–4). He graciously ceded his right to the throne to David as a result of David's heroism. He consistently stood by David's side even as he would lose the throne. One Mishnah idealizes the love between David and Jonathan as the quintessential friendship:

All love that depends on a [transient] thing, [when the] thing ceases, [the] love ceases; and [all love] that depends not on a [transient] thing, ceases not forever. Which is the [kind of] love that depends on a [transient] thing? Such as was the love of Amnon for Tamar; and [which is the kind of love] that depends not on a [transient] thing? Such as was the love of David and Jonathan. (*Avot* 5:16)

Jonathan had David swear that he would protect him and his descendants (something David kept faithfully):

Nor shall you fail to show me the Lord's faithfulness, while I am alive; nor, when I am dead, shall you ever discontinue your faithfulness to my house—not even after the Lord has wiped out every one of David's enemies from the face of the earth. Thus has Jonathan covenanted with the house of David; and may the Lord requite the enemies of David! Jonathan, out of his love for David, adjured him again, for he loved him as himself. (I Samuel 20:14–17)

Some interpret the juxtaposition of the oath and Jonathan's love for David as himself to mean that Jonathan's love for David combined interpersonal affection and an aspect of covenantal alliance. Alternatively, Abarbanel and Malbim maintain that the reference to Jonathan loving David as himself indicates that Jonathan was *not* motivated by personal gain and self-protection even in the context of such a prudent covenant.

Regardless of whether this friendship should be viewed as purely altruistic or whether it combined altruistic and utilitarian motives, Jonathan's exemplary love of David remains one of the great models of friendship in Tanakh.

FIRST DAY ROSH HA-SHANAH

(I Samuel 1:1–2:10)

The Book of Samuel opens with the story of Elkanah and his barren wife Hannah. Unable to eat as result of her sorrow, Hannah left the table. She prayed for a son whom she vowed would serve in the Tabernacle. God answered Hannah's prayer and she bore a son, Samuel, who became one of the most effective leaders in Israel's history. Samuel traveled around the country, bringing people back to God and unifying the nation.

Hannah's song of gratitude (I Samuel 2:1–10) is only tangentially about her son; it is far more about God's dominion in the world and personal righteousness. Many elders of that community believed that with a political switch to monarchy, their problems would vanish. Hannah, and later her son Samuel, disagreed. Only through national commitment to personal righteousness, self-sacrifice, and communal work can society and its cycles of trouble disappear.

The obvious parallel to the Torah reading of the day is that God gave the barren Sarah a son, as He gave the barren Hannah a son. On a deeper level, the Haftarah is about new beginnings and breaking out of seemingly endless cycles.

An important difference between the stories is that Abraham and Sarah were given divine promises of progeny. In contrast, Hannah had no reason to believe her situation would ever improve. Hannah was alone. For the first time she realized that even her beloved husband Elkanah did not understand her, and Eli the High Priest also did not understand her. She also felt alienated from God as a result of her barrenness.

Hannah stood at the Tabernacle, surrounded by people but alone, face to face with God. We are all like this, surrounded by our community, but with nobody but God who fully understands our inner state. On Rosh Ha-Shanah we stand before God, and through such personal prayer, we join together as a covenantal community.

SECOND DAY ROSH HA-SHANAH

(Jeremiah 31:1–20)

*J*eremiah began his career predicting the destruction of the Temple. Jeremiah pleaded for repentance and political loyalty to Babylonia. Most of those he was trying to help stifled his voice. The Babylonian siege of Jerusalem began. The Edomites rejoiced at the Babylonian invader. A Babylonian victory over Israel would mean more land and plunder for them (see the Haftarah of Vayishlah for Sephardim). The more cultured nation of Tyre (Phoenicia) offered no support to Israel. Jeremiah's contemporary Ezekiel describes Tyre's attitude toward Israel: The Babylonian invasion was economically beneficial for the people of Tyre, since Israel competed with them on the Mediterranean Sea routes. They, too, rejoiced over Israel's downfall.

Egypt was the regional superpower that had promised to support Israel. Egypt sent a small contingent during the Babylonian siege, but after its first setback, Egypt decided not to risk any more of its own soldiers. An isolated Israel was left to face the mighty Babylonian Empire on her own. In 586 BCE, the Babylonians breached the walls of Jerusalem. They killed thousands of Israelites and exiled much of the remaining the population, burning the Temple to the ground.

On Rosh Ha-Shanah, we read one of Jeremiah's few prophecies of consolation. This prophecy teaches something vital about Jeremiah. Despite the horrors he foresaw and witnessed, he was not filled with pessimism, but rather was a loving idealist filled with hope. He never lost sight of why he was criticizing his society, and anticipated the day when his vision would be fulfilled. Jeremiah's eternal voice continues to call to us.

> Thus said the Lord: A cry is heard in Ramah—wailing, bitter weeping—Rachel weeping for her children. She refuses to be comforted for her children, who are gone. Thus said the Lord: restrain your voice from weeping, your eyes from shedding tears; for there is a reward for your labor—declares the Lord: They shall return from the enemy's land. (Jeremiah 31:15–16)

We read of Jeremiah's positive vision for the future specifically on the day the world is judged. Never despair—do not underestimate the potential for greatness within people. There always is an opportunity for a new beginning on the individual and societal levels.

One day, the voice of Jeremiah finally will be heard and will triumph. Rachel will stop crying inconsolably and beam with delight. "Truly, Ephraim is a dear son to Me, A child that is dandled! Whenever I have turned against him, My thoughts would dwell on him still. That is why My heart yearns for him; I will receive him back in love—declares the Lord" (Jeremiah 31:20).

SHABBAT TESHUVAH ("SHUVAH")

(Hosea 14:2–10; Micah 7:18–20;
Ashkenazim also add Joel 2:15–27)

This passage contains one of Hosea's prophecies regarding the relationship between God and Israel. See the discussion in the Haftarah of Vayetzei.

YOM KIPPUR MORNING

(Isaiah 57:14–58:14)

*T*his passage pertains to false worship by fasting on Yom Kippur but then living immorally. See the discussion in the Haftarah of Tzav.

—

YOM KIPPUR MINHAH

(Book of Jonah; Micah 7:18–20)

*T*he Book of Jonah is famous for its paradoxical relationship between prophet and God. Commentators often focus on Jonah's remarkably *un*-prophet like behavior. A prophet should know that he cannot flee from God.

Furthermore, it is ironic that the one fleeing and disobeying God makes a proclamation of faith in his first words recorded in the book: "I am a Hebrew, he replied. I worship the Lord, the God of Heaven, who made both sea and land" (Jonah 1:9). In fact, as the story progresses Jonah's faith in God looks less impressive than that of the pagan sailors. As a fierce storm rages overhead, the sailors pray and call out to their gods to save them. Jonah, by comparison, does nothing but sleep. He does not pray even when the captain of the ship begs him to do so. In this episode it is the captain who sounds like a prophet, while Jonah is a rebel against God.

These acts of rebellion continue even after Jonah finds himself inside the belly of a fish. The prophet expresses a longing to return to the Temple but never apologizes for his behavior. In fact, he continues to condemn pagans as unfaithful (2:9-10). How can a rebellious Jonah go on like this when he knows the sailors on the ship acted meritoriously and that the Ninevites would repent as soon as they were told to do so?

Abarbanel and Malbim (on Jonah 4:1–2) explain Jonah's puzzling behavior as follows: Jonah was outraged that the Ninevites remained pagan after they repented from their immorality. As far as Jonah was concerned, this should have been reason enough for God to destroy them. Jonah loved God and the directive to help the Ninevites undermined his sense of God's glory. He found the act of saving those who do not recognize God belittling and insulting.

The Book of Jonah teaches that God has no patience for human immorality but will tolerate those with misguided beliefs in the hope that they can be influenced and redirected to see the truth. Ironically, Jonah *did* influence these pagans. Although he was chagrined, pagan society gained from his reluctant efforts in that they improved their behavior and came closer to God—and thus avoided being destroyed.

(Adapted from Hayyim Angel, "'I Am a Hebrew!': Jonah's Conflict with God's Mercy Toward Even the Most Worthy of Pagans," *Jewish Bible Quarterly* 34:1 [2006], pp. 3–11; reprinted in Angel, *Through an Opaque Lens* [New York: Sephardic Publication Foundation, 2006], pp. 259–269).

FIRST DAY SUKKOT

(Zechariah 14:1–21)

SHABBAT HOL HA-MO'ED SUKKOT

(Ezekiel 38:18–39:16)

*S*ukkot is known as the "season of our joy." We celebrate God's protection in the desert, the temporary dwellings the Israelites used during that time, and also the fall harvest. Although the Torah associates joy with Sukkot, there is an element of fear as well. Farmers are apprehensive about the rainfall for the coming year. Too little or too much rain can destroy their crops.

To highlight this theme of fear, two of the Haftarot chosen for Sukkot present the unnerving theme of an attack against Israel by an international coalition of enemies. The passages describe the damage these forces will inflict and God's subsequent rescue and redemption of Israel. Furthermore, Israel's enemies will recognize God, bringing peace for everyone.

There is a gentler vision of universalism on Sukkot as well. In his *Horev*, Rabbi Samson Raphael Hirsch writes that the Sukkah is the antidote to the Tower of Babel. The people built the tower as an arrogant and futile attempt at permanence, whereas the Sukkah teaches us humility and about impermanence. The Sukkah also symbolizes absolute trust in God.

In Zechariah, chapter 14 (which we read on the first day of Sukkot), non-Jews will recognize God and celebrate Sukkot, the most universalistic of all holidays, as it largely reflects rainfall and harvest. Observing that the Torah mandates 70 offerings for the seven days of the holiday, the Sages remark that they were to atone for the sins of the 70 nations (*Sukkah* 55b). We atone for ourselves on Yom Kippur and then look outwardly by taking responsibility for the world.

A midrash describes our connection with humanity in terms of rain:

> Someone asked R. Yehoshua b. Hananiah, "On what day is the entire world equal, when all nations bow before God?" He replied, ". . . when the rains fall, all celebrate and extol God. . . ." R. Tanhum says, "Greater is rain than the giving of the Torah, for the Torah made [only] Israel happy, but rain brings joy to the entire world. . . ." (*Midrash Psalms* 117)

SECOND DAY SUKKOT

(I Kings 8:2–21)

SHEMINI HAG ATZERET

(I Kings 8:54–66)

*T*hese passages pertain to King Solomon's building of the Temple. See the discussion in the Haftarah of Terumah.

SIMHAT TORAH

(Sephardim read Joshua 1:1–9; Ashkenazim add 1:10–18)

*I*n the Book of Numbers, Moses appointed his attendant Joshua as one of the spies. Surprisingly, when most of the spies expressed fears that demoralized the people, Joshua initially remained silent, leaving it to Caleb to stick his neck out and exhort the people to have faith in God's promises (Numbers 13:30). Only later did Joshua join Caleb (Numbers 14:6–10).

Most commentators leave the interpretation of this enigma to a midrashic insight that describes how Moses changed Hosea's name to Joshua. In renaming him Joshua, Moses hoped to protect him from falling prey to the negative influences of the other spies (*Sotah* 34b). Did Moses have such little confidence in his faithful student?

Talmudic wisdom penetrates into the overall portrait of Joshua. Perhaps Joshua partially agreed with the fears of the spies. Another talmudic passage expresses a related concern: "The face of Moses was like the sun; the face of Joshua was like the moon" (*Bava Batra* 75a). Joshua was a weaker reflection of his master.

God and Moses repeatedly exhorted Joshua to be strong and courageous. Evidently, Joshua lacked confidence in his ability to lead the people and therefore needed encouragement. The Haftarah of Simhat Torah, then, ostensibly sets the stage for a letdown. Moses had died, and his successor Joshua was afraid he would fail as a leader.

Despite this trepidation, however, Joshua proved to be an exceptionally effective leader. In the Torah, the Israelites regularly complained to Moses. In contrast, the people never complained to Joshua. The Book of Joshua attests to the people's righteousness throughout his tenure.

Perhaps Joshua's fears during the episode with the spies helped the people relate to him. His insecurity and fear added a human element to their new leader previously unseen during Moses' tenure. Although Moses is likened to the sun while Joshua is compared only to the moon, one cannot look directly at the sun. In fact, Moses wore a veil to conceal the bright rays that emanated from his face. True, Moses was objectively greater, but Joshua was more approachable and therefore successful at inspiring the Israelites.

When Joshua was afraid, the people knew it. When he was confident, the people knew they could trust him. The Israelites saw in Joshua a role model who could elevate them to new spiritual levels and share in their collective religious experience (see further discussion in the Haftarah of the first day of Pesah).

(Adapted from Hayyim Angel, "Moonlit Leadership: A Midrashic Reading of Joshua's Success," *Jewish Bible Quarterly* 37:3 [2009], pp. 144–152; reprinted in Angel, *Creating Space Between Peshat and Derash: A Collection of Studies on Tanakh* [Jersey City, NJ: Ktav-Sephardic Publication Foundation, 2011], pp. 64–73.)

HANUKKAH (FIRST SHABBAT)

(Zechariah 2:14–4:7)

*A*long with his contemporary Haggai, Zechariah's prophetic career was dedicated to the rebuilding of the Second Temple in 520–516 BCE. A hallmark of Zechariah's prophetic message is a series of esoteric visions. Although these visions present manifestations of the heavenly sphere, they also contain practical guidance for Zechariah's generation. Whereas Haggai concerned himself primarily with the physical rebuilding of the Temple, Zechariah focused more on the religious-political structure of the community and its responsibilities.

In the Haftarah of the first Shabbat of Hanukkah (also read for Beha'alotekha), Zechariah sees a vision of the heavenly host. During the vision, he learns about the roles of the two leaders of his generation: Zerubbabel who descended from King David and was the political head of the Jews, and Joshua the High Priest.

Joshua's role is clearly defined. He needed to be purified and would then be enabled to bring purification to the entire community. In Zechariah's vision, the angel removed Joshua's filthy garments and replaced them with clean priestly garb.

However, Zerubbabel's role was amorphous: "Hearken well, O High Priest Joshua, you and your fellow priests sitting before you! For those men are a sign that I am going to bring My servant the Branch" (Zechariah 3:8). Many commentators understand that Zerubbabel had the potential to be this "Branch." He could end up the governor of a tiny state (which sadly is what happened), or he might become the "Branch" who brings redemption. This aspect is developed with greater nuance in chapter 4.

In Zechariah's vision in chapter 4, Zerubbabel and Joshua are represented by olive trees that supply oil for the lamp which represents God. The vision teaches that both leaders must work to provide fuel for God's Presence to dwell among the people.

Zechariah states: "This is the word of the Lord to Zerubbabel: Not by might, nor by power, but by My spirit—said the Lord of Hosts" (4:6). Mordechai Zer-Kavod (*Da'at Mikra: Zechariah*) explains that this verse contains practical advice to the community. If Zerubbabel had the potential to be the Branch/redeemer, perhaps he should lead a revolt against the Persian Empire. God responds that he should not. Let God handle the political redemption in this circumstance—while Zerubbabel joins Joshua in building the Temple and sustaining God's Presence with his service of God.

~

HANUKKAH (SECOND SHABBAT)

(I Kings 7:40–50)

*I*n *Festivals of Faith: Reflections on the Jewish Holidays*, Dr. Norman Lamm asks: Hanukkah celebrates the rededication of the Second Temple. Why, however, is there no holiday commemorating the initial building of the First Temple by King Solomon?

Dr. Lamm explains that when building something new, it is easy to get energized. Not so the decision to rebuild or restore something already in existence. Although King Solomon was the original builder of the Temple, the Maccabees are "rewarded" with a holiday because they rededicated the Temple. Such an act was far more prosaic and, therefore, we celebrate this spirit of achievement.

For the Haftarah of the second Shabbat of Hanukkah, we read an excerpt from the narrative of King Solomon's building of the Temple:

Hiram also made the lavers, the scrapers, and the sprinkling bowls. So Hiram finished all the work that he had been doing for King Solomon on the House of the Lord: the two columns, the two globes of the capitals upon the columns; and the two pieces of network to cover the two globes of the capitals upon the columns; the four hundred pomegranates for the two pieces of network, two rows of pomegranates for each network, to cover the two globes of the capitals upon the columns; the ten stands and the ten lavers upon the stands; the one tank with the twelve oxen underneath the tank. . .". (I Kings 7:40–44)

This and related passages are read as the Haftarot of Vayakhel and Pekudei, as well.

Dr. Lamm derives a further lesson from the two Haftarot of Hanukkah. When building something new, one needs to temper idealistic enthusiasm with realism. Therefore the Haftarah for the second Shabbat of Hanukkah—which describes King Solomon's construction of the First Temple—focuses on technical details. The poetry of religion is meaningless without rooting it in the hard work and details that form the foundations of religious life.

In contrast, when restoring something old, one needs to be reminded of the exciting ideals that initially served as the basis for the project. For this reason the Haftarah of the first Shabbat of Hanukkah derives from the Book of Zechariah, which describes the rebuilding of the Second Temple.

The two Haftarot of Hanukkah thus complement one another, teaching the differences between building something new and restoring and rededicating the old. Both are necessary ingredients to building an enduring religious vision and lifestyle.

SHEKALIM

(Sephardim read II Kings 11:17–12:17; Ashkenazim read 12:1–17)

The Haftarah of Shekalim pertains to King Joash's Temple-building fund. Although we have been reading this Haftarah for many centuries, it took on new significance in 2001, when archaeologists discovered an ancient document describing Joash's fund.

The wealth of archaeological finds over the past two centuries has shed much light on Tanakh. Through the study of real-life artifacts, linguistics, and geography, the legal and cultural setting of Tanakh, and a host of other issues have been clarified.

How did earlier generations of rabbis approach archaeological evidence they had available to them?

After his arrival in Israel toward the end of his life, Ramban discovered an ancient coin and ascertained that it clarified a rabbinic debate over the weight of a shekel: "The words of Rashi are supported [by this coin]" (Ramban on Exodus 30:13, *Torat Hayyim* edition). Ramban's response is telling. Archaeological evidence is valuable. However, Ramban considered the coin to be only useful as a "support" of Rashi's opinion. He did not believe that Rashi's view was proven conclusively on the basis of one coin.

Rambam used archaeological evidence more widely in his writings. He had access to documents of a pagan group called the Sabeans and used these documents to speculate on the rationales behind some of the mitzvot:

> If we knew the particulars of those practices and heard details of those opinions, we would become clear regarding the wisdom manifested in the details of the practices prescribed in the commandments concerning the sacrifices and the forms of uncleanness and other matters whose reason cannot, to my mind, be easily grasped. For I for one do not doubt that all this was intended to efface those untrue opinions from the mind and to abolish those useless practices, which brought about a waste of lives in vain and futile things. (*Guide for the Perplexed* III:49)

Based on his knowledge of Sabean documents, Rambam believed that the mitzvot we could not understand likely originated as legislation to wean Israel away from paganism.

Whether one accepts the more cautious approach of Ramban or the more embracing view of Rambam, we study Tanakh not as historians but as people confronting the living word of God. Beholding artifacts from the biblical period such as Joash's Temple fund document, we can feel the biblical world coming alive. It is a blessing that the earth has provided us with so many treasures from the past, enabling us to experience a different dimension of the world of prophecy.

ZAKHOR

(I Samuel 15:1–34)

*I*n the Haftarah of Zakhor, Saul forfeits his kingship by failing to annihilate the Amalekites. However, there is an apparent redundancy since Saul already was rejected from the monarchy for his failure to wait for the prophet Samuel before making sacrificial offerings:

> But Samuel said, "What have you done…. You acted foolishly in not keeping the commandments that the Lord your God laid upon you! Otherwise the Lord would have established your dynasty over Israel forever. But now your dynasty will not endure. The Lord will seek out a man after His own heart, and the Lord will appoint him ruler over His people, because you did not abide by what the Lord had commanded you." (I Samuel 13:11–14)

Radak suggests two resolutions: (1) In chapter 13 Saul lost his dynasty; in chapter 15 Saul himself was rejected. (2) Saul still had an opportunity to repent after chapter 13, but the decree against him was sealed irrevocably after chapter 15. However, if there were no chapter 15, chapter 13 would have been understood as a permanent rejection of Saul and his dynasty.

Perhaps the following can serve as a more likely resolution. Since God never speaks in chapter 13, and the objective narrator supports Saul, it is unclear if Samuel was conveying a received prophecy or if he was speaking on his own. This ambiguity may be contrasted with chapter 15, where God explicitly told Samuel that Saul had forfeited the kingship (15:10–11). It is possible that Saul *really* lost the monarchy only after God's rejection in chapter 15 but believed that he had lost it already with Samuel's rejection in chapter 13.

This dichotomy between God's will and Samuel's also may be manifest regarding whether God can change His mind. When speaking to Saul, Samuel insisted that God does not change His mind (15:29). How does this declaration jibe with the words of God (15:11) and the narrator (15:35), where God *does* regret having appointed Saul (the same Hebrew root for regret, n-h-m, is used in all three instances)? This contradiction again may blur the boundaries between what God says and Samuel's personal views.

This passage illustrates the divide between the objective word of God and the interpretation that even one of the greatest prophets—Samuel— could inject into understanding the word of God.

(Adapted from Hayyim Angel, "'I Am the Seer': Objective and Subjective Elements of Samuel's Relationship to Saul and the Monarchy in I Samuel 8–16," *Milin Havivin: Beloved Words* 4 (2008–2010), pp. 6–18; reprinted in Angel, *Creating Space Between Peshat and Derash: A Collection of Studies on Tanakh* [Jersey City, NJ: Ktav-Sephardic Publication Foundation, 2011], pp. 84–96.)

PARAH

(Sephardim read Ezekiel 36:16–36;
Ashkenazim continue reading to v. 38)

This passage pertains to Ezekiel's vision of the restoration after the destruction of the First Temple. It is connected to Ezekiel, chapter 20. See the discussion in the Haftarah of Kedoshim for Sephardim.

HA-HODESH

(Sephardim read Ezekiel 45:18–46:15;
Ashkenazim read Ezekiel 45:16–46:18)

This passage pertains to Ezekiel's vision of the future Temple (Ezekiel, chapters 40–48). See the discussion in the Haftarah of Emor.

SHABBAT HA-GADOL

(Malachi 3:4–24)

*A*ccording to tradition, Malachi was the last prophet. Why did prophecy cease? Some sources suggest that the loss of prophecy was a punishment for sin. *Avot D'Rabbi Nathan* B:47 explains that prophecy ceased as a consequence of people mocking the prophets. Radak (on Haggai 2:5) suggests more generally that lack of fidelity to the Torah resulted in the loss of prophecy. A midrash (*Pesikta Rabbati* 35) states that many Jews failed to return to the Land of Israel after Cyrus gave them permission, and therefore prophecy ceased.

Ezekiel chapters 8–10 describe a vision wherein God shows the prophet the rampant idolatry in Jerusalem. God abandons the Temple and goes into "exile" by no longer conveying prophecies. Radak (on Ezekiel 9:3) explains that the absence of God's Presence at the time of the destruction of the First Temple ultimately contributed to the disappearance of prophecy.

Although the disappearance of prophecy was terrible, several commentators also suggest positive consequences to the transition away from prophecy. *Seder Olam Rabbah* 30 states that prophecy ceased in the time of Alexander the Great. Based on the rabbinic chronology, the Greek Empire began immediately following the biblical period, so this time frame would synchronize with Malachi. Following this chronological assumption, Rabbi Zadok HaKohen of Lublin (1823–1900) observed that a metaphysical transition to an age of reason occurred in Israel and in Greece at the same time. The development of the Oral Law was contemporaneous with the rise of the great Greek philosophers (*Resisei Laylah*, 81b).

This idea meshes with a talmudic statement that at the beginning of the Second Temple period, the temptation for idolatry ceased being the force it had been during the First Temple period (*Yoma* 69b). Rabbi Yehudah he-Hasid argued that once the urge for idolatry vanished there no longer existed the need for prophecy to counterbalance idolatry (*Sefer Hasidim*). Instead, we rely on our sacred texts and traditions to carry on the lessons taught by the prophets.

Rabbi Eliyahu Dessler suggests that prophecy and idolatry were opposite poles of a spiritual intense era that counterbalanced one another. Once the urge to idolatry had declined, prophetic revelation would have too much power if left unchecked, and people would be compelled to listen to God based on its force. To preserve free will, prophecy had to cease as well (*Mikhtav me-Eliyahu* III).

(Adapted from Hayyim Angel, "The End of Prophecy: Malachi's Position in the Spiritual Development of Israel," *Conversations* 9 [Winter 2011], pp. 112–118; reprinted in Angel, *Creating Space Between Peshat and Derash: A Collection of Studies on Tanakh* [Jersey City, NJ: Ktav-Sephardic Publication Foundation, 2011], pp. 146–153.)

FIRST DAY PESAH

(Joshua 5:2–6:1, 6:27)

*M*albim (on Exodus 3:5) contrasts the parallel scenes between Moses at the Burning Bush and Joshua with the angelic commander outside of Jericho:

And He said, "Do not come closer. Remove your sandals [*na'alekha*] from your feet, for the place on which you stand is holy ground." (Exodus 3:5)

The captain of the Lord's host answered Joshua, "Remove your sandals [*na'alkha*] from your feet, for the place where you stand is holy." And Joshua did so. (Joshua 5:15)

Standing on holy ground, both prophets were commanded to remove their sandals for their respective revelations. However, Malbim observes that in the Hebrew, Moses was commanded "*shal na'alekha* (the plural form for "sandals") *me'al raglekha*," whereas the commander ordered Joshua, "*shal na'alkha* (the singular form for "sandal") *me'al raglekha*." Malbim offers a midrashic-conceptual interpretation.

Shoes symbolize human involvement in the world. Jews are required to remove their shoes while in the Temple precincts and also on Yom Kippur to elevate themselves to the level of angels. At the other end of the spectrum, mourners remove their shoes as a sign of their debasement.

Having reached the most exalted level of revelation, Moses was completely elevated to the realm of the metaphysical in his prophecy. Therefore, he was ordered to remove both sandals. In contrast, Joshua removed only one sandal while leaving the other on. In this manner, he entered the metaphysical realm through prophecy but simultaneously remained rooted in this world.

Malbim's analysis of Joshua's "one sandal on, one sandal off" leadership captures Joshua's relationship to Moses and to the people. He had one foot in Moses' ideal world of prophecy, but at the same time kept the other with his people.

Joshua's unique combination of Moses' prophetic faith and the people's fears diminished his objective greatness in relation to Moses. His prophecy did not reach the level of Moses'. These shortcomings, however, enabled Joshua to succeed as a leader in a manner that even his master could not. Precisely these weaknesses engendered additional trust among the people. As a result, Joshua was able to bring Moses' teachings to the people, guiding a stiff-necked and rebellious people to unrivaled faithfulness as they entered the Promised Land (see further discussion in the Haftarah of Simhat Torah).

(Adapted from Hayyim Angel, "Moonlit Leadership: A Midrashic Reading of Joshua's Success," *Jewish Bible Quarterly* 37 [2009], pp. 144–152; reprinted in Angel, *Creating Space Between Peshat and Derash: A Collection of Studies on Tanakh* [Jersey City, NJ: Ktav-Sephardic Publication Foundation, 2011], pp. 64–73.)

SECOND DAY PESAH

(II Kings 23:1–9, 21–25)

Josiah (640–609 BCE) was the last righteous king in biblical history. Galvanized by the finding of a Torah scroll in the Temple precincts, he embarked on an unprecedented reformation to eradicate the idolatry that had become rampant during the reign of his wicked grandfather Manasseh. The Book of Kings underscores Josiah's unique stature by noting that he had been prophetically anticipated centuries before his birth, during the reign of Jeroboam son of Nebat (I Kings 13:2).

Unfortunately, Huldah the prophetess had informed Josiah of the sealed decree prior to his reformation (II Kings 22:15–20), and the narrative concludes that even Josiah's superior efforts could not reverse the damage of Manasseh:

> However, the Lord did not turn away from His awesome wrath that had blazed up against Judah because of all the things Manasseh did to vex Him. The Lord said, I will also banish Judah from My presence as I banished Israel; and I will reject the city of Jerusalem which I chose and the House where I said My name would abide. (II Kings 23:26–27)

Despite being told that he could not save the country from the impending destruction, Josiah did everything he could to restore the kingdom to the worship of God. The Book of Kings praises him in an unprecedented manner: "There was no king like him before who turned back to the Lord with all his heart and soul and might, in full accord with the Torah of Moses; nor did any like him arise after him" (II Kings 23:25).

Thus Josiah fulfilled the ideal set out in the Shema: "You shall love the Lord your God with all your heart and with all your soul and with all your might" (Deuteronomy 6:5). He is the only figure in biblical history who receives such praise.

As remarkable as Josiah's Reformation was in itself, it became even more admirable when he proceeded apace even with the knowledge of the impending destruction. Not expecting any concrete results, Josiah wanted his nation to serve God because it was correct to do so. He thus exemplified serving God with all his heart, soul, and might.

SHABBAT HOL HA-MO'ED PESAH

(Ezekiel 37:1–14)

*T*his passage pertains to Ezekiel's vision of the restoration after the destruction of the First Temple (Ezekiel, chapters 34–37). See the discussion in the Haftarah of Vayigash.

—

SEVENTH DAY PESAH

(II Samuel 22:1–51)

*W*e also read this Haftarah for Ha'azinu. See the discussion there.

—

EIGHTH DAY PESAH

(Isaiah 10:32–12:6)

*T*he prophets perceived a deeper beauty in the exodus from Egypt: It was the beginning of a marriage between God and the people of Israel. As expressed by Jeremiah: "I accounted to your favor the devotion of your youth, your love as a bride—how you followed Me in the wilderness, in a land not sown" (Jeremiah 2:2).

In post-talmudic times, the practice arose in many Jewish communities to read the Song of Songs on Pesah. The Song of Songs captures some of the most tender expressions of love in human literature. The Sages interpreted the Song as a reflection of the passionate love between God and Israel. On one level, then, Pesah reflects divine love.

One of the most painful of human anguishes is the broken heart. Imagine divine love being rejected! First, humanity failed: the Tree of Knowledge, Cain murdering Abel, the Flood, and the Tower of Babel. Then, Israel failed: the Golden Calf, and a history of apostasy and immorality until the destruction of the Temple and exile.

On the eighth day of Pesah, we read Isaiah's celebrated vision of a messianic king who will herald an age of morality and justice. There will be harmony in nature as there had been in the Garden of Eden. Oppressed and scattered for so long, Jewish exiles will return to Israel and live in harmony with one another. The people also will compose hymns expressing their love of God. The loving relationship will be mutual. God eternally waits for Israel to be worthy of true love despite so many setbacks.

Is it possible to have a new love as great as the first love, when everything could have been perfect? Jeremiah—the prophet at the time of the destruction of the First Temple— poignantly answers this question. When the redemption comes, it will *eclipse* the original exodus, and became the new point of reference when praising God:

> Assuredly, a time is coming—declares the Lord—when it shall no more be said, "As the Lord lives who brought the Israelites out of the land of Egypt,' but rather, 'As the Lord lives who brought the Israelites out of the northland, and out of all the lands to which He had banished them." For I will bring them back to their land, which I gave to their fathers." (Jeremiah 16:14–15)

It is in no small part thanks to the prophetic visions of love and hope that the Jewish people has survived through so many trials, and will continue to do so forever.

FIRST DAY SHAVUOT

(Ezekiel 1:1–28, 3:12)

*E*very year, we read the Ten Commandments three times in our Torah-reading cycle: Yitro, the first day of Shavuot, and Vaethannan. The creators of the Haftarah liturgy selected three different Haftarot for the three occasions.

For Yitro and Shavuot, they selected two of the most exalted visions of God and the heavenly host in prophetic literature: Isaiah, chapter 6 and Ezekiel, chapter 1. Isaiah's description of God on His throne is brief. In contrast, Ezekiel devotes an entire chapter to his vision of the Celestial Chariot. Although the two visions sound different in description and length, one Sage posits that they saw the same thing. Isaiah described his vision briefly because he was from the city, whereas Ezekiel elaborated because he was a villager (*Hagigah* 13b). Later commentators explore the meanings of being from the city versus being from a village.

Tosafot and Rambam interpret this talmudic passage with respect to audience credibility. Living in Jerusalem (the "city") in times of relative peace and widespread prophecy, Isaiah did not need to convince his audience that he had received this vision and therefore related it more tersely. In contrast, Ezekiel lived in Babylonia (away from the "city" of Jerusalem), and therefore spoke at length to convince his audience that he had indeed received prophetic revelation.

Alternatively, Rambam suggests that Isaiah had attained a higher level of prophetic experience, and therefore was less overwhelmed than Ezekiel. Consequently, he described his prophecy more briefly than did Ezekiel. Rashi submits that the cosmopolitan Isaiah was familiar with human kings, and therefore was less shocked to perceive the King of kings. Ezekiel, on the other hand, lived away from human kings. Therefore, he was completely overwhelmed by his encounter with the King of kings. From this perspective, history and personal experience color a prophet's vision in ways he does not even perceive.

No two people can perceive God in the same way. Our diverse personalities, levels of spiritual preparedness, experiences, and societal influences all impact on our perception of God. And yet, we all come together to pray to the same God and study the same Torah.

There is a blessing we recite on seeing throngs of Jews, *Barukh Hakham ha-razim*: Blessed is God, Who wisely knows the secrets of diverse people. No two people can share the identical religious outlook. At the same time, however, we share the same collective memory and destiny, which unite us as religious community.

~

SECOND DAY SHAVUOT

(Habakkuk 2:20–3:19)

*H*abakkuk lived in the seventh century BCE and prophesied the Babylonian invasion. Habakkuk could not understand God's plan. Rather than supporting any lessons of divine justice, Habakkuk feared that the success of a tyrannical nation would cause Torah to erode even further since people would conclude that the world is unfair:

> How long, O Lord, shall I cry out and You not listen, shall I shout to You, Violence! And You not save? Why do You make me see iniquity [why] do You look upon wrong?—raiding and violence are before me, strife continues and contention goes on. That is why decision fails and justice never emerges; for the villain hedges in the just man—therefore judgment emerges deformed. (Habakkuk 1:2–4)

It was unthinkable to Ibn Ezra that a prophet would speak to God so brazenly. His answer: Habakkuk is quoting other Jews living in his time. Most commentators reject this artificially imposed speaker. The majority view is that indeed Habakkuk criticizes God: He opens with a strong protest, and God responds. Habakkuk has done nothing wrong at all.

The conclusion of Habakkuk's beautiful psalm captures the tension of the prophet's experience: "I heard and my bowels quaked, my lips quivered at the sound; rot entered into my bone, I trembled where I stood. Yet I wait calmly for the day of distress, for a people to come to attack us…Yet will I rejoice in the Lord, exult in the God who delivers me. My Lord God is my strength" (3:16–18).

Habakkuk struggles with his theological problems, but rejoices in God. The conclusion of this psalm is a tribute to prophetic honesty—profound religiosity and full confrontation with God.

One ideal of the Torah is the great bliss of Ezekiel in his exalted vision. Another is the confrontation with God represented by Habakkuk. Both are aspects of what it means to receive the Torah. It therefore is fitting that Jews outside of Israel read from Ezekiel and Habakkuk on the two days of Shavuot, so that we may embrace both aspects of religious experience.

FAST DAYS MINHAH (ASHKENAZIM)
(Isaiah 55:6–56:8)

This passage pertains to the universalistic messages in the Book of Isaiah. See the discussion in the Haftarah of Rosh Hodesh.

TISHA B'AV MORNING

(Jeremiah 8:13–9:23)

This passage contains one of Jeremiah's prophecies regarding the destruction of the Temple as correlated to Israel's unfaithfulness. See the discussion in the Haftarah of Behukkotai.

TISHA B'AV MINHAH (Sephardim)

(Hosea 14:2–10; Micah 7:18–20)

This passage contains one of Hosea's prophecies regarding the relationship between God and Israel. See the discussion in the Haftarah of Vayetzei.

SELECTED BIBLIOGRAPHY:

HAFTAROT

Hayyim Angel, *Vision from the Prophet and Counsel from the Elders: A Survey of Nevi'im and Ketuvim* (New York: OU Press, 2013).

Hayyim Angel, "Moonlit Leadership: A Midrashic Reading of Joshua's Success," *Jewish Bible Quarterly* 37:3 (2009), pp. 144–152; reprinted in Angel, *Creating Space Between Peshat and Derash: A Collection of Studies on Tanakh* (Jersey City, NJ: Ktav-Sephardic Publication Foundation, 2011), pp. 64–73.

Hayyim Angel, "'I Am the Seer': Objective and Subjective Elements of Samuel's Relationship to Saul and the Monarchy in I Samuel 8–16," *Milin Havivin: Beloved Words* 4 (2008–2010), pp. 6–18; reprinted in Angel, *Creating Space Between Peshat and Derash: A Collection of Studies on Tanakh* (Jersey City, NJ: Ktav-Sephardic Publication Foundation, 2011), pp. 84–96.

Hayyim Angel, "When Love and Politics Mix: David and his Relationships with Saul, Jonathan, and Michal," *Jewish Bible Quarterly* 40:1 2012), pp. 41–51.

Hayyim Angel, "Cut the Baby in Half: Understanding Solomon's Divine Wisdom," *Jewish Bible Quarterly* 39:3 (2011), pp. 189–194.

Hayyim Angel, "Through an Opaque Lens: Non-Moshe Prophecy and Some Religious Implications," in Angel, *Through an Opaque Lens* (New York: Sephardic Publication Foundation, 2006), pp. 15–20.

Hayyim Angel, "Prophecy as Potential: The Consolations of Isaiah 1–12 in Context," *Jewish Bible Quarterly* 37:1 (2009), pp. 3–10; reprinted in Angel, *Revealed Texts, Hidden Meanings: Finding the Religious Significance in Tanakh* (Jersey City, NJ: Ktav-Sephardic Publication Foundation, 2009), pp. 117–126.

Hayyim Angel, "Jeremiah's Confrontation with the Religious Establishment: A Man of Truth in a World of Falsehood," in *Revealed Texts, Hidden Meanings: Finding the Religious Significance in Tanakh* (Jersey City, NJ: Ktav-Sephardic Publication Foundation, 2009), pp. 127–138.

Hayyim Angel, "'I Am a Hebrew!': Jonah's Conflict with God's Mercy Toward Even the Most Worthy of Pagans," *Jewish Bible Quarterly* 34:1 (2006), pp. 3–11; reprinted in Angel, *Through an Opaque Lens* (New York: Sephardic Publication Foundation, 2006), pp. 259–269.

Hayyim Angel, "God Insists on Truth: Rabbinic Evaluations of Two Audacious Biblical Prayers," *Jewish Bible Quarterly* 38:1 (2010), pp. 3–9; reprinted in Angel, *Creating Space Between Peshat and Derash: A Collection of Studies on Tanakh* (Jersey City, NJ: Ktav-Sephardic Publication Foundation, 2011), pp. 154–162.

Hayyim Angel, "The End of Prophecy: Malachi's Position in the Spiritual Development of Israel," *Conversations* 9 (Winter 2011), pp. 112–118; reprinted in Angel, *Creating Space Between Peshat and Derash* (Jersey City, NJ: Ktav-Sephardic Publication Foundation, 2011), pp. 146–153.

Hayyim Angel, "For He Is a Messenger of God: Malakhi's Prophecies to a Despairing People," in *Mitokh Ha-Ohel: From Within the Tent: The Haftarot*, ed. Daniel Z. Feldman & Stuart W. Halpern (New York: Yeshiva University Press, 2011), pp. 49–58.

Philip S. Alexander, "'A Sixtieth Part of Prophecy': The Problem of Continuing Revelation in Judaism," in *Words Remembered, Texts Renewed: Essays in Honor of John F. A. Sawyer*, ed. Jon Davies et al. (*JSOT Supp* 195, 1995), pp. 414–433.

Rabbi Yehoshua Bachrach, *Yonah ben Amitai ve-Eliyahu: Teaching the Book of Jonah According to Traditional Sources* (Hebrew) (Jerusalem: The Religious Department of the Youth and Pioneering Division of the Zionist Organization, 1967).

Umberto Cassuto, "Epic Poetry in Israel" (Hebrew), in *Biblical and Canaanite Literatures*, vol. 1 (Jerusalem: Magnes Press, 1983), pp. 62–90.

Yaakov Elman, "R. Zadok HaKohen on the History of Halakha," *Tradition* 21:4 (Fall 1985), pp. 1–26.

Rabbi Norman Lamm, *Festivals of Faith: Reflections on the Jewish Holidays* (New York: OU Press, 2011), pp. 174–178.

Rabbi Bezalel Naor, *Lights of Prophecy* (New York: Union of Orthodox Congregations, 1990).

David Neiman, "Sefarad: The Name of Spain," *Journal of Near Eastern Studies* 22 (1963), pp. 128–132.

James B. Pritchard, *Ancient Near Eastern Texts Relating to the Old Testament* (Princeton, N.J.: Princeton University Press, 1969).

Rabbi Elhanan Samet, *Pirkei Eliyahu* (Hebrew) (Jerusalem: Ma'aliyot, 2003).

Rabbi Elhanan Samet, *Pirkei Elisha* (Hebrew) (Jerusalem: Ma'aliyot, 2007), pp. 281–284.

Rabbi Moshe Sokolow, "Esav: From Edom to Rome," in *Mitokh Ha-Ohel: From Within the Tent: The Haftarot*, ed. Daniel Z. Feldman & Stuart W. Halpern (New York: Yeshiva University Press, 2011), pp. 65–77.

COMMENTARIES ON THE HAFTAROT

Michael Fishbane, *Haftarot: The Traditional Hebrew Text with the New JPS Translation* (Philadelphia: Jewish Publication Society, 2002).

Dr. Joseph H. Hertz, *The Pentateuch and Haftorahs: Hebrew Text, English Translation and Commentary* (New York: Metzudah, 1941).

Rabbi Mendel Hirsch, *Commentary on the Haftarot*, originally published in German in 1896, translated into English in 1966 by Isaac Levy, and into Hebrew in 1996 by Yitzhak Moshe Fridman.

Feivel Meltzer, *Parashat ha-Shavua ve-Haftaratah* (Hebrew) (Jerusalem: Kiryat Sefer, 1971).

Rabbi Yehuda Shaviv, *Ben Haftarah le-Parashah: Al ha-Kesharim ben ha-Haftarot le-Parashot ha-Shavua u-le Mo'adei ha-Shanah* (Hebrew) (Jerusalem: Reuven Mass, 2000).

Hayyim Angel, Review Essay: "*Ben Haftara le-Parasha*: A Glimpse into the World of Prophetic *Derush*," *Tradition* 35:4 (Winter 2001), pp. 74–87; reprinted in Angel, *Through an Opaque Lens* (New York: Sephardic Publication Foundation, 2006), pp. 77–94.

Rabbi Yissakhar Yaakovson *Hazon ha-Mikra* (Hebrew) (Tel Aviv: Sinai Publishing, 1957–1959).

ABOUT THE ORIGINS OF HAFTAROT

Rabbi Shalom Carmy, "Polyphonic Diversity and Military Music," *Tradition* 34:4 (Winter 2000), pp. 6–32.

Shlomo Katz, *The Haftarah: Laws, Customs, and History* (Silver Spring, MD: Hamaayan/The Torah Spring, 2000).

Shemuel ha-Kohen Weingarten, "The Origin of *Haftarot*: When Were They Instituted?" (Hebrew), *Sinai* 83 (1978), pp. 105–136.

Encyclopaedia Talmudit, vol. 10, pp. 1–32, s.v. *Haftarah*.

Tefillah
תפילה
Prayer

נוֹשְׂאִים
בִּתְפִילָה

Topics in
Prayer

KNOW BEFORE WHOM YOU STAND

*M*any synagogues use the talmudic expression, *da lifnei mi attah omed:* Know before Whom you stand (*Berakhot* 28b), to grace their Arks. Rambam (*Hil. Tefillah*, 4:16) writes that one must have proper intention when praying: "What is proper intention of the heart? One should remove his [other] thoughts from his heart and view himself as if he is standing before the Divine Presence."

The requirement to stand for the Amidah (literally "the standing prayer") led to its name. "Amidah" has become synonymous with prayer. In Tanakh, by contrast, there are over 100 references to prostration. "To prostrate" took on the connotation of prayer, and the word *berakhah* (blessing) may derive from *berekh*, the Hebrew word for knee, as prayer was assumed to be done in a kneeling or prostrate position.

In the biblical period, one respectfully prostrated oneself before kings and nobles. In the rabbinic period, in contrast, people rose in the presence of people of stature, such as rabbinic Sages and government officials. Similarly, the Sages ruled that when we recite the Amidah we are in God's presence and therefore must stand. *Sanhedrin* 22a remarks that one who prays is supposed to imagine that he or she is standing in the Holy of Holies and addressing God. And in *Yoma* 53b, we learn that as we conclude the Amidah, we bow to the left and then the right, as though we are backing away from God sitting on His throne.

Moreover, one may not sit within four cubits of someone else who is saying the Amidah, the central prayer where one symbolically stands before God (*Berakhot* 31b). Rabbi Menahem HaMeiri (thirteenth-century Provence) understood this ruling as teaching good manners. Sitting may distract the person who is praying. However, why would that person be less distracted by someone *standing* nearby? Therefore, Rabbi Zedekiah ben Abraham Anav (thirteenth-century Italy) in his *Shibbolei ha-Leket* quotes Rabbi Hai Gaon (tenth-century Babylonia), who explains that one may not sit in close proximity of one reciting the Amidah, as this now has become a place of God's presence. This attitude sets the proper tone of reverence and concentration during prayer.

Uri Ehrlich, "'When You Pray Know Before Whom You Are Standing' (bBer. 28b)," *Journal of Jewish Studies* 49 (1998), pp. 38–50.

————

PRAYER IN SYNAGOGUE

*A*fter the destruction of the Second Temple, synagogues became the primary centers for Jewish religious life. A new emphasis on communal prayer arose, and prayers generally were formulated with first-person plural pronouns, such as *we* and *our*, rather than *I* and *my* (*Berakhot* 29b–30a). Public prayer is less self-centered, and unites participants into a community. Even if we do not have a particular need, praying in the collective makes us conscious of the needs of others.

Jewish law favors praying in synagogue rather than in private, as individuals. Rabbi Moshe Feinstein (*Iggerot Moshe, Orah Hayyim* 3:7) ruled that even if someone is confident that he can pray with greater intention when he prays alone, it is still preferable to pray with a minyan (quorum of at least 10 Jewish males above the age of 13). If one cannot attend synagogue services, one should try to pray at the same time that the congregation is praying to retain a connection to the prayers of the community.

In a more philosophical-poetic vein, Professor Abraham Joshua Heschel wrote that it is too great a responsibility to pray without the support of a community: "It is not safe to pray alone. . . . Our share in holiness we acquire by living in the Jewish community. What we do as individuals is a trivial episode; what we attain as Israel causes us to become a part of eternity" (*Between God and Man*, pp. 209–210).

One of the most impressive aspects of communal prayer is the sanctity of the synagogue. *People* make a place holy by praying there regularly. In order to recite prayers such as Kaddish, Barekhu, and the repetition of the Amidah, a minyan is required (*Megillah* 23b). A minyan represents a community. Those prayers designated as requiring a minyan because of their sanctity are actually attempting to uncover and, in a sense, create holiness. The Kaddish begins, "May His great name be sanctified and magnified." God's name can be made greater in the presence of a community.

THE HAZZAN-SHELI'AH TZIBBUR

*I*n the Temple, the Kohanim (priests) led the rituals, and the Levites sang in a choir. People generally stood passively and watched the service. When synagogue prayer was instituted, the Sages also instituted laws for the leader of services, the *sheli'ah tzibbur*.

The *sheli'ah tzibbur* bears more of a resemblance to the prophets, who occasionally led their communities in prayer (see, for example, Jeremiah chapter 14; Joel chapter 2). The *sheli'ah tzibbur* serves as the representative of the community, rather than its functionary. We pray together. Our service is filled with antiphonal responses, reflective of our shared communal prayer relationship. The only time the Hazzan-*sheli'ah tzibbur* addresses the congregation as "you" (as opposed speaking together with them as "we")—thereby distancing himself from the crowd—is at the beginning of statutory prayer morning and evening, *barekhu et A-donai hamevorakh*. This is an invitation: Let us pray together.

It is critical to recognize the role of the Hazzan-*sheli'ah tzibbur* in a synagogue setting. The prayer services are not intended as a show, but rather a mutual prayer experience where everyone participates. The Hazzan leads as one designated by the others, rather than praying or singing on everyone's behalf.

Gerald Blidstein, "*Sheliach Tzibbur*: Historical and Phenomenological Observations," *Tradition* 12:1 (Summer 1971), pp. 69–77.

Abraham Joshua Heschel, "The Vocation of the Cantor," in *The Insecurity of Freedom* (New York: Noonday Press, 1967), pp. 242–253.

THE CHALLENGES OF PRAYER

*E*ven for those of us who attend synagogue services regularly, there are a number of impediments to prayer.

For many, the Hebrew language is a barrier. Despite the fact that Jewish law permits prayer in any language one understands, our public prayers are recited in Hebrew. Although thanking God can be understood as an expression of good manners and gratitude, what do words of praise and petition actually achieve? Furthermore, many of the concepts in our prayer book seem far removed from our experience.

Modernity favors personal autonomy and spontaneity. Halakhah (Jewish Law) often is resisted by the modern mind because it instructs us on how we should pray. We pray from a fixed text, and recite the same prayers whether at times of great joy or when we are beset by crisis.

For many, analysis is more stimulating than prayer, making Torah study a more natural religious encounter.

Even though we may confront different challenges than did earlier generations, our struggle to attain religious devotion is hardly a uniquely modern problem. Let us consider one remarkable passage from the Jerusalem Talmud (*Berakhot* 2:4, 16a):

> R. Hiyya said, "I never concentrated during prayer in all my days! Once I wanted to concentrate, but I thought about who will meet the king first: [a Persian high official] or the Exilarch." Shemuel said, "I count chicks." R. Bun b. Hiyya said, "I count bricks." R. Matnaya said, "I am grateful to my head, because it bows by itself when I reach Modim.

One commentary entitled *Toledot Yitzhak* (by Rabbi Yitzhak Karo, the brother of Rabbi Yosef Karo) explains that the Talmud includes this discussion to remind us that even the greatest Sages struggled with the issue of proper intention and focus during prayer. Their struggle should inspire us to try vigilantly to improve our focus, and not to despair when we find prayer difficult.

In addition to our efforts, we need God's help. We begin each Amidah with the introductory petition: "O Lord, open my lips, that my mouth may declare Your praise" (Psalms 51:17). We pray to God to enable us to pray!

Once we recognize some of the inherent challenges in prayer, we can begin to address those challenges and enhance our ability to pray.

THE FIXED PRAYER SERVICE

*T*he prayer book is an anthology of sacred texts, which includes passages from the Torah, later books of the Bible incorporated in the Prophets and the Holy Writings, Mishnah, Talmud, the medieval period, sixteenth-century mystical traditions—all the way to prayers for the modern State of Israel. When we pray, we transcend time by seamlessly moving through a set order of prayers.

The first written prayer book on record was composed by Rabbi Amram Gaon (c. 875, Babylonia) as a response to a request from Jews in Spain to elucidate the proper order of the prayers. Since then, many editions of the prayer book have been published. The prayer book represents a fixed ritual, operating under several widely held principles. Go to any synagogue in the world that is faithful to tradition, and the underlying structure of the services is essentially the same.

The Sages of the Talmud insisted that all Jews should follow their prescribed prayer formulations. Simultaneously, however, they warned against making prayer overly routinized, as it should be true worship of the heart: "From where do we derive prayer? As it says in a Baraita: 'To love the Lord your God and to worship Him with all your heart' (Deuteronomy 11:13)—what is worship of the heart? This is prayer" (*Ta'anit* 2b).

Although prayer should contain a spontaneous element, there are advantages to having a fixed text. Rabbi Marc D. Angel observes that "there is a profundity about this kind of prayer. We recognize our limitations. Whatever we say is inadequate. We cannot have confidence in our own abilities to generate proper prayers." Furthermore, a fixed liturgy links us with all communities everywhere and across time. Without a fixed text, we would have lost our shared identity long ago (*Seeking Good, Speaking Peace*, 1994, pp. 40–42).

A fixed text allows us to enter a meditative state precisely because it is familiar. Additionally, though the text may remain constant, it speaks to us differently every day, since *we* are different. Finally, the Talmud and later rabbinic traditions encourage us to add our own personal prayers to each Amidah, and at any time throughout the day. By maintaining a fixed structure of the prayer service, we gain confidence in the words we say as they have the weight of tradition behind them. Simultaneously, we do not fully relinquish our personal dialogue with God, since we may add our own words to our prayers.

The Talmud strikes this balance:

> Rabbi Eliezer says: Whoever makes his prayer a fixed task (*keva*), his prayers are not supplications. What is meant by "a fixed task"? Rabbi Yaakov son of Idi said in the name of Rabbi Oshaya: Anyone whose prayer is like a heavy burden upon him. The rabbis say: Whoever does not say it in the manner of supplication. Rabba and Rav Yosef both say: Whoever is not able to insert something fresh into it. (*Berakhot* 29b)

PETITION AND PRAISE

One of the great debates over prayer concerns the source of the mitzvah. Rambam (Maimonides) was the first to rule that there is a Torah commandment to pray daily. Ramban (Nahmanides) disagreed, insisting that the Torah obligation to pray applies only in times of acute distress. However, the obligation of daily prayer is rabbinic in origin. In a novel interpretation, Rabbi Joseph Soloveitchik proposed that Rambam actually agrees with Ramban that what obligates one to pray is the sense of distress. According to Rambam, however, *every* day is a time of existential distress.

For Rabbi Soloveitchik, then, the defining characteristic of prayer is crying out from distress. The focus of prayer is the middle section of the daily Amidah: the petition. We request the fulfillment of our needs, spiritual as well as material. Although prayer also includes praise and thanksgiving, the power and vitality of prayer lies in petition. Only in that way can a person truly serve God with his or her entire being:

> The aim of worship of the heart is the offering of sacrifice through the total surrender of body and soul to God...The hymn, embroidered with aesthetic experience is confined to the private domain of the elite. It is pleasing only to mystics, who are characteristically anti-social... Halakhah cannot be confined within the domain of spiritual nobility. Only petition can bring prayer to the public domain. (*Worship of the Heart*, p. 174)

In contrast, Professor Abraham Joshua Heschel believed that the primary purpose of prayer is to transcend oneself. Praise is the only selfless component of prayer, reflecting the pure joy of being in a relationship with God. In contrast, the petition and thanksgiving aspects of prayer focus more on our personal needs, and therefore are less ideal, according to Prof. Heschel.

Rabbi Soloveitchik vigorously rejected that argumentation, and insisted that petition, rather than praise, represents the central aspect of prayer. In the Talmud (*Berakhot* 32a), "Rabbi Simlai expounded: One should always first recount the praise of the Holy One, blessed be He, and then pray." In this passage, it is clear that "prayer" refers to petition. We transcend ourselves not by being selfless and only praising God, but precisely by attempting to present our true selves with all our needs before God and pray from a full heart.

David Hartman, "Prayer and Religious Consciousness: An Analysis of Jewish Prayer in the Works of Joseph B. Soloveitchik, Yeshayahu Leibowitz, and Abraham Joshua Heschel," *Modern Judaism* 23 (2003), pp. 105–125.

THE PARADOX OF PRAYER

*T*here is a paradox inherent in prayer: Do we really hope to influence God? God knows what we lack without our needing to inform Him. Moreover, God will not necessarily respond to our petitions, and certainly does not need our words of praise.

A rationalist would say that we cannot influence God at all; prayer is primarily intended to remind us of our complete reliance on God. A kabbalist would say that God allows human prayer to change the course of events. Many biblical narratives give this impression as well, as God often responds to prayers.

A problem with the rationalist view is the dissonance that ensues, since our prayers are in fact largely comprised of praise and petition. In the kabbalistic approach, it is all too easy for prayer to take on a pagan character where we think we are manipulating God, treating Him like an unusually well-stocked vending machine. Additionally, many prayers are not answered as one would have liked. The false expectation that prayer achieves direct positive results may cause one to lose faith.

The Talmud (*Berakhot* 32a) presents a healthier approach: "Rabbi Simlai expounded: One should always first recount the praise of the Holy One, blessed be He, and then pray. From where do we know this? From Moses' plea to enter the Land" (Deuteronomy 3:23–24). Ironically, the Talmud cites the classic example of a prayer that was *not* accepted! And of all people, Moses was praying! As heartbreaking as that episode is, it presents a vital lesson showing that even Moses did not always get what he wanted when he prayed.

Following this lead, Rabbi Joseph Soloveitchik explains that "The foundation of prayer is not the conviction of its effectiveness but the belief that through it we approach God intimately and the miraculous community embracing finite man and his Creator is born. The basic function of prayer is not its practical consequences but the metaphysical formation of a fellowship consisting of God and man" (*Worship of the Heart*, p. 35).

MORE ON PETITIONARY PRAYER

*T*he Talmud reports an unusual anecdote about petitionary prayer that contains important insight into the nature of asking things of God:

> Rabbi Mani often used to attend [the discourses] of Rabbi Yitzhak ben Eliashab, and he complained: The rich members of the family of my father-in-law are annoying me. The latter exclaimed: May they become poor! They became poor. Later on [Rabbi Mani] complained: Now they press me [for support], and Rabbi Isaac exclaimed: Let them become rich! They became rich.
>
> [On another occasion] he complained: My wife is no longer attractive to me. Rabbi Isaac asked: What is her name? He replied: Hannah. Whereupon Rabbi Isaac exclaimed: May Hannah become beautiful! And she became beautiful. He then complained: She now has become too arrogant [from her beauty], whereupon Rabbi Isaac exclaimed: If that is so, let Hannah revert to her [former] ugliness! And she became once again ugly.
>
> Two disciples used to attend [the discourses of] Rabbi Isaac ben Eliashab, and they said to him, Master, pray that we may become very wise. He replied: Once I had the power to do this, but now I no longer possess this power. (*Ta'anit* 23b)

Rabbi Yitzchak Blau addresses different levels of this fascinating and somewhat troubling story. At its surface, the Talmud teaches that we should pray for what really matters most, rather than getting caught up in trivial matters. Additionally, we often want things that contain mixed blessings. What initially seems best for us in one area often comes at high price in another.

At another level, the final component of the narrative—the disciples who requested a prayer for wisdom and were rebuffed—teaches that even matters that are truly important cannot be corrected with the use of prayer as a magic wand. To attain wisdom, one must devote oneself to study, rather than praying for instant knowledge and judgment. The talmudic anecdote, then, teaches that first, we must be careful what we pray for, and second, that we must look inward and work to achieve genuine change, rather than depending exclusively on prayer.

Rabbi Yitzchak Blau, *Fresh Fruit & Vintage Wine: The Ethics and Wisdom of the Aggada* (Jersey City, NJ: Ktav, 2009), pp. 219–221.

BIBLICAL VERSUS PAGAN PRAYER

ometimes, we can better appreciate what the Bible contributed to the world by understanding it against its ancient Near Eastern backdrop. In biblical prayer, God is presented as the Creator-King and is all good. Therefore, we owe God loyalty out of gratitude and dependence. The relationship between God and humanity is often cast as a slave-master relationship, creating a tone of greater subservience and reliance. Unlike pagans, who believed that their gods needed the meat of their sacrifices for sustenance, the Bible teaches an absolute sense of human dependence, wherein God does not need human offerings to satisfy His hunger. Worship is not a barter system where God and people each gain something, but rather was instituted to create a vehicle for people to serve God.

On a higher plane, the relationship between God and humanity is depicted using marriage imagery. Just as God loves us, our service of God is returned love. We attain joy from praising God for the sake of praise. Biblical praise does not always precede petition. We say every weekday morning: "A Psalm of thanksgiving. Make a joyful noise to the Lord, all the earth. Serve the Lord with gladness; come before His presence with singing" (Psalms 100:1–2). Biblical praise of God has nothing to do with the flattery or appeasement that was prevalent in the pagan barter system of prayer. Our praise of God is an expression of our genuine love. In fact, our love of God is so great that we want to share that love with the wider community and ultimately with the whole world.

Moshe Greenberg, "On the Refinement of the Conception of Prayer in Hebrew Scriptures," *AJS Review* 1 (1976), pp. 57–92.

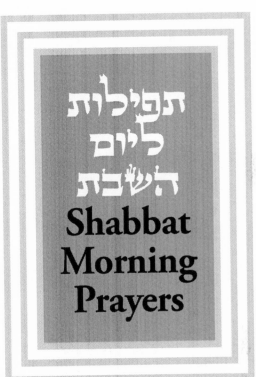

תְּפִלּוֹת לְיוֹם הַשַּׁבָּת

Shabbat
Morning
Prayers

OVERVIEW OF THE
SHABBAT MORNING SERVICE

*T*he Shabbat service begins with morning blessings, Psalms and verses of song called *Pesukei de-Zimra* (or *Zemirot*), followed by the Shaharit (morning service). The main features of the Shaharit are the Shema and the Amidah. After the repetition of the Amidah, the Torah scroll is then taken from the Ark and brought in procession to the reader's desk. The Torah reading is followed by a prophetic reading called the Haftarah. Communities recite special prayers for the welfare of their government, the Congregation, and the State of Israel either before the Torah reading or after the Haftarah.

After the completion of the reading of the Torah and Haftarah, Ashrei (Psalm 145) and some other prayers are recited and these are followed by the returning of the Torah to the Ark. The Ark is closed, and there often is a sermon by the rabbi.

After the sermon, Musaf (additional service) is recited, followed by concluding prayers, including En Ke-Elohenu, Alenu, and Adon Olam.

EARLY MORNING BLESSINGS

*R*abbi Yosef Karo's *Shulhan Arukh* opens with a mishnaic statement to set the tone for serving God: "Yehudah ben Tema said: Be bold as a leopard, swift as an eagle, fleet as a hart, and strong as a lion, to do the will of your Father who is in Heaven" (Mishnah *Avot* 5:20).

One of the first early morning blessings is the *E-lohai neshamah*: "My God, the soul with which You have endowed me is pure...So long as there is soul within me, I avow before You, Lord my God and God of My ancestors, that You are the Sovereign of all creation, the Ruler of all living, the

Lord of all souls." What a beautiful prayer to begin each day! Not only do we thank God for returning us to a conscious state from our sleep, but we also optimistically proclaim that God gave us all pure souls.

Jakob J. Petuchowski relates a famous anecdote:

> When Samuel Morse, in 1843, got his telegraph line working between Washington and Baltimore, it was a tremendous achievement, of which Morse could have been inordinately proud. No doubt he was. But the first message he sent was: "What hath God wrought!". . . Man's prayer of thanksgiving addressed to God has never been taken to imply that God does not work through human channels. But man's self-congratulatory prayer, addressed to man, is idolatry. (*Understanding Jewish Prayer*, p. 60)

There is a very wide variety of blessings to cover all aspects of life. For example, the blessing to be recited after using the bathroom (*asher yatzar*) is remarkable. We do not take *anything* for granted, and thank God when our bodies function properly. We also recite blessings over Torah study, such as, "May these teachings of Your Torah be pleasant in our mouth and in the mouth of all Your people the household of Israel, that we, our children and children's children may all know You and learn Your Torah for the love of it."

Blessings are short, easy to learn, and give us God-consciousness for everything from the most mundane to the most transcendent; from the moment we wake up until the moment we go to sleep; from day-to-day occurrences to the most unusual occasions; from the happiest times to the saddest. They provide us with opportunities to connect with God on a regular basis.

KORBANOT-OFFERINGS

After the Temple was destroyed, the sacrificial order prescribed by the Torah was abolished, and prayer became the central form of worship. The Sages cited and adapted a verse in Hosea, "Accept our good sacrifices of praise instead of bulls"

(Hosea 14:3). They interpreted this verse to mean that if we read the order of sacrifices, God will consider it as though we have brought them (*Ta'anit* 27b).

The chapter of Mishnah read from tractate *Zevahim* also is the only chapter in the entire Mishnah that contains no rabbinic disagreements. It therefore represents pristine oral law (*Bet Yosef*).

Our early morning prayers contain selections from the Torah, the Mishnah, Talmud, and midrash. These selections are followed by the Rabbis' Kaddish, which is recited after a public study session.

PESUKEI DE-ZIMRA

he Talmud (*Berakhot* 32b) relates that pious Jews in olden times would sit for an hour before praying, pray for an hour, and then sit for another hour afterward. Although most of us do not have this much time nor the spiritual stamina required, it is proper to consider the *Pesukei de-Zimra* as a spiritual warm-up before the mandatory prayers (Rabbi Haim David Halevi, *Mekor Hayyim* vol. 1, p. 174).

G. K. Chesterton stated that "The difference between the philosopher and the poet is that the philosopher tries to get the heavens into his head while the poet tries to get his head into the heavens" (quoted in Louis Jacobs, *Their Heads in Heaven*, introduction). Philosophers try to translate God and revelation into terms people can understand. Poets instead try to transcend human limitations. Our daily reading of Psalms helps us achieve the poetic spiritual mindset.

PSALM 30

*I*n Psalm 30, it appears that the psalmist has already been saved from his woes and then expresses gratitude to God: "Lord, I would extol You, for You have raised me up and have not suffered my foes to exult over me." Later in the Psalm, the psalmist flashes back, remembering his unwarranted self-confidence prior to his woes: "As for me, I had thought in my security I shall never be moved...But You hid Your face, I was dismayed. . . ." Once he recalls this crisis the psalmist can thank God more fully by learning and growing from his experiences. The spiritual journey and self-reflection contained in this Psalm are important aspects of prayer.

Let us return to the opening verse. "A Psalm. A song at the dedication of the House. Of David." It seems that the dedication of the "House" refers to the Temple. Additionally, it sounds like the psalmist already has achieved salvation. However, King David did not witness the building of the First Temple. More significantly, the body of the Psalm does not appear related to a Temple dedication ceremony. These questions led to many centuries of interpretation by classical commentators without a clear resolution.

Troubled by these questions, a few commentators including Ibn Ezra and Meiri suggested that David referred to his own palace, rather than the Temple. Two alternative approaches to the Psalm's introductory verse recently have been suggested. The simpler response is that "*le-David*" does not necessarily mean "of David," i.e., that he authored this Psalm. Perhaps a later writer dedicated this Psalm *to* David at the beginning of the Second Temple period. He metaphorically referred to the enemies who had exiled the Jews as an "illness": "I cried out to You, and You healed me" (30:3).

Alternatively, an earlier psalmist could have composed this Psalm to thank God for saving him from an actual illness or from enemies (or both). At the dedication of the Second Temple, a later writer may have allegorized "illness" to the exile or another national disaster. In this latter reading, there is a transition of meaning from the personal to the national (Nahum Sarna, *On the Book of Psalms*).

Rabbi Eli Munk suggests that we read this Psalm early in the morning liturgy as a preface to praising God. Many may be suffering personally, or have people close to them who are. Therefore, we initiate the service with this prayer to approach God from where we really are. We then may join in the communal chorus from our straits (*World of Prayer*, p. 60).

~

PSALM 103

*M*ost congregations worldwide do not include Psalm 103 in their regular liturgy, but a few recite it daily, including Spanish and Portuguese communities. It is not a prayer in the sense of a person addressing God directly. The psalmist instead speaks *about* God. The opening five verses capture a glimpse of the psalmist in an intimate conversation with himself, encouraging himself to praise God: "O my soul, bless the Lord, and all that is within me, bless His holy name." The Psalm is an inspirational expression of the deep desire to cultivate the God-human relationship.

Verses 6–10 turn to members of the community, teaching them about God's kindnesses. Once he finds himself, the psalmist can look outward to others. This is how we grow into a covenantal community through prayer.

Verses 11–16 then focus on the question of why God is good to us, given that we sin. God relates to us as parents love their children, and also realizes that we are frail. Verses 17–18 extend and modify that idea by stating that God is merciful to those who pursue a relationship with Him: "But the mercy of the Lord on those who revere Him is from everlasting to everlasting, and His righteous dealing unto children's children." By praying with the community and observing the commandments, we may transmit these values to future generations.

The Psalm turns to cosmic praise of God. Angels and nature fulfill God's will, and so do we. One cannot talk about a universal vision without being personally connected to God. This Psalm begins with ourselves and then works outward to the community, to future generations, and finally to the cosmos.

At the conclusion of the Psalm, the psalmist returns to himself: "Bless the Lord, all His works, in all the places of His dominion. O my soul, bless you the Lord." We do not forfeit our individuality when we see ourselves as part of a community, a link in a generational chain, or the cosmos. On the contrary, when we add our own voices to the voice of the community, we are fulfilled as individuals.

—

PSALM 19

*P*salm 19 describes two pathways to loving God—through nature and through Torah: "The heavens declare the glory of God, and the firmament tells His handiwork. . . . The Torah of the Lord is faithful, rejoicing the heart."

Dr. Norman Lamm discusses an apparent conflict within Rambam's writings. In his *Mishneh Torah* (*Yesodei ha-Torah* 2:2) Rambam writes that one attains love of God through contemplating nature; he takes the same view in his *Guide for the Perplexed*. In his *Sefer ha-Mitzvot*, however, Rambam includes both mitzvah observance and contemplation of nature as means to attaining love of God.

Dr. Lamm adopts a common approach in Rambam scholarship, and distinguishes between the masses and the intellectual elite. The masses love God through observance of the mitzvot, whereas the philosophical elite love God through nature. The *Guide* is elitist, whereas *Sefer ha-Mitzvot* was written as a popular work. What about the *Mishneh Torah*, a work similarly intended for everyone? Dr. Lamm answers that its opening chapters are philosophical, and therefore can be understood properly only by an exclusive elite audience ("Maimonides on the Love of God," *Maimonidean Studies* 3 [1992–1993], pp. 131–142).

One may question this solution. Even the simplest soul can be overwhelmed by the natural world. Several Psalms—Psalm 19 included—express that sentiment. Perhaps the discrepancy in Rambam's writings has more to do with the context of each book. *Sefer ha-Mitzvot* teaches how Jews develop a love of God—through the Torah's commandments and the contemplation of nature. In contrast, the *Mishneh Torah* and the *Guide* focus on how any religious *person* attains the love and fear of God.

In his book *Torah u-Madda* (pp. 146–147), Dr. Lamm quotes Mishnah *Avot* 3:7, "Rabbi Yaakov used to say: One who is studying Torah as he walks by the way, and who interrupts his studies to say, 'How beautiful is this tree,' or 'how beautiful is this furrow,' it is as though he is guilty with his life." Dr. Lamm adopts Rashi's interpretation: nature certainly helps us appreciate God, but Torah is God's word and therefore it has primacy.

Rabbi Marc Angel suggests an alternate interpretation. One who views nature as an *interruption* from Torah errs. One who perceives nature as part of a Torah worldview has a proper understanding. As Psalm 19 teaches, Torah and nature are different manifestations of God's voice. Of course they are different, and the Psalm therefore separates them. But they are two means of hearing God's voice that work together in harmony.

Hayyim Angel, "Perspectives on *Tehillim* 19," forthcoming in *Mi-Tokh Ha-Ohel: Shabbat Prayer Volume* (Jerusalem: Maggid, 2014).

PSALMS 145–150:
"EVERYDAY HALLEL"

Rabbi Yosei said: May my portion be of those who recite the entire Hallel every day. But that is not so, for a Master said: He who reads Hallel every day blasphemes and reproaches [the Divine Name]? We refer to the Verses of Song (*Pesukei de-Zimra*). (*Shabbat* 118b)

Why would someone who recites the *Hallel* (Psalms 113–118) each day be considered a blasphemer? R. Yitzchak Etshalom quotes R. Joseph Soloveitchik, who taught that the *Hallel* includes praise for God for His miracles. We risk lessening the impact of God's acts if we equate all miracles—daily and supernatural. Daily recital of *Hallel* would be a form of blasphemy. In contrast, *Tehillim* chapters 145–150 praise God for daily miracles such as sustaining creation and natural phenomena. R. Yosei wishes that his portion would be among those who sing God's praises for the miracles we enjoy and appreciate every day.

Similarly, the Talmud suggests that the ideal praises bless God for the mundane:

> Rabbi Eleazar b. Avina says: Whoever recites [the psalm] Praise of David (Psalm 145) three times daily, is sure to inherit the world to come. What is the reason? Shall I say it is because it has an alphabetical arrangement? Then let him recite, Happy are they that are upright in the way (Psalm 119), which has an eightfold alphabetical arrangement. Again, is it because it contains [the verse], You open Your hand [*pote'ah et yadekha*]? Then let him recite the great *Hallel* (Psalm 136), where it is written: Who gives food to all flesh! (136:25). Rather, [the reason is] because it contains both. (*Berakhot* 4b)

Replete with praise for God for the Creation and exodus, chapter 136 receives honorable mention for its penultimate verse that praises God for day-to-day sustenance. Human nature revels in the supernatural and finds little to get excited about in the mundane. In contrast, Jewish thought gives primacy to the miracles of every day, rather than the extraordinary. The *Tur* (*Orah Hayyim* 51) explains that the verse "*pote'ah et yadekha*" is the primary reason that the Sages mandated reading Psalm 145 each day. The *Shulhan Arukh* rules that if one does not have proper intention when reading this verse, he should return to recite it again (*Orah Hayyim* 51:7).

Hayyim Angel, "Perspectives on *Tehillim* 145," forthcoming in *Mi-Tokh Ha-Ohel: Weekday Prayer Volume* (Jerusalem: Maggid, 2014).

Rabbi Yitzchak Etshalom, http://www.torah.org/advanced/mikra/5762/hagim/Hallel1.pdf.

⟶

BARUKH SHE-AMAR THROUGH YISHTABAH

*B*arukh she-amar serves as the opening blessing for the Psalms we recite each day and on Shabbat. Rabbi Haim David Halevi explains that the brief paragraph that follows Psalms 145–150 (*barukh A-donai le-olam amen ve-amen*) serves as a concluding blessing formula to the Psalms. We then begin a new section that opens with a new "blessing," *va-yevarekh David*, and culminates with the Song at the Sea (*Mekor Hayyim* vol. 1, pp. 172–173). Rabbi Jonathan Sacks observes that these passages reflect historical moments when Israel pledged to be defined as a nation bound as a community of prayer, rather than the individual prayers we have recited thus far. This section transitions us to the public prayers that follow (*Koren Rosh HaShana Mahzor*, pp. 336–339).

We conclude the *Pesukei de-Zimra* with the *Yishtabah* as the closing blessing for the entire section. Rabbi Haim David Halevi notes that the *Barukh she-amar* ends with the formula, "*Melekh mehullal ba-tishbahot*" (divine Ruler exalted with psalms of praise). We travel higher on the spiritual ladder through our recital of the Psalms and then the Song at the Sea, until we close with the formula at the end of the Yishtabah, "*Melekh **gadol** u-mehullal ba-tishbahot*" (divine Ruler, **great**, exalted with psalms of praise). After having immersed ourselves in the beautiful praises that begin our services, we are elevated in our appreciation of God's grandeur, so we add "*gadol*" (great) in recognition of our own spiritual growth through reciting the *Pesukei de-Zimra* (*Mekor Hayyim* vol. 1, p. 176).

NISHMAT KOL HAI

*T*he prayers recited every Shabbat and holiday after *Pesukei de-Zimra* begin with the Nishmat praise. Several components of these prayers trace back to the talmudic period, but it appears that they entered the Shabbat liturgy in the Geonic period.

A Mishnah refers to "the grace of song" to be recited at the Passover Seder after the Hallel (*Pesahim* 117b). The Talmud asks, "What is 'the grace of song?' Rab Judah said: They shall praise You, O Lord our God (*yehallelukha*, the blessing at the conclusion of the Hallel); while R. Johanan said: The breath of all living (*nishmat kol hai*)" (*Pesahim* 118a).

The second paragraph of this prayer (*ve-ilu pinu*) may have originated as a prayer over rain: "What blessing do they say [over rain]? . . . R. Johanan concluded thus: If our mouths were full of song like the sea . . . we could not sufficiently give thanks unto You, O Lord our God, etc., up to 'shall prostrate itself before You.' Blessed are You, O Lord, to whom abundant thanksgivings are due" (*Berakhot* 59b).

After reciting the Psalms and other prayers in *Pesukei de-Zimra*, the Nishmat elevates us even further, helping us to approach the climactic prayers of the Shema, Amidah, and their accompanying blessings. While we offer many praises to God throughout *Pesukei de-Zimra*, the Nishmat section also reminds us that we truly are incapable of adequately praising God

---

THE KADDISH: PART 1

The Kaddish is one of the most misunderstood prayers. Contrary to popular perception, it was not initially composed as a prayer of mourning. The Kaddish is a prayer for God's well-being during our exile. God's existence is a reality, but His immanence depends on whether we want Him manifest in this world or not. Professor Abraham Joshua Heschel offers a similar idea about the Kaddish: "God is in need of man: His being immanent depends upon us . . . *Yitgadal ve-yitkadash*: may there be more of God in this world" (*Man's Quest for God*, p. 62).

The Talmud reports a remarkable story related to the Kaddish:

R. Yosei entered into one of the ruins of Jerusalem to pray. Elijah appeared . . . . He asked me, what did you hear in this ruin? I replied: I heard a divine voice, cooing like a dove, and saying: Woe to the children, on account of whose sins I destroyed My house and burnt My temple and exiled them among the nations of the world! He said to me: . . . Not in this moment alone does it so exclaim, but three times each day it says this! And more than that, whenever the Israelites go into the synagogues and schoolhouses and respond: May His great name be blessed (*yehei shemei ha-gadol mevorakh*), God shakes His head and says: Happy is the King who is thus praised in this house! Woe to the Father who had to banish His children, and woe to the children who had to be banished from the table of their Father! (*Berakhot* 3a)

Rabbi Haim David Halevi explains that when reciting the Kaddish, we feel anguish and devastation over the continued lack of our Temple in

Jerusalem and also over the desecration of God's Name as a result of Israel's exile. The Kaddish simultaneously serves as a call to action: We need to sanctify God's Name so that God will again have a home in this world.

Using the Kaddish as a mourners' prayer seems to have begun in France-Germany after the First Crusade. When a mourner recites the Kaddish for his or her parents (or other close relatives), this expression of belief is a tribute to the success of the parent in transmitting the highest values of our faith to the next generation.

THE KADDISH: PART 2

The great Hasidic master Rabbi Levi Yitzhak of Berditchev (1740–1810) composed a variation of the Kaddish, which he recited on Rosh HaShanah:

Good morning to You, Lord, Master of the Universe.
I, Levi Yitzhak, son of Sarah of Berditchev,
I come to You with a complaint from Your people Israel.

What do You want of Your people Israel?
What have You demanded of Your people Israel?
For everywhere I look it says, "Say to the children of Israel,"
And every other verse says, "Speak to the children of Israel,"
And over and over, "Command the children of Israel."

Father, sweet Father in heaven,
How many nations are there in the world?
Persians, Babylonians, Edomites.

The Russians, what do they say?
That their Czar is the only ruler.
The Prussians, what do they say?
That their Kaiser is supreme.

And the English, what do they say?
That George the Third is the sovereign.

And I, Levi Yitzhak, son of Sarah of Berditchev, say,
Lo azuz mi-mekomi; from my stand I will not waver,
And from my place I shall not move
Until there be an end to all this.
Yitgadal ve-yitkadash shemei rabbah—
Magnified and sanctified is only Your Name.

(Translation in Seth Kadish, *Kavvana*, p. 252)

We envision the day when a perfected humanity will adopt the Torah's noble vision. At the same time, we express anguish over the immorality so pervasive in the world.

Through the recital of the Kaddish, we address God: Look at us, who have suffered for millennia, all because we have remained faithful to You. Please help us and our world so that Your Name will be sanctified.

THE BLESSINGS PRECEDING SHEMA

*T*he *Pesukei de-Zimra* awaken our spirits for the core of the prayer service, which consists of two blessings before Shema, the Shema, a blessing after the Shema, and the Amidah. The first blessing preceding the Shema focuses on God as the universal Creator, whereas the second focuses on God's particular relationship with Israel.

Dr. Norman Lamm writes that "a truly religious Jew, devoted to his own people in keen attachment to both their physical and spiritual welfare, must at the same time be deeply concerned with all human beings. Paradoxically, the more particularistic a Jew is, the more universal must be his concerns" (*Shema*, p. 35).

The contemplation of nature draws us into a relationship with God. We recognize our dependence on God, but simultaneously function as partners in creation. Staring at a starry sky, one psalmist captures these two elements:

When I look at Your heavens, the work of Your fingers, the moon and the stars, which You have established; What is man, that You are mindful of him? And the son of man, that You visit him? For You have made him a little lower than the angels, and have crowned him with glory and honor. You made him to have dominion over the works of Your hands; you have put all things under his feet. (Psalms 8:4–7).

Rabbi Jonathan Sacks expresses the Jewish relationship to creation as one of the high points of human philosophy. Modernity summarizes the history of the world by saying that first there were many gods; monotheism taught that there was one God; then science came and people believed in no God. We have a different way of telling the story: pagans saw the world in terms of vast impersonal forces to which we are all subjected. Today is no different—we have a global economy, the internet, and international politics—none of which care about what we do. The Torah, on the other hand, teaches that creation is an act of God's love and purpose. Human self-consciousness lies at the center of this enterprise (*A Letter in the Scroll*, pp. 70–76).

Rabbi Sacks also observes that the blessings that surround the Shema express the three most basic elements of Jewish faith: creation, revelation, and redemption. For the most part Jews did not write books of theology; they composed prayers. We do not speak about God as much as we speak to God. Faith is our relationship with God best expressed through prayer (*Koren Rosh HaShana Mahzor*, 2011, pp. 55–56).

THE SHEMA: PART 1

*T*he Talmud (*Sukkah* 42a) instructs parents to teach their children two verses as soon as they learn to speak: (1) "Moses commanded us the Torah, a heritage for the congregation of Jacob" (Deuteronomy 33:4). (2) The Shema (Deuteronomy 6:4). The Shema is so central to Jewish life that the corpus of the Talmud begins with the laws of the Shema.

Although the Shema lies at the heart of our prayer service, it is not really a prayer at all. It is an address to the nation, and we use it as a proclamation of faith. Accordingly, the Sages of the Talmud do not use the verb *le-hitpallel* ("to pray") regarding the Shema. Rather, they refer to it as *keri'at Shema* (reading, reciting, or proclaiming the Shema). Similarly, we refer to our public Torah reading as *keri'at ha-Torah*, since it, too, is not formal prayer.

Dr. Norman Lamm quotes the Hasidic Rabbi Zvi Elimelech Shapira of Dinov, who explains that seeing is rational, empirical. In contrast, hearing represents tradition. There is a time for intellectual study and a time for questioning. Shema (literally, listen, hear), however, is the time to be childlike in purity and focus.

Rashi explains the third verse of the Shema in a similar vein. "And these words which I command you *today* shall be in your heart." We must view the Torah as freshly as though it were given today. This attitude enables us to accept the Torah with adult sophistication and childlike enthusiasm.

Read literally, that verse reads that "the words...shall be *upon* your heart." Why not *in* your heart? The Hasidic Rabbi Menahem Mendel of Kotzk explained that it would be preposterous to demand that Torah reside in the heart. Moreover, how could the words of the Torah penetrate hearts that were spiritually blocked and ossified? Rather, we should place the words of the Torah upon our heart. There are moments when the heart does open up. If the words of the Torah lie upon it, they might seep in (in Heschel, *A Passion for Truth*, pp. 17–18).

THE SHEMA: PART 2

*I*n the Shema, we proclaim that God is *ehad*, one. Commentators adopt different understandings of the precise meaning of "one." Rashbam, Ibn Ezra, and Rabbi Yosef Albo explain that the verse refers to God's uniqueness: *alone* is God. *Sifrei Vaethannan* 31 offers a messianic interpretation: "'The Lord is our God'—in this world; 'the Lord is one'—in the world to come [i.e., the Messianic era, when God's unity will be universally acknowledged]. Therefore is it said, 'And the Lord shall be king over all the earth; on that day shall the Lord be one and His name one' (Zechariah 14:9)."

The Shema also came to be understood as a call to publicly sanctify God's Name. The Talmud relates that when Rabbi Akiva was taken out by the Romans for execution, it was time to recite the Shema. "While they combed his flesh with iron combs, he was accepting upon himself the kingship of heaven (i.e., reciting the Shema). His disciples said to him: Our teacher, even to this point? He said to them: All my days I have been troubled by this verse, 'with all your soul,' [which I interpret,] even if He takes your soul. I said: When shall I have the opportunity to fulfill this? Now that I have the opportunity shall I not fulfill it? He prolonged the word *ehad* until he expired while saying it. A voice from heaven proclaimed: Happy are you, Akiva that your soul has departed with the word *ehad!*" (*Berakhot* 61b).

In an age where too many so-called advocates of religion actively promote murder, hatred, and discrimination, may we cause God's name to be beloved by living truly exemplary lives, so that all can see the highest level of human conduct and character emanating from our most basic desire that God's name will be one.

THE SHEMA: PART 3

*T*he Talmud relates a fascinating story:

> [On his deathbed, Jacob was worried:] Perhaps, Heaven forbid, there is one unfit among my children, like Abraham, from whom there issued Ishmael, or like my father Isaac, from whom there issued Esau. [But] his sons answered him, Hear O Israel, the Lord our God the Lord is One . . . Jacob exclaimed, Blessed be the name of His glorious kingdom for ever and ever. (*Pesahim* 56a)

What is the Talmud trying to teach by projecting the reading of Shema back to the Patriarchs?

Rabbi Haim David Halevi understands the passage as teaching a basic lesson of faith: Jacob's ultimate concern on his deathbed was that his children should be God-fearing. One's religious will and testament is far more important than one's property will (*Mekor Hayyim* vol. 1, pp. 182–183).

Rabbi Joseph Soloveitchik adds another dimension. This story teaches that the creed of the Shema goes back to the foundation of our nation. It is a living doctrine that unites us with our Patriarchs, creating a timeless connection. The story similarly teaches that the revelation of the Shema in Moses' time simply confirms what human intellect attained in the time of the Patriarchs. "Hence, the experience connected with Shema is not something mysterious and paradoxical, which man can only accept but not comprehend. It is an august truth rooted in the logos and reaching out to the deepest strata of the human personality" (*Worship of the Heart*, pp. 110–113).

Although the recital of the Shema is a positive commandment, we do not say a blessing preceding its recital. In the Cairo Genizah, scholars found a blessing that some communities once recited before the Shema: "Blessed are You, O Lord our God, Sovereign of the Universe, Who has sanctified us through His commandments, and has commanded us the commandment of the Proclamation of the Shema, so that we may proclaim His Kingship with a perfect heart, declare His unity with a single mind, and serve Him with a fervent heart" (in Petuchowski, "The Liturgy of the Synagogue," pp. 26–27).

This blessing is understood by most scholars to be a later invention, as most mitzvot do not use this particular formula. Although we do not recite this blessing in our liturgy, it conveys a beautiful sentiment we should feel and experience.

THE AMIDAH: PART 1

*I*t is noteworthy that the heart of our prayer service—the Amidah—was composed by the Sages of the Talmud, rather than deriving from the Torah or later parts of the Bible. In the medieval period, Karaites attacked believers in Rabbinic Judaism for supplanting the beautiful prayers of the Bible—particularly the Psalms—with a prayer that is rabbinic in origin.

One explanation of the rabbinic logic is that the lofty poetry in Psalms often is difficult to understand. In contrast, the Amidah focuses clearly and directly on the themes in our daily lives, and was written in a lucid style that is accessible to all.

There is a deeper rationale behind the rabbinic composition of the Amidah, as well. Several Psalms call to sing new songs to God (Psalms 33:3; 40:4; 96:1; 98:1; 144:9; 149:1). By composing the Amidah, the Sages of the Talmud captured the spirit of prayer of the Psalms. By placing rabbinic prayers at the center of our liturgy, the Sages demonstrated the need for human input and personalization of prayers, rather than allowing them to become fossilized texts.

Amos Hakham (*Da'at Mikra* commentary on Psalm 149) observes that the last "real" Psalm (Psalm 149; Psalm 150 is a dramatic finale to the entire book) opens with a call for a new song: "Sing to the Lord a new song; sing His praise in the meeting of the pious." Although the Book of Psalms may be concluding, we are reminded to compose new prayers as worship of the heart.

Finally, we envelop the Amidah with verses from Psalms, creating continuity with the biblical world. We open with, "O Lord, open my lips, that my mouth may declare Your praise" (Psalms 51:17). When we begin the Amidah, we implore God to help us pray. At the conclusion of the Amidah, we add, "May the words of my mouth and the prayer of my heart be acceptable to You, o Lord, my rock and redeemer" (Psalms 19:15).

THE AMIDAH: PART 2

*T*he first blessing of the Amidah invokes our ancestors: "God of our fathers, God of Abraham, God of Isaac, and God of Jacob." Professor Abraham Joshua Heschel explains that "Abraham, Isaac, and Jacob do not signify ideas, principles, or abstract values...The categories of the Bible are not principles to be comprehended but events to be continued. The life of him who joins the covenant of Abraham continues the life of Abraham" (*Moral Grandeur and Spiritual Audacity*, p. 125).

The founder of modern Hasidism, the Baal Shem Tov (1700–1760), observed that we say "God of Abraham, God of Isaac, and God of Jacob," instead of the more concise "God of Abraham, Isaac, and Jacob." Isaac and Jacob did not rely on Abraham's tradition, but rather forged their own personal relationships with God.

Rabbi Ezra Bick calls attention to the unusual appellation, *El Elyon* ("God sublime"). This uncommon name of God appears only four times in the Torah and all in one place—during the dialogue between Abraham and Melchizedek, a God-fearing person outside of the Patriarchal family (Genesis chapter 14). In this blessing, then, we stand in the tradition of our ancestors and simultaneously recognize God's universality (Yeshivat Har Etzion, lecture 4; at http://www.vbm-torah.org/archive/18/).

Rabbi Aryeh Kaplan observed that the end of this blessing refers to God as King, Helper, Savior, and Shield (*Melekh Ozer u-Moshia u-Magen*). God begins as a very distant King; He then answers us if we call; He then actually saves; finally, He is a shield, something we hold very close to ourselves. While all four expressions describe God's protection, they progressively bring God from far away into a close personal relationship.

In just one blessing, then, we connect to the tradition of our ancestors and to God as Master of all humanity. We pray for redemption. God begins transcendent, but we bring Him closer to us as we continue praying. By connecting to God and our roots, we are elevated through our prayer as we stand silently and forge our own personal relationships with God.

THE AMIDAH: PART 3

*R*abbi Marvin Luban notes a distinction between the Kaddish and the Kedushah. In the Kedushah, we sanctify God's Name in tandem with the angels. In the Kaddish, we cry over the absence of God's presence in the world.

The medieval French rabbis who wrote the Tosafot glosses on *Sanhedrin* 37b refer to an early Geonic custom where Kedushah was recited only on Shabbat, whereas Kaddish was recited only on weekdays.

Although we do not follow this practice (we recite both Kaddish and Kedushah on weekdays and Shabbat), it makes excellent conceptual sense. Kedushah conveys a sense of serenity, setting a perfect tone for Shabbat. In contrast, Kaddish reflects distress over the exile, which is better suited for weekdays.

A relic of this practice distinguishes the Kedushah read by Sephardim and Ashkenazim for Shaharit on Shabbat. Ashkenazim merge the language of Kaddish into the Kedushah: "From Your place, our King, You will appear and reign over us, for we await You. When will You reign in Zion? Soon, in our days, forever and ever, may You dwell there. May You be exalted and sanctified (*titgaddal ve-titkaddash*) within Jerusalem Your city, from generation to generation and for all eternity. May our eyes see Your kingdom, as it is expressed in the songs of Your might, written by David, Your righteous anointed" (ArtScroll translation).

In contrast, Sephardim keep the Kaddish and the Kedushah separate—there is a time and a place for each type of prayer.

Rabbi Marvin Luban, "The Kaddish: Man's Reply to the Problem of Evil," in *Studies in Torah Judaism*, ed. Leon Stitskin (New York: Yeshiva University Press, 1969), pp. 191–234.

THE AMIDAH: PART 4

The weekday Amidah has 19 blessings. The first three are blessings of praise, and the final three are blessings of gratitude. The middle 13 blessings are petitions. On Shabbat, the first three and final three blessings are the same as those of the weekday Amidah, but there is only one middle blessing pertaining to Shabbat. This middle blessing varies for each of the four Shabbat services.

Rabbi Aharon Lichtenstein makes the surprising observation that there is a genuine problem of prayer on Shabbat. Although "prayer" can broadly refer to all forms of verbal worship, the essence of prayer lies in petition. "Rabbi Simlai said: One should always first set forth God's praises, and then let him pray (i.e., petition God)" (*Berakhot* 32a).

Petition arises from our needs, frustrations, inadequacies, and anxieties. In contrast, Shabbat strikes a note of serenity and gives us a taste of an ideal world. Rabbi Lichtenstein observes that Rambam repeatedly cites the prohibition to fast, cry out, plead, or to beg mercy on Shabbat.

In fact, our true prayer is *shorter* on Shabbat than on weekdays. Do not be fooled by the considerably longer time we spend in synagogue. Most of the added time on Shabbat comes from the Torah-Haftarah-Sermon, which comprise elements of public Torah study rather than prayer. We also tend to sing more and move at a slower pace than on weekdays.

The middle 13 weekday blessings of petition are replaced by one blessing that captures themes of Shabbat. In some sense the middle blessing is still a request, but not one emerging from distress. Rabbi Lichtenstein writes,

> On Shabbat, then, we do not escape either the state of the sense of need. That would deny our creaturely humanity. We do, however, reorient our needs. As regards prayer, they are reduced to one: Shabbat. We plead for nothing else. . . . Striving through prayer toward maximal realization of the day's sanctity, we thus assert both our weakness and our strength—the inability to go it alone, and the capacity for spiritual flight. (p. 171)

In Rabbi Lichtenstein's analysis, then, we *do* petition God on Shabbat, thereby achieving the essence of prayer. However, we suspend our usual requests and petition God for greater serenity and spiritual connection to God on Shabbat.

Rabbi Aharon Lichtenstein, "Prayer on Shabbat," in *Leaves of Faith*, vol. 2 (Hoboken, NJ: Ktav, 2004), pp. 153–177.

THE TORAH READING

he public Torah reading in synagogue reenacts the Revelation at Mount Sinai. There are antecedents to our practice in the Torah. Moses publicly read "the Book of the Covenant" (Exodus 24:7). There also is a commandment to gather all men, women, and children to Jerusalem (*hakhel*) every seven years where the Torah would be read publicly on Sukkot (Deuteronomy 31:10–13).

HAGBAHAH: The Torah is lifted so that all may see it (*Soferim*, chapter 14). This practice often is explained as stemming from the principle that the Torah must be accessible to everyone. Sephardim typically lift the Torah before the portion is read, whereas Ashkenazim typically lift the Torah after it has been read.

BLESSINGS BEFORE AND AFTER THE TORAH IS READ: The Talmud (*Nedarim* 81a) states that the Temple was destroyed because people did not recite blessings over the Torah. Rabbi Haim David Halevi (*Mekor Hayyim* vol. 1, p. 70) explains that people learned Torah but viewed it as they would any other subject. Our recital of blessings before and after each reading is a means of demonstrating the Torah's unique status.

THE TORAH READING: The Torah reading is considered as being akin to the revelation of the Torah at Sinai. Some, therefore, have the custom to stand during all Torah readings. Most communities felt that this was too great a burden to impose on the public, and therefore the common practice is to remain seated.

TORAH STUDY AND PRAYER: The Torah-Haftarah-Sermon elements of our Shabbat morning services enable us to receive the Torah and apply it to our lives. They comprise a dominant portion of the second half of morning services. These two experiences are the complementary cornerstones of relating to God on a mutual plane. Torah study represents hearing God's voice speaking to us, whereas prayer conveys our voice to God.

REPETITION OF THE AMIDAH FOR SHAHARIT VERSUS READING IT ONCE ALOUD FOR MUSAF

*I*n talmudic times, there were no compiled prayer books. The Hazzan read the Amidah aloud, and the congregation listened and then responded *Amen* (i.e., I agree and accept what the Hazzan said as true) after each blessing. In this way, they fulfilled the obligation of saying the Amidah.

Over time, when most synagogue-goers became familiar with the prayers, there was no need to continue this practice, as people now recited the Amidah themselves. However, the original practice remained in force, both for the sake of retaining the original practice, and also because there may be congregants who are unfamiliar with the prayers and still benefit from the Hazzan reciting the Amidah aloud. Therefore, the widespread practice became to have a silent Amidah, and then the Hazzan would repeat the Amidah aloud with congregants responding *Amen* after each blessing.

A negative consequence of retaining this practice is that the repetition became idle time for congregants who already had said the Amidah themselves. When Rambam arrived in Cairo, he was outraged by the chatting, spitting, and nose-wiping that took place during the repetition of the Amidah. Consequently, he ruled that the Amidah be read once aloud for Musaf, and the practice was eventually extended to Minhah as well. Rambam advocated this practice in order to maintain the decorum and sanctity of the synagogue.

Many congregations retain the original practice and read a silent Amidah followed by the repetition. In communities who follow Rambam's ruling and read the Amidah together out loud, congregants should read along silently with the Hazzan, and not answer *Amen* (as opposed to when there is a repetition, in which case they do respond). Since they are reading themselves, they should not answer *Amen* to their own blessings. Those who read ahead silently after the Kedushah may respond *Amen* after they complete the Amidah, but of course should not talk since others are still in the middle of the Amidah.

DAILY MINYAN

A Hasidic tale tells of a girl who would go into the woods to pray. Her father was concerned about the dangers of the woods. "Why do you go to the woods to pray?" "I go to find God," was her reply. "But God is the same everywhere—even at home!" "Yes Daddy, but *I'm* not the same everywhere."

God is everywhere, and we say the same words of prayer each day. However, our lives are constantly changing. The more regularly we pray, the more we feel that the same words mean different things to us at different times.

In addition to our praying together and building life-long relationships with one another, daily minyan regulars also provide constant *hesed* to their communities and to visitors. Congregants who attend daily services when they need to say Kaddish or to celebrate a special occasion expect a minyan. Visitors likewise attend with the hopes of finding a minyan. It is the daily minyan regulars who enable communal prayer for everyone.

The best example of the value of daily services occurs at the conclusion of Yom Kippur. With a packed synagogue, we blow the shofar at the end of Neilah with great drama. Rather than ending the services there, we immediately pray the regular weekday Arvit. The lesson is clear. We need exceptional days such as Yom Kippur. However, it is the day-to-day rhythm of prayer, Torah study, acts of kindness to others, and building community that ultimately create a House of God.

Rabbi Joseph Soloveitchik observes that the Talmud (*Megillah* 23b) surprisingly derives the law of a minyan as requiring at least ten men from the sin of the ten wicked spies, who were called an "evil congregation" (Numbers 14:27). Why would the law of having a quorum derive from such negative figures? He answers that these ten individuals were called a "congregation" because they had the power to influence the entire Israelite community. So too, a small group of ten who are dedicated to attending synagogue services can upgrade the religiosity of an entire community. Those who dedicate themselves to daily minyan change the nature of the entire society for the good by becoming the spiritual backbone of a community (Aharon Ziegler, *Halakhic Positions of Rabbi Joseph B. Soloveitchik*, vol. 6, pp. 19–20).

—

CONCLUDING THOUGHTS

*U*pon entering a synagogue, Rabbi Yitzhak Luria would say, "I now am ready to fulfill the commandment of loving my neighbor as myself." Prayer is the purest expression of the relationship between God and people, yet specifically here is where we can realize the importance of good relationships among human beings. Communal prayer means creating shared lives built around dialogue with God, Torah, education, and community service. If we truly can pray, we truly can love others.

Prayer is not intended to be a spiritual experience in a vacuum. We are supposed to carry our religious experiences from the synagogue to sanctify every aspect of our lives. In the words of Rabbi Joseph Soloveitchik:

> What is sacred and profane in Judaism depends upon man's actions. If man so desires, God will abide in his office, on the assembly line, or in the halls of Congress. No boundaries will keep God out if man wants His presence. But, if man does not want His presence, God will absent Himself even from the synagogue, even from the Holy of Holies. (*Insights of R. Joseph B. Soloveitchik*, pp. 41–42)

Rabbi Marc D. Angel composed the following poem on prayer:

Prayer, a still small voice in the darkness;
A light; the earthly shadow of man's soul,
A whispered song that climbs beyond stars;
The innermost core of man's thinking heart.
Weapon against God, a sinner's last toll,
Thunderous lightning flashed from man heavenward,
A subtle melody that all things hear.
Softness, and calm, and bliss, and thoughtfulness;

The body sanctified, the world made pure;
A mystical transfusion, the eye's gleam,
A graceful swan swerving in a green pond;
Spices and stars, crackling woodlands, a dream,
A vision of perfect greatness perceived,
A happy mood, something felt and believed.

May we merit growth in prayer, bonding more deeply as a community with each other, with the community of Israel, with humanity, and with God—and carry this energy into every aspect of our lives.

—

Selected Bibliography:

Prayer

Books

Rabbi David Brofsky, *Hilchot Tefilla: A Comprehensive Guide to the Laws of Daily Prayer* (New York: OU Press, in association with Yeshivat Har Etzion, 2010).

Rabbi Hayim Donin, *To Pray as a Jew: A Guide to the Prayer Book and the Synagogue Service* (New York: Basic Books, 1980).

Ismar Elbogen, *Jewish Liturgy: A Comprehensive History*, translated by Raymond P. Scheindlin (Philadelphia: Jewish Publication Society, 1993).

Rabbi Shemtob Gaguine, *Keter Shem Tov* (seven volumes, Hebrew), 1934.

Amos Hakham, *Da'at Mikra: Psalms* (Hebrew) (Jerusalem: Mossad HaRav Kook, 1979).

Rabbi Aviyah HaKohen, *Tefillah le-El Hai: the Journey of the Soul and the Spirit of the Song in the Book of Psalms* (Hebrew) (En Tzurim: Yeshivat HaKibbutz HaDati, 2007).

Rabbi Haim David Halevi, *Mekor Hayyim ha-Shalem* (Hebrew), 1966.

Joseph Heinemann, *Prayer in the Talmud: Forms and Patterns* (Berlin: de Gruyter, 1977).

Joseph Heinemann, *Prayer in the Thought of the Sages* (Hebrew) (Jerusalem: Emunah, 1960).

Abraham Joshua Heschel, *Man's Quest for God: Studies in Prayer and Symbolism* (New York: Scribner, 1954).

Seth Kadish, *Kavvana: Directing the Heart in Jewish Prayer* (Northvale, NJ: Jason Aronson, 1997).

Rabbi Norman Lamm, *The Shema: Spirituality and Law in Judaism* (Philadelphia: Jewish Publication Society, 1998).

Ruth Langer & Steven Fine (eds.), *Liturgy in the Life of the Synagogue: Studies in the History of Jewish Prayer* (Winona Lake, IN: Eisenbrauns, 2005).

Rabbi Elie Munk, *The World of Prayer: Commentary and Translation of the Siddur* (two volumes) (Jerusalem: Feldheim, 1963).

Jakob J. Petuchowski, *Understanding Jewish Prayer* (New York: Ktav, 1972).

Dov Rappel, *Pithei She'arim: Studies on the Topic of Prayer* (Hebrew) (Tel Aviv: Yediot Aharonot, 2001).

Stefan C. Reif, *Judaism and Hebrew Prayer* (Cambridge: Cambridge University Press, 1993).

Nahum M. Sarna, *On the Book of Psalms: Exploring the Prayers of Ancient Israel* (New York: Schocken Books, 1993).

Rav [Shimon] Schwab on Prayer (Brooklyn, NY: Mesorah Publications, 2001).

Rabbi Joseph B. Soloveitchik, *Worship of the Heart: Essays on Jewish Prayer*, ed. Shalom Carmy (Hoboken, NJ: Ktav, 2003).

Rabbi Adin Steinsaltz, *A Guide to Jewish Prayer* (New York: Schocken Books, 2000).

Moshe Weinfeld, *Early Jewish Liturgy: From the Psalms to the Prayers in the Qumran Scrolls and in Rabbinic Literature* (Hebrew) (Jerusalem: Magnes Press, 2004).

ARTICLES

Hayyim Angel, "Review Essay: *Ben Haftarah le-Parashah:* A Glimpse into the World of Prophetic *Derush*," *Tradition* 35:4 (Winter 2001), pp. 74–87; reprinted in Angel, *Through an Opaque Lens* (New York: Sephardic Publication Foundation, 2006), pp. 77–94.

Hayyim Angel, "Perspectives on *Tehillim* 19," forthcoming in *Mi-Tokh Ha-Ohel: Shabbat Prayer Volume* (Jerusalem: Maggid, 2014).

Hayyim Angel, "Perspectives on *Tehillim* 145," forthcoming in *Mi-Tokh Ha-Ohel: Weekday Prayer Volume* (Jerusalem: Maggid, 2014).

Rabbi Marc D. Angel, "Thoughts about Prayer," in *Seeking Good, Speaking Peace*, ed. Hayyim Angel (Hoboken, NJ: Ktav, 1994), pp. 36–49.

Rabbi Eliezer Berkovits, "Prayer," in *Studies in Torah Judaism*, ed. Leon Stitskin (New York: Yeshiva University Press, 1969), pp. 81–189, esp. pp. 130–137 on communal prayer.

Rabbi Ezra Bick, "Understanding the Shemona Esrei," at http://www.vbm-torah.org/archive/18/.

Rabbi Yitzchak Blau, *Fresh Fruit & Vintage Wine: The Ethics and Wisdom of the Aggada* (Jersey City, NJ: Ktav, 2009), pp. 219–221.

Gerald Blidstein, "*Sheliach Tzibbur*: Historical and Phenomenological Observations," *Tradition* 12:1 (Summer 1971), pp. 69–77.

Rabbi Shalom Carmy, "Destiny, Freedom, and the Logic of Petition," *Tradition* 24:2 (Winter 1989), pp. 17–37.

Uri Ehrlich, "'When You Pray Know Before Whom You Are Standing' (bBer. 28b)," *Journal of Jewish Studies* 49 (1998), pp. 38–50.

Rabbi Yitzhak Etshalom, essays on *Tehillim* 113–118, at http://www.torah.org/advanced/mikra/hagim.htm.

Rabbi Yitzchak Etshalom, http://www.torah.org/advanced/mikra/5762/hagim/Hallel1.pdf.

Moshe Greenberg, "On the Refinement of the Conception of Prayer in Hebrew Scriptures," *AJS Review* 1 (1976), pp. 57–92.

David Hartman, "Prayer and Religious Consciousness: An Analysis of Jewish Prayer in the Works of Joseph B. Soloveitchik, Yeshayahu Leibowitz, and Abraham Joshua Heschel," *Modern Judaism* 23 (2003), pp. 105–125.

Abraham Joshua Heschel, "The Vocation of the Cantor," in *The Insecurity of Freedom* (New York: Noonday Press, 1967), pp. 242–253.

Rabbi Aharon Lichtenstein, "Prayer on Shabbat," in *Leaves of Faith*, vol. 2 (Hoboken, NJ: Ktav, 2004), pp. 153–177.

Rabbi Marvin Luban, "The Kaddish: Man's Reply to the Problem of Evil," in *Studies in Torah Judaism*, ed. Leon Stitskin (New York: Yeshiva University Press, 1969), pp. 191–234.

Jakob J. Petuchowski, "The Liturgy of the Synagogue: History, Structure, and Contents," in *Approaches to Ancient Judaism*, vol. 4, ed. William Scott Green (Atlanta, GA: Scholars Press, 1990), pp. 1–64.

Rabbi Joseph B. Soloveitchik, "Redemption, Prayer and Talmud Torah," *Tradition* 17:2 (1978), pp. 55–72.

Rabbi Joseph B. Soloveitchik, "Thoughts on Prayer" (Hebrew), in *Ish ha-Halakhah: Galuy ve-Nistar* (Jerusalem: World Zionist Organization, 1979), pp. 239–271.

Shubert Spero, "From Tabernacle (*Mishkan*) and Temple (*Mikdash*) to Synagogue (*Bet Keneset*)," *Tradition* 38:3 (Fall 2004), pp. 60–85.

Made in the USA
Lexington, KY
23 March 2014